First Edition

The Postcard Price Guide

A Comprehensive Listing

J.L. Mashburn

Thousands of Prices, Representing Millions of Cards

WorldComm™
a division of Creativity, Inc.

Publisher: Ralph Roberts

Editor: Emma Mashburn

Assistant Editor: Kathryn L. Hall

Cover Design: WorldComm™

Interior Design and Electronic Page Assembly: WorldComm™

A Colonial House Production

Printed in the United States of America

First Edition

10 9 8 7 6 5 4 3 2 1

ISBN 1-56664-009-1

WorldComm Press—a Division of Creativity, Inc., 65 Macedonia Road, Alexander, North Carolina 28701, (704) 252-9515—is a full service publisher.

AN IMPORTANT NOTICE TO THE READERS OF THIS PRICE GUIDE:

The comprehensive nature of compiling data and prices on the thousands of cards, sets and series in this publication gives many probabilities for error. Although all information has been compiled from reliable sources, experienced collectors and dealers, some data may still be questionable. The author and publisher will not be held responsible for any losses that might occur in the purchase or sale of cards because of the information contained herein.

The author will be most pleased to receive notice of errors so that they may be corrected in future editions.

Contact: J.L. Mashburn, P.O. Box 609, Enka NC 28728 USA.

Contents

DEDICATION

To Emma
My Love, My Life

ACKNOWLEDGEMENTS

Many individuals have made countless valuable contributions which have been incorporated into this publication. While all cannot be acknowledged, appreciation is extended to the following contributors who have exhibited a special dedication by creating, revising or verifying checklists or lending cards for photography.

To **Audrey Buffington,** the long-time collector and lover of the works of F. Earl Christy, for her invaluable checklist and her concise editing of the complete works of the artist.

To **Gordon Gesner** for his tremendous help in providing the checklist and information on the works of his favorite artist, Philip Boileau.

To **Fred Kahn,** fellow North Carolina Dealer-Collector, who provided many of the cards for photographing, and also helped with pricing information. All the beautiful Mermaid photos are from cards in his personal collection.

To **Ted Holmes,** the prolific Collector-Historian of artist-signed cards, for providing checklists and information on Howard Chandler Christy, Clarence Underwood, R. Ford Harper, Coles Phillips, Archie Gunn, Lester Ralph, and additions to others that were incomplete.

And finally, to the many thousands of collectors and dealers that have made this hobby so fantastic.

A Word About Color: The many cards depicted in this book to aid you in identification are obviously in black and white. The actual cards, such as the German one above, are very colorful. This little Teutonic lady is dressed in vivid green, her hat is a bright red, her soft hair is blonde, and the background behind her is a lustrous gold. A good part of the joy and magic in collecting postcards is color. Postcards are truly art. Seek them out and let their beauty warm your heart.

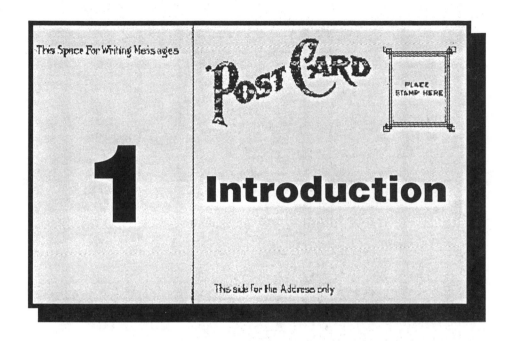

Through all of my years as a postcard collector-dealer I have felt a great need for a good, comprehensive postcard price guide. Today, even more than before, that need exists. Although there have been several good price guides published—and certainly they served their purpose for the times—they were not comprehensive enough for today's tremendous wealth of available material. Most were rarely ever updated for price appreciation (or depreciation) or for new additions as warranted.

I believe that this publication, **The Postcard Price Guide—A Comprehensive Listing,** is the missing link. Never has a price guide publisher attempted to list complete, or near complete, checklists of some of the more prominent and widely collected artists; nor have complete sections on all important Fantasy, Deco, French Glamour, Nudes, and so on, been listed before.

It has been unfair to list a price range of an artist's work; e.g., "$3 to $40 each." Which cards are $3 and which are worth $40? This leaves an unmistakable void. With the help of many collectors, dealers and postcard historians, this guide has addressed the missing listings and similar problems. By continuous updating and problem eliminations, it should prove to be a very valuable tool for all deltiologists.

The tremendous American collector demand for European cards, especially Artist-Signed, Art Deco, Art Nouveau, Animals, Erotic, Nudes, Fantasy, and French Glamour, has caused a great influx of highly collectible cards in the 1980's and 90's. Only the very knowledgeable dealers and advanced collectors know the true values of this wealth of beautiful material.

The issues of hundreds of foreign artists, various publishers, and diverse topics are listed and priced to better inform the collector of the cards now available in the U.S. Whether buying or selling, it is always best to know what is available and also to know the true value.

This influx has also revealed the existence of rare and unrecorded issues of the works of many American artists. The foreign issues of Harrison Fisher, Philip Boileau, Frances Brundage, Bessie Pease Gutmann, and others have opened up new worlds for specialist collectors. Many of these, with approximate values, are listed here for the first time. Hopefully, this information will be of benefit to the collectors trying to build a complete collection of cards by their favorite artists.

As years go by, new collectors enter the hobby with varying interests. Cards that had great appeal just a few years ago may have temporarily lost their glamour and may lie dormant until their cycle rolls around to make them popular once again.

No longer are ladies content to collect only Santas and beautiful children by the Clapsaddles, Brundages and Wiederseims. This will continue, but their interests have widened to include Italian Art Deco and Fashions of Busi, Nanni, Colombo and Corbella; the intriguing Fantasy of beautifully dressed Frogs and Mushroom People and Thiele animals; colorful Nursery Rhymes and dainty Fairies.

No longer are men in the hobby collecting only Ocean Liners, Zeppelins, Advertising, Street Scenes and Town Views...and the glamorous ladies of Boileau, Fisher and Christy. Much of their new interest lies in Real Photo Topicals, Roadside America, the beautiful and colorful Nudes and Fantasy Nudes of European artists ... the exotic French glamour of Susan Meunier and Jean Tam, and the equally delightful French Real Photo Nudes. These are popular new additions now widely collected and the cards that are in vogue today—the great collectibles of the early 1990's. These, plus other equally popular topics, are well represented in this first edition.

Joseph Lee Mashburn
July, 1992

HOW TO USE THIS PRICE GUIDE

We have tried to uniquely design this price guide to serve the needs of both the beginning and advanced collector, as well as the established postcard dealer. Our attempt to provide a comprehensive guide to postcards dating from 1900 through the 1940's makes it possible for even the novice collector to consult it with confidence and ease in finding each particular listing. The following important explanations summarize the general practices that will help in getting the most benefits from its use.

CATEGORICAL ARRANGEMENT

Cards are arranged by category, and each category is listed in the Table of Contents. All Artist-Signed cards are listed under a particular type or theme. If an artist painted both cats and dogs, he/she will be listed under both "Cats" and "Dogs," etc. Artists are always listed alphabetically, as are the publishers if the cards are unsigned.

Topical cards are listed alphabetically with individual listings of some of the most prominent cards and their values. Otherwise, the prices listed are for generalized cards in the particular topic or theme.

LISTINGS

Listings may be identified as follows:

1. **SECTION** (Artist-Signed, Fantasy, etc.).
2. **TOPIC** (Beautiful Women, Cats, Dogs, etc.).
3. **ARTIST** (Listed in Bold Capital Letters) when available.
4. **PUBLISHER** (Listed in Bold, Lower Case Letters).
5. **NAME OF SERIES; OR SERIES NUMBER.**
6. **NUMBER OF CARDS IN SET OR SERIES** (Enclosed in Parentheses) when available.
7. **CAPTION OR TITLE OF CARD** (Enclosed in Quotation Marks).
8. **PRICE OF 1 CARD IN VERY GOOD CONDITION**
9. **PRICE OF 1 CARD IN EXCELLENT CONDITION**

Example of above:

1. **ARTIST-SIGNED**
2. **BEAUTIFUL WOMEN**
3. **HARRISON FISHER**
4. **Reinthal & Newman**
5. 101 Series
6. (12)
7. "American Beauties"
8. $10 - 15
9. $15 - 18

CONDITION AND GRADING OF POSTCARDS

The condition of a postcard, as with old coins, stamps, books, etc., is an extremely important factor in pricing it for the collector, the dealer, and for those having found cards to sell. Damaged, worn, creased, or dirty cards —cards in less than Very Good condition—are almost uncollectible unless they are to be used as a space filler until a better one is found. Never buy a damaged card if you expect to sell it later on.

It is necessary that some sort of card grading standard be used so that buyer and seller may come to an informed agreement on the value of a card. Two different collectible conditions, **Very Good** and **Excellent,** are used in **THE POST CARD PRICE GUIDE.** There are, of course, higher and lower grades, but these two will be most normally seen and most normally quoted for postcards sold throughout the hobby.

The standard grading system adapted by most dealers and by the leading postcard hobby publications in the field, *Barr's Post Card News* and *Post Card Collector*, is listed below with their permission:

M—MINT. A perfect card just as it comes from the printing press. No marks, bends, or creases. No writing or postmarks. A clean and fresh card. Seldom seen.

NM—NEAR MINT. Like Mint but very light aging or very slight discoloration from being in an album for many years. Not as sharp or crisp.

EX—EXCELLENT. Like mint in appearance with no bends or creases, or rounded or blunt corners. May be postally used or unused and with writing and postmark only on the address side. A clean, fresh card on the picture side.

VG—VERY GOOD. Corners may be just a bit blunt or rounded. Almost undetectable crease or bend that does not detract from overall appearance of the picture side. May have writing or postally used on address side. A very collectible card.

G—GOOD. Corners may be noticeably blunt or rounded with noticeably slight bends or creases. May be postally used or have writing on address side. Less than VG.

FR—FAIR. Card is intact. Excess soil, stains, creases, writing, or cancellation may affect picture. Could be a scarce card that is difficult to find in any condition.

Postcard dealers will always want better condition cards that have no defects. If you have cards to sell, please keep this in mind. If you are building a collection you should also maintain a standard for condition and stick to it. Even if the asking price is a little higher, it will pay you when or if you should decide to dispose of it.

VALUATIONS

The postcard values quoted in this publication represent the current retail market. They were compiled from dealer pricing at shows, personal dealer communications, from the author's personal purchasing, both in the U.S. and throughout Europe, from his approval sales and more than 100 mail auctions, and from his active day-to-day involvement in the postcard field.

Some values were also compiled from observations of listings in auctions, auction catalogs (U.S., Europe, and Great Britain), prices realized and fixed price sales in the fine hobby publications, *Barr's Post Card News* and *Postcard Collector*, and other related publications. **In all instances, listings of high and low values were taken for each observation, and these were averaged to obtain the "VG" and "Excellent" prices quoted.**

It must be stressed that this price guide is intended to serve only as an aid in evaluating postcards. It should not be used otherwise. As we all know, actual market conditions change constantly, and prices may fluctuate. The trend for postcards seems to always be to the upside.

Publication of this price guide is not intended to be a solicitation to buy or sell any of the cards listed.

Price ranges for cards in both **Very Good** and **Excellent** conditions are found at the end of each listing. Prices for cards in less than Very Good condition would be much lower, while those grading above Excellent might command relatively higher prices.

Without exception, prices quoted are for **one** card, whether it be a single entity or one card in a complete set or series. Note that after many entries a number is enclosed in parentheses; e.g., (6). This number indicates the total number of cards in a set or in a series. The price listed is for one card in the set and is multiplied by this number to determine the value of a complete set.

WHY PRICE RANGES ARE QUOTED

For cards graded both **VG** and **Excellent**, price ranges are quoted for four major reasons. Any one, or more, of the following can determine the difference in the high or low prices in each of the listing ranges.

1. Prices vary in different geographical areas across the United States. At this time, they are somewhat higher on the Pacific coast and other western states. They tend to be a little lower in the East and somewhere in-between in the central and midwestern states. For instance, a card with a price range of $6.00-8.00 might sell for $6.00 in the East, $7.00 in the Mid-West and $8.00 in the Far West.

2. Dealer price valuations also vary. Those who continually set up at postcard shows seem to have a better feel for prices and know which cards are selling well and, therefore, can adjust their prices accordingly. Dealers who sell only by mail, or by mail auction, tend to price their cards (or list estimated values in their auctions) just a bit higher. They usually are able to get these prices because of a wider collector market base obtained by the large number of subscribers served by the nationally distributed postcard auction publications. The publications also reach collectors who are unable to attend shows.

3. Cards that are in great demand, or "hot" topics, also have wider price ranges; as collector interests rise there is a greater disparity in values because of supply and demand. If a dealer has only a small number of big demand cards he will almost automatically elevate his prices. Those who have a large supply will probably not go as high.

4. Card appearance and the subject in a set or series can also cause a variance in the price range. Printing quality, more beautiful and varied colors, and sharpness of the image may make a particular card much more desirable and, therefore, it will command a higher price.

Cards that have a wide price range usually are those that are presently the "most wanted" and best sellers. Dealers, most often, will only offer a small discount when selling these because they know there is a good market for them. Cards listed with a narrow price range are usually those that have been "hot" but have settled down and established a more competitive trading range. Dealer discounting on these slow-movers tends to be much more prevalent than those in the wide price ranges.

GUIDELINES FOR BUYING AND SELLING CARDS

As noted above, the prices listed in this price guide are retail prices—prices that a collector can expect to pay when buying a card from a dealer. It is up to the collectors to bargain for any available discount from the dealer.

The wholesale price is the price which a collector can expect from a dealer when selling cards. This price will be significantly lower than the retail price. Most dealers try to operate on a 100% mark-up and will normally pay around 50% of a card's low retail value. On some high-demand cards, he might pay up to 60% or 75% if he wants them badly enough.

Dealers are always interested in purchasing collections and accumulations of cards. They are primarily interested in those that were issued before 1915, but may be induced to take those issued afterwards if they are clean and in good condition.

Collections: Normally, collections are a specialized group or groups of cards that a person has built over the years. They will be in nice condition, without any damage, and may contain some rarities or high-demand cards.

If the collection is a group of views from your home town or state it would be to your advantage, pricewise, to sell them to a collector or dealer near you. You might place an ad in your daily paper; you will be surprised at the interest it creates. Set your price a little high. You can always come down.

If the collection contains artist-signed, topicals, and complete sets, as well as views, etc., you may need to contact a dealer in order to dispose of them. As noted above, be prepared to sell to the dealer at around 50% of the value of the collection. If you do not know of any dealers, write the **International Federation**

of Postcard Dealers, to the attention of John McClintock, Executive Secretary, P.O. Box 1765, Manassas, VA 22110 and enclose a stamped, self-addressed #10 envelope for a list of members.

You might also dispose of your collection by writing to the dealers who advertise in *Barr's Post Card News,* 70 South 6th St., Lansing, IA 52151 or *Postcard Collector,* P.O. Box 37, Iola, WI 54945. Write to either for a sample copy and information on subscriptions.

Accumulations: Accumulations are usually groups of many different kinds, many different eras, and many different topics ... with the good usually mixed in with the bad. If you have a large accumulation that you wish to dispose of, your best bet is to contact a dealer as noted above. You may expect only 20% to 30% of value on a group such as this. Many low demand cards are non-sellers and are worthless to a dealer, but he may take them if there are some good cards in the accumulation.

Buying: Without doubt, the best way to buy postcards is to attend a show where there is a large group of dealers. Compare prices among dealers on cards that are of interest to you, and return to those who have the best cards at the lowest price for your purchases.

Buy from a dealer in your area if there is one. A good dealer will help you with your collection by searching for cards you need or want. If none are available, many dealers listed in *Barr's Post Card News* and *Postcard Collector* run auctions or will send cards on approval.

It is also possible to find cards at Antique Shows, Flea Markets and Antique Shops. You can, however, waste a lot of time and never find suitable cards. It is best to go direct to the source and that would be a postcard dealer or auctioneer. Here you can find a great variety and almost always cards of interest to you.

IDENTIFYING THE AGE OF POSTCARDS

The dating of postcards for years or eras of issue can be accurately determined if the card is studied for identity points. Research has already been done by earlier historians and guidelines have been put into place.

There were seven eras for the postcard industry and each one has distinguishing points to help establish its respective identity. The following helps determine the era of the card in question:

PIONEER ERA (1893-1898)

The Pioneer Era began when picture postcards were placed on sale by vendors and exhibitors at the Columbian Exposition in Chicago, May, 1893. These were very popular and proved to be a great success. The profitable and lasting future of the postcard was greatly enhanced.

Pioneer cards are relatively scarce and hard to find. They can be identified by combinations of the following:

- All have undivided backs.

- None show the "Authorized by Act of Congress" byline.

- Postal cards will have the Grant or Jefferson head stamp.

- Most, but not all, will be multiple view cards.

- The words "Souvenir of ..." or "Greetings from ..." will appear on many.

- Postage rate, if listed, is 2 cents.

- The most common titles will be "Souvenir Card" or "Mail Card."

- Appeared mostly in the big Eastern cities.

PRIVATE MAILING CARD ERA (1898-1901)

The government, on May 19, 1898, gave private printers permission to print and sell postcards. The cards were all issued with the inscription "Private Mailing Card," and today they are referred to as PMC's. It is very easy to identify these because of the inscription. It may be noted that many of the early Pioneer views were reprinted as Private Mailing Cards.

POST CARD ERA (1901-1907)

On December 24, 1901, permission was given for use of the wording "Post Card" to be imprinted on the backs of privately printed cards. All cards during this era had undivided backs and only the address was to appear on the back. The message, therefore, had to be written on the front (picture side) of the card. For this reason many cards have writing on the face of the card. This fault is becoming more acceptable as time goes on.

DIVIDED BACK ERA (1907-1915)

This era came into being on March 1, 1907. The divided back made it possible for both the address and the message to be on the back of the card. This prevented the face of the card from being written on and proved to be a great boon for collectors. Normally the view colors or images filled the entire card with no white border.

WHITE BORDER ERA (1915-1930)

The White Border Era brought an end to the postcard craze era. The golden age ended as imports from Germany ceased and publishers in the U.S. began printing postcards to try to fill the void. The cards were very poor quality and many were reprints of earlier Divided Back Era cards. These are easily distinguished by the white border around the pictured area.

LINEN ERA (1930-1945)

Improvements in American printing technology brought improved card quality. Publishers began using a linen-like paper containing a high rag content but used very cheap inks in most instances. Until recently, these cards were considered very cheap by collectors. Now they are very popular with collectors of Roadside America, Blacks, Comics, and Advertising. Views are also becoming more popular as collectors realize that this era too is a part of our history, and these cards help to illustrate the changes in the geographic structure of America.

PHOTOCHROME ERA (1939 to present day)

"Modern Chromes," as they are now called by the postcard fraternity, were first introduced in 1939. Publishers, such as

Mike Roberts, Dexter Press, Curt Teich, and **Plastichrome,** began producing cards that had very beautiful chrome colors and were very appealing to collectors. The growth of this group has been spectacular in recent years, so much so that there are now many postcard dealers who specialize only in chromes.

REAL PHOTO POSTCARDS (1900 to present day)

Real Photo postcards were in use as early as 1900. It is sometimes very hard to date a card unless it has been postally used or dated by the photographer. The stamp box will usually show the process by which it was printed—AZO, EKC, KODAK, VELOX, and KRUXO are some of the principal ones. Careful study of photo cards is essential to make sure they have not been reproduced.

An example of a Real Photo postcard, the Graf Zeppelin. *Photo by AZO.*

This Space For Writing Messages

POST CARD

PLACE STAMP HERE

2 Artist-Signed

This side for the Address only

If you ask a postcard collector "What do you collect?" he will invariably answer, "I collect views of my home town," and then continues ... with a gleam in his eye ... "and cards signed by Harrison Fisher"... or Philip Boileau, or Earl Christy, Frances Brundage, Pauli Ebner, and so on.

The Artist-Signed postcard is overwhelmingly the favorite type to collect in the entire postcard field. The beauty and elegance of several cards, or a group or set of cards by a great artist, makes the pulse quicken and creates the desire to possess them for one's own.

Since Artist-Signed cards are so popular, we are listing almost all major and many minor artists in the U.S.A. in all fields. Included are the complete, or near complete, checklists (with all cards priced) of Harrison Fisher, Philip Boileau, Earl Christy, Howard Chandler Christy, Clarence Underwood, Coles Phillips, and others. This is a major accomplishment and, to my knowledge, has never been attempted in the postcard field. Separate checklists have been made but never all together ... and never priced.

Listed also are major and minor foreign artists and their works in the important topics of Art Deco, Art Nouveau, Fantasy, Fantasy Nudes, Color Nudes, Nursery Rhymes, Fairy Tales, Animals, French Fashion, and others. This is the type of information today's collectors and dealers desire.

What is an Artist-Signed card? It is any card bearing an artist's signature or initials. If you have never collected them, you have much to look forward to.

BEAUTIFUL LADIES

	VG	EX
ABEILLE, JACK (France)		
Lady/Flower Series	$35 - 40	$40 - 45
ANICHINI, E. (Italy) See Art Deco		
ARMSTRONG, ROLF (U.S.A.)		
K. Co., N.Y.		
Water Color Ser. 101 - 112	10 - 15	15 - 20
ASTI, ANGELO (Italy)		
Raphael Tuck		
Connoisseur Series 2731		
"Beatrice"	8 - 12	12 - 16

Rolf Armstrong
K. Co. Inc., 108

Rolf Armstrong
K. Co. Inc., 109

"Gladys"	8 - 12	12 - 16
"Irene"	8 - 12	12 - 16
"Juliet"	8 - 12	12 - 16
"Marguerite"	8 - 12	12 - 16
"Rosalind"	8 - 12	12 - 16
Connoisseur Series 2743		
"Helena"	8 - 12	12 - 16
"Madeline"	8 - 12	12 - 16
"Muriel"	8 - 12	12 - 16
"Phyllis"	8 - 12	12 - 16
"Portia"	8 - 12	12 - 16
"Sylvia"	8 - 12	12 - 16
Rotograph Co., N.Y.		
Series T. 5268		
"Beatrice"	7 - 10	10 - 15
"Gladys"	7 - 10	10 - 15
"Irene"	7 - 10	10 - 15
"Juliet"	7 - 10	10 - 15
"Marguerite"	7 - 10	10 - 15
"Rosalind"	7 - 10	10 - 15
T.S.N. (Theo Stroefer)		
Series 505 (8) No Captions	6 - 8	8 - 10
Semi-Nude Real Photo Series		
"Epanouissment"	15 - 18	18 - 22
"Fantasie"	15 - 18	18 - 22
"Solitude"	15 - 18	18 - 22
"Une Favorite"	15 - 18	18 - 22
"Volupte"	15 - 18	18 - 22
Others	15 - 18	18 - 22
AXENTOWICZ		
Heads	8 - 10	12 - 15
Fantasy	12 - 15	15 - 20
Nudes	12 - 15	15 - 20
AZZONI, N. (Italy) See Art Deco		
BARBER, COURT (U.S.A.)		
B.K.W.I. Series 683 (6)	6 - 8	8 - 10
B.K.W.I. Series 686 (6)	8 - 10	10 - 12
B.K.W.I. Series 1200	6 - 8	8 - 10
Others	6 - 8	8 - 10
J.W. & Co. Series	6 - 8	8 - 9
S.S.S.B. Series	6 - 8	8 - 9
BARBER, C. W. (U.S.A.)		
B.K.W.I. Series 861 (12)	8 - 10	10 - 14
B.K.W.I. Series 2128 (8)	8 - 10	10 - 14
Carleton Publishing Co.		

Series 676, 678	8 - 9	9 - 12
Series 709, 716	8 - 9	9 - 12
Series 735, 861	8 - 10	10 - 14

BARRIBAL, L. (GB)
   International Art Pub. Co.

"Artisque" Series	8 - 10	10 - 12

   Valentine Co.

"Flags of Nation" Series	6 - 8	8 - 10

   "Great Britain"
   "Japan"
   "Scotland"
   "Ireland"
   "Germany"
   "Russia"

BACHRICH, M. See Art Deco
BALOTINI (Italy) See Art Deco
BASCH, ARPAD (Hungary) See Art Nouveau
BERTIGLIA, A. (Italy) See Art Deco
BIANCHI (Italy) See Art Deco
BIRI, S. (Italy) See Art Deco
BOILEAU, PHILIP (Canada-U.S.A.)

Philip Boileau, born in Canada but finally settling in New York, was another of the great painters and illustrators of beautiful women. His works are collected world-wide and are in great demand by all who love the facial beauty of the selected fair.

Most of his images on postcards were published in the U.S.A. by the New York firm of Reinthal & Newman during the "postcard craze" years of 1905-1918. Other principal publishers were Osborne Calendar Co., with their printings of the rare Boileau calendar cards, National Art Co. and their advertising cards, and The Taylor, Platt Co. and their scarce flower-decorated cards and valentine head issues.

Minor issuers were advertising cards by Flood & Conklin, Soapine Mfg. Co., S.E. Perlberg Tailors, and others. These various issues, as well as his other advertising card issues, are extremely hard to find and are very high priced when they surface.

British, European and Finnish publishers issued Boileau cards which are very elusive and also command high prices. The Tuck Connoisseur Series 2819 and the German K N G Schoen Frauen, along with the KOY Finnish Series, are among those sought after by collectors worldwide.

PHILIP BOILEAU

AMERICAN PUBLISHERS

Reinthal & Newman
Series 94 *

"At the Opera"	10 - 15	15 - 20
"Peggy"	10 - 15	15 - 20
"Schooldays"	10 - 15	15 - 20
"Sweethearts"	10 - 15	15 - 20
"Thinking of You"	10 - 15	15 - 20
"Twins"	10 - 15	15 - 20

* Card w/Series No. on back, add $5
Series 95 *

"A Mischiefmaker"	10 - 15	15 - 20
"Anticipation"	10 - 15	15 - 20
"Forever"	10 - 15	15 - 20
"Little Lady Demure"	10 - 15	15 - 20
"My Chauffeur"	10 - 15	15 - 20
"Nocturne"	10 - 15	15 - 20

P. Boileau
R&N 208, "Miss America"

P. Boileau
KKOY N:O 1/20, No Caption

"Passing Shadow"	12 - 18	18 - 22
"Spring Song"	12 - 18	18 - 22
"Today"	10 - 15	15 - 20
"Tomorrow"	10 - 15	15 - 20
"Winter Whispers"	12 - 18	18 - 22
"Yesterday"	10 - 15	15 - 20
* Cards w/Series No. on back add $5		
Series 109 *		
"Evening and You"	20 - 25	25 - 30
"Girl in Black"	20 - 25	25 - 30
"Her Soul With Purity Possessed"	22 - 27	27 - 32
"In Maiden Meditation"	22 - 27	27 - 32
"June, Blessed June"	20 - 25	25 - 30
"My Moonbeam"	20 - 25	25 - 30
"My One Rose"	20 - 25	25 - 30
"Ready for Mischief"	20 - 25	25 - 30
"The Secret of the Flowers"	22 - 27	27 - 32
"True as the Blue Above"	22 - 27	27 - 32
"Twixt Doubt and Hope"	20 - 25	25 - 30
"Waiting for You"	20 - 25	25 - 30
"With Care for None"	20 - 25	25 - 30
* Cards w/Series No. on back add $5		
200 Series		
204 "Rings on Her Fingers"	10 - 15	15 - 20
205 "Question"	10 - 15	15 - 20
205 "Chrysanthemums"	15 - 20	20 - 25
206 "The Enchantress"	10 - 15	15 - 20
207 "A Hundred Years Ago"	10 - 15	15 - 20
208 "Miss America"	12 - 16	16 - 22
209 "Youth"	10 - 15	15 - 20
210 "Joyful Calm"	10 - 15	15 - 20
211 "Chums"	10 - 15	15 - 20
212 "Sweet Lips of Coral Hue"	10 - 15	15 - 20
213 "His First Love"	10 - 15	15 - 20
214 "For Him"	10 - 15	15 - 20
215 "I Wonder"	10 - 15	15 - 20
282 "Ready for the Meeting"	12 - 16	16 - 22
283 "Miss Pat"	12 - 16	16 - 22
284 "Old Home Farewell"	10 - 15	15 - 20
285 "A Serious Thought"	10 - 15	15 - 20
286 "I Don't Care"	12 - 16	16 - 22
287 "The Eyes Say No, The Lips Say Yes"	12 - 16	16 - 22

294 "Blue Ribbons"	15 - 20	20 - 25
295 "A Little Devil"	15 - 20	20 - 25
296 "Once Upon A Time"	10 - 15	15 - 20
297 "My Big Brother"	10 - 15	15 - 20
298 "My Boy"	10 - 15	15 - 20
299 "Baby Mine"	15 - 20	20 - 25

Water Color Series 369-380 *

369 "Vanity"	15 - 22	30 - 40
370 "Haughtiness"	20 - 25	30 - 40
371 "Purity"	15 - 22	30 - 40
372 "Loneliness"	20 - 25	40 - 45
373 "Happiness"	20 - 25	30 - 40
374 "Queenliness"	20 - 25	30 - 40
375 "Whisperings of Love" (Annunciation)	20 - 25	30 - 40
376 "Fairy Tales" (Girlhood)	20 - 25	30 - 40
377 "Parting of the Ways" (Maidenhood)	20 - 25	30 - 40
378 "Here Comes Daddy"	15 - 20	30 - 40
379 "Lullabye" (Motherhood)	20 - 25	30 - 40
380 "Don't Wake the Baby"	15 - 20	30 - 40

* Cards without Subtitle - add $5

445 Series *

1 "Spring Song"	18 - 22	25 - 30
2 "Today"	18 - 22	25 - 30
3 "Tomorrow"	18 - 22	25 - 30
4 "Forever"	18 - 22	25 - 30
5 "My Chauffeur"	18 - 22	25 - 30
6 "Nocturne"	18 - 22	25 - 30

* With German caption - add $5 to prices.

474 Series *

1 "Spring Song"	20 - 25	30 - 35
2 "A Passing Shadow"	20 - 25	30 - 35
3 "Mischiefmaker"	20 - 25	30 - 35
4 "Anticipating"	20 - 25	30 - 35
5 "Yesterday"	20 - 25	30 - 35
6 "Little Lady Demure"	20 - 25	30 - 35

* With German caption - add $5 to prices.

700 Series

750 "Be Prepared" *	12 - 15	15 - 20
751 "Absence Cannot Hearts Divide" *	12 - 15	15 - 20
752 "A Neutral" *	12 - 15	15 - 20
753 "The Chrysalis" *	12 - 15	15 - 20
754 "Pensive" *	12 - 15	15 - 20
755 "The Girl of the Golden West" *	12 - 15	15 - 20
756 "Pebbles on the Beach" *	15 - 18	18 - 26
757 "Snowbirds" *	15 - 18	18 - 26

758 "One Kind Act a Day" *	12 - 15	15 - 20
759 "The Flirt" *	12 - 15	15 - 20
760 "In Confidence" *	12 - 15	15 - 20
761 "The Coming Storm" *	15 - 18	18 - 26

* With German Caption - add $5 to prices.

800 Series

820 "Devotion"	25 - 30	35 - 40
821 "Golden Dreams"	20 - 25	35 - 40
822 "Every Breeze Carries My Thoughts..."	18 - 22	22 - 26
823 "Priscilla"	25 - 30	35 - 45
824 "Fruit of the Vine"	18 - 22	22 - 26
825 "Butterfly"	25 - 30	35 - 45
826 "When Dreams Come True" *	12 - 15	15 - 20
827 "Sister's First Love" *	12 - 15	15 - 20
828 "The Little Neighbors" *	12 - 15	15 - 20
829 "Peach Blossoms" *	15 - 20	20 - 25
830 "When His Ship Comes In" *	12 - 15	15 - 20
831 "Need a Lassie Cry" *	12 - 15	15 - 20

* With German Caption - add $5 to prices.

Water Color Series 936-941

936 "A Bit of Heaven"	18 - 22	35 - 40
937 "Chic"	18 - 22	35 - 40
938 "Have a Care"		
also "Hav a Care"	20 - 25	35 - 40
939 "Just a Wearying for You"	20 - 25	35 - 40
940 "Sunshine"	25 - 30	35 - 40
941 "Sincerely Yours"	20 - 25	35 - 40

2000 Series

2052 "Thinking of You"	20 - 25	25 - 30
2063 "Chums"	20 - 25	25 - 30
2064 "His First Love"	20 - 25	25 - 30
2065 "Question"	20 - 25	25 - 30
2066 "From Him"	20 - 25	25 - 30
2067 "The Enchantress"	20 - 25	25 - 30
2068 "Joyful Calm"	20 - 25	25 - 30
Others	20 - 25	25 - 30

Unnumbered Series

"The Dreamy Hour"	15 - 20	25 - 35
"Out for Fun"	15 - 20	25 - 35

Osborne Calendar Co. *

940 "A Fair Debutante"	75 - 100	100 - 150
941 "The Blonde"	75 - 100	100 - 150
942 "Phyllis"	75 - 100	100 - 150
943 "Pansies"	75 - 100	100 - 150

P. Boileau
R&N No Number, "To-day?"

P. Boileau
R&N 282, "Ready for the Meeting"

P. Boileau
R&N 285, "A Serious Thought"

P. Boileau
KNG 8011, Schöne Frauen

944 "True Blue"	75 - 100	100 - 150
945 "Army Girl"	75 - 100	100 - 150
946 "Day Dreams"	75 - 100	100 - 150
947 "Passing Shadow"	75 - 100	100 - 150
948 "The Girl in Brown"	75 - 100	100 - 150
949 "Goodbye"	75 - 100	100 - 150
950 "Passing Glance"	75 - 100	100 - 150
951 "A Winter Girl"	75 - 100	100 - 150
459 "Winifred"	100 - 125	125 - 150
1459 "Rhododendrons"	100 - 125	125 - 150
1489 "At Play"	125 - 150	150 - 175
2076 "Suzanne"	125 - 150	150 - 175
3525 "Autumn"	125 - 150	150 - 175
3625 "Chrysanthemums"	125 - 150	150 - 175

* The Osborne Calendar Cards are the rarest
U.S. series. Price quotes may be too low!

National Art Company

17 "Spring"	70 - 80	80 - 90
18 "Summer"	70 - 80	80 - 90
19 "Autumn"	70 - 80	80 - 90
20 "Winter"	70 - 80	80 - 90
150 "The Debutantes"	65 - 70	75 - 100
160 "Summer"	70 - 80	80 - 90
161 "Autumn"	70 - 80	80 - 90
162 "Spring"	70 - 80	80 - 90
163 "Winter"	70 - 80	80 - 90
230 "Spring"	80 - 90	90 - 100
231 "Summer"	80 - 90	90 - 100
232 "Autumn"	80 - 90	90 - 100
233 "Winter"	80 - 90	90 - 100

C.N. Snyder Art

"Spring Song"	65 - 75	75 - 85

S.E. Perlberg Co., Tailors   Ad on Back

"My Moonbeam"	65 - 75	75 - 85
"My One Rose"	65 - 75	75 - 85
"Secret of the Flowers"	65 - 75	75 - 85
"True as the Blue Above"	65 - 75	75 - 85
"Twixt Doubt and Hope"	65 - 75	75 - 85

Flood & Conklin

"Girl in Blue"	75 - 85	85 - 95
"The Girl in Brown"	75 - 85	85 - 95

"His First Love"	75 - 85	85 - 95
Others	75 - 85	85 - 95
Soapine Advertising	75 - 85	85 - 95
Sparks Tailoring Ad on Back **(R&N)**		
"Tomorrow"	65 - 75	75 - 85
A. P. Co. Advertising	75 - 85	85 - 95
Holland Magazine Ad on Back		
"Miss Pat"	65 - 75	75 - 85
"Ready for the Meeting"	65 - 75	75 - 85
Metropolitan Life Advertising	35 - 40	50 - 60
Will's Embassy Pipe Tobacco Mixtures		
"Nocturne"	65 - 75	75 - 85
Worthmore Tay Tailors, Chicago		
"Ready for Mischief"	65 - 75	75 - 85
First Nat. Bank, Cripple Creek, CO		
"Virginia"	65 - 75	75 - 85
Taylor, Platt *		
"Chrysanthemums"	70 - 80	80 - 100
"Poppies"	70 - 80	80 - 100
"Violets"	70 - 80	80 - 100
"Wild Roses"	70 - 80	80 - 100
* 12 cards supposedly issued.		
Only 4 above have been seen.		
Unsigned, Unknown Publisher *		
"Chrysanthemums" **	30 - 35	35 - 45
(To My Sweetheart)		
"Poppies"	30 - 35	35 - 45
(A Greeting from St. Valentine)		
(A Token of Love) 2 types		
"Violets"	30 - 35	35 - 45
(A Gift of Love)		
"Wild Roses"	30 - 35	35 - 45
(To My Valentine)		
* Others may exist.		
** Embossed and un-embossed varieties		
exist, and possibly in all four cards.		
Wolfe & Co.		
"Fancy Free" (Silk)	150 - 200	200 - 250

FOREIGN PHILIP BOILEAU

MEU Publisher Logo on Back		
Untitled, Dated 1905 - Woman/Dark Hat	65 - 75	75 - 85
R. Tuck		

P. Boileau
Russian-Polish Back
"The Enchantress"

P. Boileau
KNG 8010, Schöne Frauen

Connoisseur Ser. 2819

"At Home"	125 - 150	150 - 175
"Au Revoir"	125 - 150	150 - 175
"Fancy Free"	125 - 150	150 - 175
"I Am Late"	125 - 150	150 - 175
"Paying a Call"	125 - 150	150 - 175
"Summer Breezes"	125 - 150	150 - 175

K. K. OY, Finland

"Baby Mine"	125 - 150	150 - 175
"Sister's First Love"	125 - 150	150 - 175
"Snowbirds"	125 - 150	150 - 175
"Here Comes Daddy" (Light Pastels)	125 - 150	150 - 175

KNG, Germany

Schöne Frauen Ser. 8010

"I am Late" (No border)	75 - 100	100 - 125
"Paying a Call" (No border)	75 - 100	100 - 125
"Summer Breezes" (No border)	75 - 100	100 - 125
"Fancy Free"	100 - 125	125 - 150
"Au Revoir"	100 - 125	125 - 150
"At Home"	100 - 125	125 - 150

Schoen Frauen Ser. 8011

116	125 - 150	150 - 175
Unknown Publisher, Russia		
Real-Photo Type, Russian-Polish back		
"The Enchantress"	125 - 150	150 - 175
Pebbled Grain Paper		
18 "A Brotherly Kiss"	125 - 150	150 - 175
AWE - W/Russian-Polish Back		
Real Photo Series		
"Miss America"	125 - 150	150 - 175
Unknown Publisher Probably Dutch		
Series R		
R.236 "Miss America"	50 - 75	75 - 95
R.238 "His First Love"	50 - 75	75 - 95
R.239 "Chums"	50 - 75	75 - 95
Unsigned		
"Miss America"	50 - 75	75 - 95
"Miss America" (signed, 1910, blue ink)	50 - 75	75 - 95
"Rings on Her Fingers"	50 - 75	75 - 95
Series 682 (6)		
682-1 "Anticipation"	50 - 60	60 - 75
682-2 "True as the Blue Above"	50 - 60	60 - 75
682-3 "In Maiden Meditation"	50 - 60	60 - 75
682-4 Unknown	175 - 200	200 - 225
682-5 "Twins"	50 - 60	60 - 75
682-6 "The Girl in Black"	50 - 60	60 - 75
BOMPARD, S. (Italy) See Art Deco		
BONORA (Italy) See Art Deco		
BOTTARO (Italy) See Art Deco		
BROWN, J. FRANCIS (U.S.A.)	4 - 5	5 - 6
BRUNELLESCHI (Italy) See Deco, Fr. Glamour		
BUSI, ADOLFO (Italy) See Art Deco		
BUTCHER, ARTHUR (GB)		
United Six Girls Series		
"Belgium"	10 - 12	12 - 15
"Britain"	10 - 12	12 - 15
"France"	10 - 12	12 - 15
"Japan"	10 - 12	12 - 15
"Russia"	12 - 15	15 - 18
"Serbia"	12 - 15	15 - 18
"Artisque" Series 1509 (6)	8 - 10	10 - 12
A.R.i.B. Series 1963 (6)	8 - 10	10 - 12
CALDONA (Italy) See Art Deco		
CASTELLI (Italy) See Art Deco		
CHERUBINI (Italy) See Art Deco		

CHIOSTRI (Italy) See Art Deco
CHRISTY, F. EARL (U.S.A.)

F. Earl Christy was one of the leading artists who depicted the beauty of the American girl, especially of the college and university varieties. Most of his early works were in this category, as he helped start the tradition of glorifying the beauties of the era.

He pictured them as high classed, always beautifully dressed, and seemingly in complete command of the situation. These were the girls who attended football games, played golf and tennis, rode in new automobiles and were gifted with musical talent. His was the *All-American Girl*.

His first College Girl series was published by the U.S.S. Postcard Co. in 1905. This series revealed an artist with promising talents, and he went on to design many of the "College Girl" series for numerous publishers. Among his most popular works were the Raphael Tuck College Queens and College Kings series.

After the college/university girl fad had run its course, Christy used his many talents to paint beautiful ladies and man/woman lover types. The Reinthal & Newman Co. of New York was his major publisher; however, he did many fine sets for the Knapp Co., Edward Gross, and others. His images were also published and distributed in Europe and Scandinavia.

F. EARL CHRISTY

Reinthal & Newman
No Number

"Love"		12 - 15	15 - 18
"A Sandwich"		12 - 15	15 - 18
"Be With You in a Minute"		10 - 12	12 - 15
"Always Winning"		15 - 18	18 - 22
"Love Dreams"		10 - 12	12 - 15
"Lovingly Yours"		10 - 12	12 - 15
"Swimming"		12 - 15	15 - 18
"A Sweet Surrender" Series			
168	"A Sweet Surrender"	12 - 15	15 - 18
169	"The Pilot"	12 - 15	15 - 18
170	"My Love is Like a Red, Red Rose"	12 - 15	15 - 18
171	"Come Sit Beside Me"	10 - 12	12 - 15
172	"Come With Me"	10 - 12	12 - 15

173	"Love All"	15 - 18	18 - 22

"The Siren" Series

228	"Masks Off!"	10 - 12	12 - 15
229	"Lovingly Yours"	10 - 12	12 - 15
230	"Be With You in a Minute"	10 - 12	12 - 15
231	"The Rose Maid"	10 - 12	12 - 15
232	"The Siren"	12 - 15	15 - 18
233	"Roses are Always in Season"	10 - 12	12 - 15

"The Path of Love" Series

276	"The Love Song"	10 - 12	12 - 15
277	"Love Dreams"	10 - 12	12 - 15
278	"The Love Story"	10 - 12	12 - 15
279	"The Love Match"	10 - 12	12 - 15
280	"The Love Waltz"	10 - 12	12 - 15
281	"Love"	10 - 12	12 - 15

Water Color Series

363	"A Bit of Tea & Gossip"	12 - 15	15 - 18
364	"The Sweetest of All"	12 - 15	15 - 18
365	"For the Wedding Chest"	12 - 15	15 - 18
366	"The Message of Love"	12 - 15	15 - 18
367	"The Day's Work"	15 - 18	18 - 22
368	"A Finishing Touch"	12 - 15	15 - 18

Series 428-433

428	"What Shall I Answer?"	10 - 12	12 - 15
429	"I'm Waiting for You"	10 - 12	12 - 15
430	"Tender Memories"	10 - 12	12 - 15
431	"A Message of Love"	10 - 12	12 - 15
432	"On the Bridal Path"	10 - 12	12 - 15
433	"Always Winning"	15 - 18	18 - 22

Series 618-623

618	"The Girl I Like"	10 - 12	12 - 15
619	"The Girl I Like to Chat With"	10 - 12	12 - 14
620	"The Girl I Like to Walk With"	10 - 12	12 - 15
621	"The Girl I Like to Flirt With"	10 - 12	12 - 15
622	"The Girl I Like to Play With"	15 - 18	18 - 22
623	"The Girl I Like to Sing With"	10 - 12	12 - 15

Series 624-629

624	"By Appointment"	12 - 15	15 - 18
625	"As Promised"	12 - 15	15 - 18
626	"What Shall I Say?"	10 - 12	12 - 15
627	"A Sandwitch"	12 - 15	15 - 18
628	"With Fond Love"	10 - 12	12 - 15
629	"Nearest Her Heart"	10 - 12	12 - 15

Water Color Series 942-947

Earl Christy
Ullman 1499, "Columbia"

Earl Christy
FAS 199, No Caption

Earl Christy, Illustrated Postcard Co.,
198-6, "Hockey is not the only game"

942	"Protected"	10 - 12	12 - 15
943	"Someone is Thinking of You"	10 - 12	12 - 15
944	"Are You There?"	10 - 12	12 - 15
945	"Love, Here is My Heart"	10 - 12	12 - 15
946	"Worth Waiting For"	10 - 12	12 - 15
947	"Not Forgotten"	10 - 12	12 - 15

ENGLISH REPRINTS

2106	"On the Bridal Path"	12 - 15	15 - 18
2107	"Tender Memories"	12 - 15	15 - 18
2109	"Nearest Her Heart"	12 - 15	15 - 18

FAS (F.A. Schneider)

197	Horseback Riding	15 - 18	18 - 25
198	Skates	15 - 18	18 - 25
199	Tennis	20 - 25	25 - 30
200	Golf	20 - 25	25 - 30
201	In an Auto	15 - 18	18 - 25
202	"What the Waves are Saying"	15 - 18	18 - 25
203	Daisies	15 - 18	18 - 25

Edward Gross

Series 3

"Black Eyed Susan"	10 - 12	12 - 15
"God is not All"	10 - 12	12 - 15
"Her Pilot"	10 - 12	12 - 15
"In Deep Water"	10 - 12	12 - 15
"Oldest Trust Co."	10 - 12	12 - 15
"World Before Them"	10 - 12	12 - 15

Knapp Co., N.Y. © **W.M. Sanford**

Paul Heckscher Imp. Ser. 304

1	"Annie Laurie"	10 - 12	12 - 15
2	"The Lost Chord"	10 - 12	12 - 15
3	"Louisiana Lou"	10 - 12	12 - 15
4	"The Rosary"	10 - 12	12 - 15
5	"The Largo"	10 - 12	12 - 15
6	"Love's Old Sweet Song"	10 - 12	12 - 15
7	"Daughter of the Regiment"	10 - 12	12 - 15
8	"Good Night, Beloved"	10 - 12	12 - 15
9	"The Gypsy Maid"	10 - 12	12 - 15
10	"Maryland, My Maryland"	10 - 12	12 - 15
11	"Home, Sweet Home"	10 - 12	12 - 15
12	"Wish I was in Dixie"	10 - 12	12 - 15

Paul Hecksher Imp. Ser. 304
   © **W.M. Sanford**

Earl Christy
R&N 2106, "On the Bridal Path"

Earl Christy
Ill. P.C. Silk 150-2, "Harvard"

Earl Christy
R&N 628, "With Fond Love"

Earl Christy
R&N 228, "Masks Off"

MINIATURE IMAGES
Same as above but different numbers.

371	"Annie Laurie"	12 - 15	15 - 18
381	"The Lost Chord"	12 - 15	15 - 18
391	"Louisiana Lou"	12 - 15	15 - 18
401	"The Rosary"	12 - 15	15 - 18
411	"The Largo"	12 - 15	15 - 18
421	"Love's Old Sweet Song"	12 - 15	15 - 18
431	"Daughters of the Regiment"	12 - 15	15 - 18
441	"Good Night, Beloved"	12 - 15	15 - 18
451	"The Gypsy Maid"	12 - 15	15 - 18
461	"Maryland, My Maryland"	12 - 15	15 - 18
471	"Home, Sweet Home"	12 - 15	15 - 18
481	"Wish I was in Dixie"	12 - 15	15 - 18

Paul Hecksher Import

1025-3	"I'm Ready"	12 - 15	15 - 18

K. Co. (Continued)

103	Girl in Sailor Blouse/Hat	12 - 15	15 - 18
105	Girl W/Lace Collar	12 - 15	15 - 18
114	Girl in Sailor Blouse	12 - 15	15 - 18
115	Beauty, W/Pearl Necklace	12 - 15	15 - 18
116	Sweet Girl W/Long Curl	12 - 15	15 - 18
119	Blonde Girl W/Black Pearls	12 - 15	15 - 18
124	"Prudence"	10 - 12	12 - 15
169	"Let's Go"	12 - 15	15 - 18
176	"Skipper's Mate"	12 - 15	15 - 18
215	"Beauty"	10 - 12	12 - 15
219	"Anna Belle"	10 - 12	12 - 15

Note: There may be cards missing from 103 through 219.

Knapp Co. H. Import Series 318

"The Best of Chums"	12 - 15	15 - 18
"Blossoming Affection"	12 - 15	15 - 18
"Goodbye Summer"	12 - 15	15 - 18
"The Springtime of Friendship"	12 - 15	15 - 18

Knapp Co. H. Import Series 319

"Embracing the Opportunity"	12 - 15	15 - 18
"In Sweet Accord"	12 - 15	15 - 18
"The Message of the Rose"	12 - 15	15 - 18
"Tempting Fate"	12 - 15	15 - 18

1916 Calendar, **Knapp** card by **Sanford**

"I Wish I Was in Dixie"	15 - 18	18 - 22

Jules Bien, 1907
"College" Series 95

Girl and Boy on Football

950	"Yale"	12 - 15	15 - 18
951	"Harvard"	12 - 15	15 - 18
952	"Columbia"	12 - 15	15 - 18
953	"Penn"	12 - 15	15 - 18
954	"Princeton"	12 - 15	15 - 18
955	"Cornell"	12 - 15	15 - 18

Chapman, N.Y., 1910

1032	"A Brisk Walk"	8 - 10	10 - 12
1034	"Waiting Their Turn"	8 - 10	10 - 12
1039	"At the Horse Show"	8 - 10	10 - 12

William B. Christy (His Father)

Unnumbered Series

"Harvard"	12 - 15	15 - 18
"Michigan"	12 - 15	15 - 18
"Penn"	12 - 15	15 - 18
"Princeton"	12 - 15	15 - 18
"Yale"	12 - 15	15 - 18

EAS (Ea. Schwerd Teger)

Girl on Brick Wall Series

"Columbia"	8 - 10	10 - 12
"Cornell"	8 - 10	10 - 12
"Harvard"	8 - 10	10 - 12
"Penn"	8 - 10	10 - 12
"Princeton"	8 - 10	10 - 12
"Yale"	8 - 10	10 - 12

H. Henninger Co.

40 Driving	8 - 10	10 - 12
44 In an Auto (Same as **FAS** 201)	10 - 12	12 - 15
45 Daisies	10 - 12	12 - 15

Illustrated Postal Card & Novelty Co.

Series 133 *

1	"Cornell"	8 - 10	10 - 12
2	"Harvard"	8 - 10	10 - 12
3	"Yale"	8 - 10	10 - 12
4	"Penn"	8 - 10	10 - 12
5	"Princeton"	8 - 10	10 - 12
6	"Columbia"	8 - 10	10 - 12

* W/Silk Applique Dress - add $10-15.

Series 150 *

1	"Cornell"	8 - 10	10 - 12
2	"Harvard"	8 - 10	10 - 12
3	"Yale"	8 - 10	10 - 12
4	"Penn"	8 - 10	10 - 12

5	"Princeton"	8 - 10	10 - 12
6	"Columbia"	8 - 10	10 - 12

* W/Silk Applique Dress - add $10-15.

Note: Numbers are shown on backs of some cards.

Series 160, 1907

160-1	"A Drama"	8 - 10	10 - 12
160-2	"A Critical Moment"	8 - 10	10 - 12
160-3	"The World was Made ..."	8 - 10	10 - 12
160-4	"An Attractive Parasol"	8 - 10	10 - 12
160-5	"Getting Acquainted"	8 - 10	10 - 12
160-6		8 - 10	10 - 12

"Sports" Series

552D	Swinging	6 - 8	8 - 10
554	Bowling	6 - 8	8 - 10
557	Rowing	6 - 8	8 - 10
562	Swimming	6 - 8	8 - 10
567	Driving Old Car	6 - 8	8 - 10
572	Golf	10 - 12	12 - 15
577	Buggy	6 - 8	8 - 10
584	Tennis	10 - 12	12 - 15

Ill. P.C. & Novelty Co.

Series 5006

1			
2			
3	"Swinging"	6 - 8	8 - 10
4			
5			
6			
7			
8	Horse & Buggy	6 - 8	8 - 10
9	Old Car-Harvard	6 - 8	8 - 10
10	Old Car-Yale	6 - 8	8 - 10
11	Old Car-Princeton	6 - 8	8 - 10
12	Old Car-Penn	6 - 8	8 - 10

Platinachrome, 1907

Girl/Pennant form Letter, W/College Yell

"Chicago"	15 - 18	18 - 25
"Columbia"	15 - 18	18 - 25
"Cornell"	15 - 18	18 - 25
"Harvard"	15 - 18	18 - 25
"Michigan"	15 - 18	18 - 25
"Penn"	15 - 18	18 - 25
"Princeton"	15 - 18	18 - 25
"Yale"	15 - 18	18 - 25

Earl Christy
K. Co. Inc. 114, No Caption

Earl Christy
FAS 197, No Caption

Earl Christy
R&N 431, "A Message of Love"

Earl Christy
P. Sander, New York 1908

Platinachrome, © 1905 **F. Earl Christy**
No Numbers or Captions

Two Women in a Car	8 - 10	10 - 12
Woman Golfing	12 - 15	15 - 18
Woman Bowling	8 - 10	10 - 12
Woman-Ice Hockey	8 - 10	10 - 12

P. Sander, N.Y., 1907 (Ill. P.C. Co.)
Series 198

1	"Is a Caddie always Necessary"	12 - 15	15 - 18
2	"Is horseback riding ..."	10 - 12	12 - 15
3	"Trying to make a hit"	10 - 12	12 - 15
4	Tennis	12 - 15	15 - 18
5	"Out for a catch"	10 - 12	12 - 15
6	"Hockey is not the only game"	12 - 15	15 - 18

P. Sander, N.Y., 1908
Series 246 (6) Large Hats *

1	Full Photo	6 - 8	8 - 12
2	1910 Calendar	10 - 12	12 - 15
3	Christmas, Silver	5 - 6	6 - 8
4	Christmas, Gold	5 - 6	6 - 8
5	Woman in Easter Egg	5 - 6	6 - 8
6	Valentine	5 - 6	6 - 8

* Full card is signed. Others cropped & uns.
Note: There are 6 diff. cards of each image!
Series 304-A (6) Signed, 1908

1	Full Card	8 - 10	10 - 12
2	Birthday, White	6 - 8	8 - 10
3	Birthday, Gold	6 - 8	8 - 10
4	Birthday, Silver	6 - 8	8 - 10
5	Woman in Egg	6 - 8	8 - 10
6	Valentine, Checkered	6 - 8	8 - 10
7	Valentine, Gold	6 - 8	8 - 10
8	Horse Shoe, B-day, White	6 - 8	8 - 10
9	Horse Shoe, B-day, Gold	6 - 8	8 - 10
10	Horse Shoe, B-day, Silver	6 - 8	8 - 10

Note: There are 10 diff. cards of each image!
W.H. Sanford   Series 371

"Goodbye Summer"	12 - 15	15 - 18
"Tempting Fate"	12 - 15	15 - 18

Stecher Litho Co., N.Y.
Series 618, Valentines

A	"To My Sweetheart"	8 - 10	10 - 12
C	"To My Valentine" (uns.)	8 - 10	10 - 12
D	"A Valentine Greeting"	8 - 10	10 - 12

F	"A Valentine Greeting"	8 - 10	10 - 12

Souvenir Postcard Co., © 1907 F. Earl Christy
Girl and Football Player W/Banner

1	"Michigan"	10 - 12	12 - 15
2	"Chicago"	10 - 12	12 - 15
3	"Princeton"	10 - 12	12 - 15
4	"Penn"	10 - 12	12 - 15
5	"Cornell"	10 - 12	12 - 15
6	"Yale"	10 - 12	12 - 15
7	"Harvard"	10 - 12	12 - 15
8	"Columbia"	10 - 12	12 - 15

Raphael Tuck
University Girl Series 2453

"Oberlin College"	20 - 22	22 - 25
"West Point"	20 - 22	22 - 25
"Syracuse U."	20 - 22	22 - 25
"Georgetown"	20 - 22	22 - 25
"U.S. Naval Academy"	20 - 22	22 - 25
"Tennessee"	20 - 22	22 - 25

Series 2590

"Iowa"	20 - 22	22 - 25
"U. of Arkansas"	20 - 22	22 - 25
"Valparaiso U."	20 - 22	22 - 25
"Ames"	20 - 22	22 - 25
"Kentucky"	20 - 22	22 - 25
"Penn State"	20 - 22	22 - 25

Series 2593

"Bucknell"	15 - 18	18 - 22
"Colby"	15 - 18	18 - 22
"U. of Maine"	15 - 18	18 - 22
"U. of Notre Dame"	15 - 18	18 - 22

Series 2717

"Mary Baldwin Seminary"	15 - 18	18 - 22

University Girl Series 2625

"Columbia"	15 - 18	18 - 22
"Cornell"	15 - 18	18 - 22
"Harvard"	15 - 18	18 - 22
"Penn"	15 - 18	18 - 22
"Princeton"	15 - 18	18 - 22
"Yale"	15 - 18	18 - 22

Series 2626

"U. of Chicago"	15 - 18	18 - 22
"U. of Illinois"	15 - 18	18 - 22
"Indiana U."	15 - 18	18 - 22

"U. of Michigan"		15 - 18	18 - 22
"U. of Minnesota"		15 - 18	18 - 22
"U. of Wisconsin"		15 - 18	18 - 22
Series 2627			
"Brown U."		15 - 18	18 - 22
"Tulane of La."		15 - 18	18 - 22
"Vanderbilt U."		15 - 18	18 - 22
"U. of Virginia"		15 - 18	18 - 22
"Williston Seminary"		15 - 18	18 - 22
"McGill College"		15 - 18	18 - 22
Series 2766 College Kings			
"Columbia"		60 - 70	70 - 80
"Cornell"		60 - 70	70 - 80
"Chicago"		60 - 70	70 - 80
"Michigan"		60 - 70	70 - 80
Series 2767 College Queens			
"Yale"		60 - 70	70 - 80
"Penn"		60 - 70	70 - 80
"Harvard"		60 - 70	70 - 80
"Princeton"		60 - 70	70 - 80
"Good Luck" Series 2769			
"Not only for today ..."		10 - 12	12 - 15
"Good luck attend you ..."		10 - 12	12 - 15
"Good wishes greet thee ..."		10 - 12	12 - 15
"May Fortune spin ..."		10 - 12	12 - 15
Ullman Mfg. Co.			
College Girls, Ser. 24, © 1905 (uns.)			
1498	"Penn"	6 - 8	8 - 10
1499	"Columbia"	6 - 8	8 - 10
1512	"Yale"	6 - 8	8 - 10
1513	"Harvard"	6 - 8	8 - 10
1514	"Leland Stanford"	6 - 8	8 - 10
1515	"Cornell"	6 - 8	8 - 10
1516	"Princeton"	6 - 8	8 - 10
1517	"Chicago"	6 - 8	8 - 10
College Football Players,			
Ser. 24, © 1905 (uns.)			
1464	"Harvard"	6 - 8	8 - 10
1465	"Princeton"	12 - 15	15 - 18
1466	"Penn"	12 - 15	15 - 18
1467	"Yale"	12 - 15	15 - 18
1518	"Columbia"	12 - 15	15 - 18
1519	"Leland Stanford"	12 - 15	15 - 18
1520	"Chicago"	12 - 15	15 - 18

1521	"Cornell"	12 - 15	15 - 18

Ullman 1907   Girl in Big College Letter Ser.

1990	"Chicago"	10 - 12	12 - 15
1991	"Cornell"	10 - 12	12 - 15
1992	"Michigan"	10 - 12	12 - 15
1993	"Columbia"	10 - 12	12 - 15
1994	"Penn"	10 - 12	12 - 15
1995	"Yale"	10 - 12	12 - 15
1996	"Princeton"	10 - 12	12 - 15
1997	"Harvard"	10 - 12	12 - 15

Other **Ullman** College Girls

569	"Princeton"	6 - 8	8 - 10
574	"Penn"	6 - 8	8 - 10
575	"Harvard"	6 - 8	8 - 10
582	"Yale"	6 - 8	8 - 10

Ullman Co., 1905, N.Y.

501	"Golf"	10 - 12	12 - 15
506	"A Pleasant Ride"	4 - 6	6 - 8
507	"In Fair Japan"	4 - 6	6 - 8
1583	"The Graduate"	8 - 10	10 - 12

U.S.S.P.C. Co. 1905 College Seal Series

1	"Penn"	10 - 12	12 - 14
2	"Princeton"	10 - 12	12 - 14
3	"Harvard" (also leather) *	10 - 12	12 - 14
4	"Yale"	10 - 12	12 - 14
5	"Michigan"	10 - 12	12 - 14
6	"Chicago"	10 - 12	12 - 14
7	"Columbia"	10 - 12	12 - 14
8	"Cornell"	10 - 12	12 - 14

* Add $5-10 for leather cards.

Valentine & Sons
"Artotype" Series, No Numbers

"Columbia"	15 - 18	18 - 22
"Penn"	15 - 18	18 - 22

Friedman-Shelby Shoe Co.
Big Hat Series

Shoe Style 3324	20 - 25	25 - 30
Shoe Style 3332	20 - 25	25 - 30
The Style 3151	20 - 25	25 - 30
Red Goose School Shoes	20 - 25	25 - 30
Shoe Style 3339	20 - 25	25 - 30

Greenfield's Delatour Chocolates, 1911

Girl W/Big Hat, Walks Right	25 - 30	30 - 35
Bulls-Eye Overalls	20 - 25	25 - 30

UNKNOWN
© 1910 F. Earl Christy
Bust of woman w/nosegay & big hat

tied under chin.	8 - 10	10 - 12
Blue dress and pink flowers	8 - 10	10 - 12
Blue hat and red flowers	8 - 10	10 - 12
Orange hat and yellow flowers	8 - 10	10 - 12

Water Colors

650-5	"Embracing the Opportunity"	10 - 12	12 - 15
656-5	"In Sweet Accord"	10 - 12	12 - 15
657-5	"Vacation Days"	10 - 12	12 - 15

FINLAND ISSUES

Pain. Karjalan Kirjap. Oy, Viipuri
N:0 12   Unsigned, No Caption

Same as R&N 173, "Love All"	35 - 40	40 - 50

N:0 6   Signed, No Caption

Girl in white, w/big red umbrella	35 - 40	40 - 45

No Identification Series
   Unsigned, no caption. Same as

R&N 365, "For the Wedding Chest"	30 - 35	35 - 40

W. & G. American Series N:0 7001/1-35
   Girl w/long stemmed roses handing

one to man behind the chair.	35 - 40	40 - 50

CHRISTY, HOWARD CHANDLER (U.S.A.)

Howard Chandler Christy, although of no relation to F. Earl Christy, was also one of the more prominent illustrators of the 1900-1920 era. He did illustrations for many magazines and paintings of "famous people" portraits, but probably gained most fame from his World War I Posters.

Among the paintings he was commissioned to do were those of Presidents Harding and Coolidge, Mussolini, Will Rogers, and Amelia Earhart. His historical painting of "Signing the Constitution" now hangs in the Capitol in Washington, D.C.

For the postcard collectors of today he left many renderings of beautiful ladies. These became known as the "Christy Girls" and were adapted from his magazine illustrations and posters to postcards. His most famous cards were those of "The Army Girl" and "The Navy Girl" published for the Jamestown Exposition of 1907.

HOWARD CHANDLER CHRISTY

Moffat, Yard, & Co., N.Y., 1905			
"The Christy Post Card"		8 - 10	10 - 12
1 "Arbutus" B&W			
2 "At the Opera"			
3 "A City Girl" B&W			
Also appears in partial color.			
4 "The Dance"			
5 "The Debutante"			
6 "Encore"			
7 "Mistletoe" B&W			
Also appears in partial color.			
8 "A Moment of Reflection"			
9 "Reverie" B&W			
10 "A Suburban Girl" B&W			
11 "The Summer Girl" B&W			
12 "Violets" B&W			
Also appears in partial color.			
13 "Waiting"			
14 "Water Lilies" B&W			
15 "The Winter Girl" B&W			
Unnumbered Series, 1908		10 - 12	12 - 14
"The American Queen"			
"American Beauties"			
"At the Theater"			
"Canoe Mates"			
"Drifting"			
"Excess Baggage"			
"A Fisherman's Luck"			
"The Golf Girl"			
"Lilies"			
"On the Beach"			
"Sailing Close"			
"A Summer Girl"			
"Teasing"			
"A Winning Hand"			
Series 3, 1909		10 - 12	12 - 14
"Black-Eyed Susan"			
"Gold is Not All"			
"Her Pilot"			
"In Deep Water"			

"Miss Demure"
"The Oldest Trust Company"
"A Plea For Arbitration"
"The Sweet Girl Graduate"
"The Teasing Girl"

Series 4, 1909	10 - 12	12 - 14

"Au Revoir"
"Congratulations"
"Happiest Hours"
"The Heart of America"
"Her Gift"
"Honeymoon"
"Into the Future"
"Life's Beginning"
"Love Spats"
"Mistletoe"
"Overpowering Beauty"
"A Rose on the Lips"

Edward Gross (6)	10 - 12	12 - 14
Scribner's (8)	10 - 12	12 - 14
Armour & Co, Chicago, 1901, Advertising		
"The Howard Chandler Christy Girl"	15 - 20	20 - 25
A & V. Jamestown Expo., 1907		
"The Army Girl"	60 - 70	70 - 80
"The Navy Girl"	60 - 70	70 - 80
Curt Teich & Co.		
"Boy Scout Jamboree" Linen Card, 1937	10 - 12	12 - 15
FOREIGN		
Novitas Series 21655	12 - 14	14 - 18

"City Girl"
"Drifting"
"Reverie"
"A Summer Girl"
"Violets"
"The World Before Them"

Series 21657 (6)	12 - 14	14 - 18
CLAY, JOHN C. (U.S.A.)		
Detroit Pub. Co.	6 - 8	8 - 10
Rotograph Co. Water colors, Ser. 160	10 - 12	12 - 15
Armour & Co. Advertising		
"The John C. Clay Girl"	10 - 12	12 - 15
CLIRIO, L. (Italy) See Art Deco		
COFFIN, HASKELL (U.S.A.)		
R. C. Co. - Series 205		

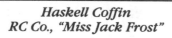

Haskell Coffin
RC Co., "Miss Jack Frost"

Haskell Coffin
K. Co. Inc. 215, "Beauty"

"A Modern Eve"	12 - 15	15 - 20
"An American Queen"	12 - 15	15 - 20
"The Glory of Autumn"	12 - 15	15 - 20
"The Lure of the Poppies"	12 - 15	15 - 20
"Miss Jack Frost"	15 - 18	18 - 20
"Motherhood"	12 - 15	15 - 20
"Queen of the Court"	18 - 20	20 - 22
"The Spring Maid"	15 - 18	18 - 20
"Vanity Fair"	15 - 18	18 - 20
"Winter's Charm"	15 - 18	18 - 20
K. Co. Water Color Series		
215 "Beauty"	15 - 18	18 - 20
216 "Sally"	15 - 18	18 - 20
217 "Ruth"	15 - 18	18 - 20
218 "Billy"	15 - 18	18 - 20
Photo Color Graph Co.		
Ser. 205 "Art Studies"		
1 "Bohemia"	12 - 13	13 - 16
2 "Miss Knickerbocker"	12 - 13	13 - 16
3 "Her First Love Letter"	12 - 13	13 - 16
4 "The Final Touch"	12 - 13	13 - 16

5 "Sweet Sixteen"	14 - 16	16 - 18
6 "Girl From the Golden West"	12 - 14	14 - 16
8 "Pride of the Orient"	12 - 14	14 - 16
9 "News from the Sunny South"	12 - 14	14 - 16
Others	12 - 13	13 - 16
"Flower & Figure" Series 280	10 - 12	12 - 14
1 Iris		
2 Violet		
3 Poppies		
4 Narcissus		
5 Goldenrod		
6 Daffodils		
7 Hollyhock		
8 Water Lily		
9 Nasturtium		
10 Rose		
11 Sweet Pea		
12 Morning Glory		
Fantasy Women Ser. "Celia" Semi-nude	15 - 18	18 - 22
Advertising Cards		
Blue Bell Brand Candies (2)	15 - 18	18 - 22
A. R. & C.i.B. Co.		
417 "An American Queen"	12 - 15	15 - 18
"The Glory of Autumn"	12 - 15	15 - 18
"The Joy of the Hunt"	12 - 15	15 - 18
"Miss Jack Frost"	12 - 15	15 - 18
"Ruth"	12 - 15	15 - 18
"Winter's Charm"	12 - 15	15 - 18
"Vanity Fair"	12 - 15	15 - 18
H & S Company		
1551 D 3 "A New York Belle"	10 - 12	12 - 14
1551 D 6 "Thoughtful"	10 - 12	12 - 14
Others, W/Captions	10 - 12	12 - 14
Others, No Captions	8 - 10	10 - 12
Advertising - Hires Root Beer Girl	15 - 20	20 - 25
COLOMBO (Italy) See Art Deco		
CORBELLA, T. (Italy) See Art Deco		
CREMIEUX, ED. (France) See French Glamour		
CYRANICUS (Italy)		
CRANDALL, JOHN BRADSHAW		
K. Co., N.Y.	7 - 8	8 - 10
DANIELL, EVA See Art Nouveau		
DAY, FRANCES	4 - 5	5 - 6
DAVIS, STANLEY (U.S.A.)	8 - 10	10 - 12

Frank Desch
K. Co. 309-2, "Virginia"

Frank Desch
K. Co. Inc. 309-4, "Diana"

DAY, FRANCES (U.S.A.)	5 - 6	6 - 7
DEGAMI (Italy) See Art Deco		
DERNINI (Italy) See Art Deco		
DERRANTI, D. (Italy) See Art Deco		
DESCH, FRANK (U.S.A.)		
Knapp Co. Series 303	12 - 15	15 - 18
"Annette"		
"Diana"		
"Eloise"		
"Flora"		
"Florence"		
"Grace"		
"Ida"		
"Isabel"		
"Laura"		
"Lillian"		
"Virginia"		
"Violet"		
Knapp Co. Series 309	12 - 15	15 - 18
Knapp Co. Series 50	10 - 12	12 - 15
Knapp Co. Others	12 - 15	15 - 18

Knapp Co. Calendars		
9443 "Grace"	15 - 18	18 - 22
9453 "Rosina"	15 - 18	18 - 22
9503 "Laura"	15 - 18	18 - 22
9513 "Felicia	15 - 18	18 - 22
H. Import Co. Series 300	10 - 12	12 - 15
DEWEY, ALFRED (U.S.A.)		
Boston Sunday Post		
Romantic Baseball - Ser. 22	7 - 10	10 - 12
"Caught Stealing"		
"A Costly Error"		
"A Double Play"		
"A Sacrifice"		
"A Single"		
"A Shut-Out"		
Reinthal & Newman		
"Weather Forecast" Ser. 221 (12)	7 - 8	8 - 10
"Eventful Hours" Ser. 270-275	8 - 10	10 - 12
"Mother & Child" Ser. 450-455	7 - 8	8 - 10
"Love Signal" Ser. 456-461	7 - 8	8 - 10
"Moon" Ser. 462-467	8 - 10	10 - 12
"Smoke" Ser. 668-673	8 - 10	10 - 12
"Love & Nature" Ser. 807-812	7 - 8	8 - 10
DIHLEN, H.N. (U.S.A.)	5 - 6	6 - 7
DITZLER, H.N. (U.S.A.)	6 - 7	7 - 9
DOUBECK		
Ackerman Co.		
"Historic Ladies" Series	10 - 12	12 - 15
DUDOVICH, M. (Italy) See Art Deco		
"Eureka" Series IV (6)	12 - 15	15 - 20
DUNCAN, FREDERICK (U.S.A.)		
Reinthal & Newman		
Water color Ser. 930-935	12 - 15	15 - 18
K. Co.	12 - 15	15 - 18
ELLIOTT, KATHRYN (U.S.A.)		
Gartner & Bender Issues	4 - 5	5 - 8
ELLKA		
M. Munk, Vienna		
Head Studies	10 - 12	12 - 18
FABIANO (Italy) See Art Deco, French Glamour		
FARINI, MAY L. (U.S.A.)	6 - 8	12 - 18
FIDLER ALICE LOUELLA (U.S.A.)	6 - 8	12 - 18
FIDLER, PEARL EUGENIA	6 - 8	8 - 12
LEMUNYAN, PEARL FIDLER	6 - 8	8 - 12

FISCHER, C. (U.S.A.)	6 - 8	8 - 10
FISHER, HARRISON (U.S.A.)		

Harrison Fisher was one of the most prolific of all American illustrators. His works, mainly of beautiful women of the era, are desired by collectors throughout the world. The values of his postcards tend to rise almost yearly.

The principal publisher of Fisher postcards was the New York firm of Reinthal & Newman. They published many of his cards in various series ranging from the No-Numbered, the 100's and on through the rare and final 900 series, and then did the English reprints in the 1000 and 2000 series.

The Detroit Publishing Company, beginning around 1905, published a small group of Fisher cards from what were originally illustrations in stories in the old *LIFE* magazine. The cards were numbered in the Detroit 14,000 series and were printed mainly in sepia, with a few being in black and white.

The American book publishers who used Fisher's illustrations in their novels issued postcards to advertise their books. These advertising postcards usually showed a beautiful Fisher lady on one-half of the double cards and an order form on the other half. These cards are among the most sought after and most expensive of his American-published cards.

Foreign publishers also did several series which are very much in demand. Among the most elusive, and those commanding the highest prices, are the cards produced in Finland and Russia.

Detroit Publishing Co.	10 - 12	12 - 14
14028 "I don't see ..."		
14036 "An Important ..."		
14037 "So you don't Kiss ..."		
14038 "Between Themselves ..."		
14039 "Can you give your Answer?"		
14040 "I suppose you Lost ..."		
14041 "It's just Horrid ..."		
14042 "Wasn't There ..."		
14043 "And shall we Never ..."		
14044 "I fear there is no Hope"		
Book Adv. Cards (G&D, Dodd-Mead, etc.)		
Double-folded Cards	85 - 90	90 - 100

W/Reply section missing	60 - 70	75 - 85
"The Bill Tippers"		
"Featherbone Girl"		
"54-40 or Fight"		
"Half A Rogue"		
"The Hungry Heart"		
"Jane Cable"		
"Jewel Weed"		
"The Man From Brodney's"		
"My Lady of Cleeve"		
"Nedra"		
"The One Way Out"		
"A Taste of Paradise"		
"The Title Market"		
"To My Valentine"		
"Goose Girl"		
Armour & Co., U.S.	50 - 60	60 - 70
Armour & Co., Germany	70 - 75	75 - 80
Reinthal & Newman		

Harrison Fisher
R&N 979, "Somewhere in France"

Harrison Fisher
R&N 845, "Sparring for Time"

Unnumbered

"After the Dance"	10 - 15	15 - 18
"The Critical Moment"	10 - 15	15 - 18
"The Motor Girl"	12 - 18	18 - 22
"Ready for the Run"	10 - 15	15 - 18
"Ruth"	10 - 15	15 - 18
"A Tennis Champion"	15 - 18	18 - 22
"The Winter Girl"	15 - 18	18 - 22

101 Series (12)

"American Beauties"	10 - 15	15 - 18
"Anticipation"	10 - 15	15 - 18
"Beauties"	12 - 15	15 - 18
"Danger"	10 - 12	12 - 15
"A Fair Driver"	15 - 18	18 - 22
"Odd Moments"	12 - 15	15 - 18
"The Old Miniature"	12 - 15	15 - 18
"Over the Tea Cup"	15 - 18	18 - 22
"Reflections"	15 - 18	18 - 22
"The Study Hour"	12 - 15	15 - 18
"A Thoroughbred"	15 - 18	15 - 18
"Those Bewitching Eyes"	12 - 15	15 - 18

102 Series (6)

"American Girl in England"	10 - 15	15 - 18
"American Girl in France"	10 - 15	15 - 18
"American Girl in Ireland"	10 - 15	15 - 18
"American Girl in Italy"	10 - 15	15 - 18
"American Girl in Japan"	10 - 15	15 - 18
"American Girl in Netherlands"	10 - 15	15 - 18

103 Series (6)

"At Home with Art"	10 - 12	12 - 15
"The Canoe"	10 - 12	12 - 15
"Engagement Days"	12 - 15	15 - 18
"Fisherman's Luck"	12 - 15	15 - 18
"Fore"	18 - 22	22 - 26
"Wanted, an Answer"	12 - 15	15 - 18

108 Series (12)

"An Old Song"	12 - 15	15 - 18
"The Ambush"	12 - 15	15 - 18
"The Artist"	12 - 15	15 - 18
"The Bride"	20 - 22	22 - 26
"The Debutante"	15 - 18	18 - 22
"Dumb Luck"	15 - 18	18 - 22
"He's Only Joking"	15 - 18	18 - 22
"His Gift"	15 - 18	18 - 22

Harrison Fisher
R&N 261, "Girlie"

Harrison Fisher
R&N Ser. 108, "Dumb Luck"

"The Kiss"	12 - 15	15 - 18
"Lost?"	15 - 18	18 - 22
"Oh! Promise Me"	15 - 18	18 - 22
"Song of the Soul"	15 - 18	18 - 22
"Two Up"	18 - 22	22 - 25
123 Series (6)		
"Making Hay"	10 - 12	12 - 15
"A Modern Eve"	12 - 15	15 - 18
"Taking Toll"	10 - 12	12 - 15
"You Will Marry a Dark Man"	10 - 12	12 - 15
"The Fudge Party"	12 - 15	15 - 18
"In Clover"	12 - 15	15 - 18
180-191 Series		
180 "Well Protected"	15 - 18	18 - 22
181 "The Rose"	15 - 18	18 - 22
182 "Miss Santa Claus"	22 - 25	25 - 30
183 "Miss Knickerbocker"	15 - 18	18 - 22
184 "Following the Race"	15 - 18	18 - 22
185 "Naughty, Naughty!"	20 - 22	22 - 25
186 "The Proposal"	10 - 12	12 - 15
187 "The Trousseau"	10 - 12	12 - 15

188 "The Wedding"	12 - 15	15 - 18
189 "The Honeymoon"	10 - 12	12 - 15
190 "The First Evening ..."	10 - 12	12 - 15
191 "Their New Love"	10 - 12	12 - 15
192-203 Series		
192 "Cherry Ripe"	15 - 18	18 - 22
193 "Undue Haste"	15 - 18	18 - 22
194 "Sweetheart"	15 - 18	18 - 22
195 "Vanity"	15 - 18	18 - 22
196 "Beauties"	15 - 18	18 - 22
197 "Lips for Kisses"	15 - 18	18 - 22
198 "Bewitching Maiden"	15 - 18	18 - 22
199 "Leisure Moments"	15 - 18	18 - 22
200 "And Yet Her Eyes..."	15 - 18	18 - 22
201 "Roses"	15 - 18	18 - 22
202 "In the Toils"	15 - 18	18 - 22
203 "Maid to Worship"	20 - 22	22 - 25
252-263 Series		
252 "Dreaming of You"	15 - 18	18 - 22
253 "Luxury"	15 - 18	18 - 22
254 "Pals"	15 - 18	18 - 22
255 "Homeward Bound"	12 - 15	15 - 18
256 "Preparing to Conquer"	15 - 18	18 - 22
257 "Love Lyrics"	15 - 18	18 - 22
258 "Tempting Lips"	15 - 18	18 - 22
259 "Good Night"	12 - 15	15 - 18
260 "Bows Attract Beaus"	15 - 18	18 - 22
261 "Girlie"	15 - 18	18 - 22
262 "Beauty and Value"	15 - 18	18 - 22
263 "A Prairie Belle"	15 - 18	18 - 22
300 Series		
300 "Auto Kiss"	15 - 18	18 - 22
301 "Sweethearts Asleep"	22 - 25	25 - 30
302 "Behave!"	15 - 18	18 - 22
303 "All Mine!"	12 - 15	15 - 18
304 "Thoroughbreds"	20 - 22	22 - 25
305 "The Laugh is on You"	15 - 18	18 - 22
Water Color Ser.		
381 "All's Well"	15 - 18	18 - 25
382 "Two Roses"	15 - 18	18 - 25
383 "Contentment"	15 - 18	18 - 22
384 "Not Yet - But Soon"	12 - 15	15 - 18
385 "Smile Even if it Hurts"	15 - 18	18 - 22
386 "Speak!"	15 - 18	18 - 25

Harrison Fisher
R&N No #, "Over the Teacup"

Harrison Fisher
R&N 846, "Confidences"

387 "Welcome Home"	12 - 15	15 - 18
388 "A Helping Hand"	15 - 18	18 - 22
389 "Undecided"	15 - 18	18 - 25
390 "Well Guarded"	15 - 18	18 - 25
391 "My Lady Waits"	15 - 18	18 - 25
392 "Gathering Honey"	15 - 18	18 - 22
400-423 Series		
400 "Looking Backward"	18 - 20	20 - 25
401 "Art and Beauty"	15 - 20	20 - 25
402 "The Chief Interest"	15 - 20	20 - 25
403 "Passing Fancies"	15 - 20	20 - 25
404 "The Pink of Perfection"	15 - 20	20 - 25
405 "He Won't Bite"	15 - 20	20 - 25
406 "Refreshments"	15 - 20	20 - 25
407 "Princess Pat"	18 - 22	22 - 28
408 "Fine Feathers"	15 - 20	20 - 25
409 "Isn't He Sweet?"	18 - 22	22 - 28
410 "Maid at Arms"	18 - 22	22 - 28
411 "He Cometh Not"	15 - 20	20 - 25
412 "Can't You Speak?"	18 - 22	22 - 28
413 "What Will She Say?"	15 - 20	20 - 25

414 "Music Hath Charm"	15 - 20	20 - 25
415 "Do I Intrude"	15 - 20	20 - 25
416 "My Queen"	18 - 22	22 - 28
417 "My Lady Drives"	18 - 22	22 - 25
418 "Ready and Waiting"	15 - 20	20 - 25
419 "The Parasol"	15 - 20	20 - 25
420 "Tempting Lips"	15 - 20	20 - 25
421 "Mary"	18 - 22	22 - 25
422 "Courting Attention"	15 - 20	20 - 25
423 "My Pretty Neighbor"	18 - 22	22 - 28

600-617 Series

600 "A Winter Sport"	20 - 25	25 - 30
601 "Winter Whispers"	20 - 25	25 - 30
602 "A Christmas Him"	20 - 25	25 - 30
603 "A Sprig of Holly"	20 - 25	25 - 30
604 "Snow Birds"	20 - 25	25 - 30
605 "A Christmas Belle"	20 - 25	25 - 30
606 "The Serenade"	20 - 25	25 - 30
607 "The Secret"	20 - 25	25 - 30
608 "Good Morning, Mama"	20 - 25	25 - 30
609 "A Passing Glance"	20 - 25	25 - 30
610 "A Fair Exhibitor"	20 - 25	25 - 30
611 "Paddling Their Own Canoe"	18 - 20	20 - 25
612 "Tea Time"	20 - 25	25 - 30
613 "The Favorite Pillow"	20 - 25	25 - 30
614 "Don't Worry"	20 - 25	25 - 30
615 "June"	20 - 25	25 - 30
616 "Sketching"	20 - 25	25 - 30
617 "Chocolate"	20 - 25	25 - 30

700-705 Water Color Series
"The Senses"

700 "The First Meeting" Sight	20 - 25	25 - 30
701 "Falling in Love" Smell	20 - 25	25 - 30
702 "Making Progress" Taste	20 - 25	25 - 30
703 "Anxious Moments" Hearing	20 - 25	25 - 30
704 "To Love and Cherish" Touch	20 - 25	25 - 30
705 "The Greatest Joy" Common Sense	20 - 25	25 - 30

762-773 Series

762 "Alone at Last"	12 - 15	15 - 18
763 "Alert"	15 - 18	18 - 22
764 "Close to Shore"	15 - 18	18 - 22
765 "Looks Good to Me"	12 - 15	15 - 18
766 "Passers By"	12 - 15	15 - 18
767 "At the Toilet"	15 - 18	18 - 22

768 "Drifting" *	12 - 15	15 - 18
769 "Her Favorite Him" *	12 - 15	15 - 18
770 "The Third Party" *	12 - 15	15 - 18
771 "Inspiration" *	15 - 18	18 - 22
772 "Dangers of the Deep" *	12 - 15	15 - 18
773 "Farewell" *	12 - 15	15 - 18

* Add $5 to prices if German caption.
Cards usually are slightly oversized
and have Universal copyright.

800 Series

819 "Here's Happiness"	15 - 18	18 - 22

Cosmopolitan/Star
800 Series

832 "Wireless"	20 - 25	25 - 30
833 "Neptune's Daughter"	20 - 25	25 - 30
834 "Her Game"	20 - 25	25 - 30
835 "All Mine"	18 - 20	20 - 25
836 "On Summer Seas"	20 - 25	25 - 30
837 "Autumn's Beauty"	20 - 25	25 - 30
838 "The Only Pebble"	20 - 25	25 - 30
839 "A Love Score"	25 - 30	30 - 35
840 "Spring Business"	20 - 25	25 - 30
841 "The King of Hearts"	20 - 25	25 - 30
842 "Fair and Warmer"	20 - 25	25 - 30
843 "Baby Mine"	20 - 25	25 - 30
844 "Compensation"	20 - 25	25 - 30
845 "Sparring for Time"	20 - 25	25 - 30
846 "Confidences"	20 - 25	25 - 30
847 "Her Future"	20 - 25	25 - 30
848 "Day Dreams"	20 - 25	25 - 30
849 "Muriel"	20 - 25	25 - 30
856 "Song of the Soul"	15 - 20	20 - 25
860 "By Right of Conquest" *	18 - 22	22 - 25
861 "The Evening Hour" *	18 - 22	22 - 25
862 "Caught Napping" *	20 - 25	25 - 30
863 "A Novice" *	20 - 25	25 - 30
864 "Winners" *	20 - 25	25 - 30
865 "A Midsummer Reverie" *	25 - 30	30 - 35
866 "When the Leaves Turn" *	20 - 25	25 - 30
867 "Over the Teacup" *	20 - 25	25 - 30
868 "A Ripening Bud" *	20 - 25	25 - 30
869 "I'm Ready" *	20 - 25	25 - 30
870 "Reflections" *	20 - 25	25 - 30

Harrison Fisher
R&N 198, "Bewitching Maiden"

Harrison Fisher
R&N 408, "Fine Feathers"

Harrison Fisher
30/25-10-US, "My Man"

H. Fisher, Publisher at Polyphot,
"The Eavesdropper"

871 "Peggy" *	20 - 25	25 - 30
872 "Penseroso" *	20 - 25	25 - 30
873 "The Girl He Left Behind" *	20 - 25	25 - 30
874 "A Spring Blossom" *	20 - 25	25 - 30
875 "A Study in Contentment" *	20 - 25	25 - 30
876 "A Lucky Beggar" *	20 - 25	25 - 30
877 "Roses" *	20 - 25	25 - 30

* With Cosmopolitan Print Dept. byline add $5

900-979 Series

970 "Chums"	50 - 75	75 - 100
971 "Cynthia"	50 - 75	75 - 100
972 "A Forest Flower"	50 - 75	75 - 100
973 "The Dancing Girl"	50 - 75	75 - 100
974 "Each Stitch a Prayer"	50 - 100	100 - 125
975 "The Sailor Maid"	75 - 100	100 - 125
976 "My Man"	75 - 100	100 - 125
977 "My Hero"	75 - 100	100 - 125
978 "Her Heart's in Service"	75 - 100	100 - 125
979 "Somewhere in France"	100 - 125	125 - 150

1001-1005 Series
English Reprints

1001 "Cherry Ripe"	20 - 25	25 - 30
1002 "Beauties"	20 - 25	25 - 30
1003 "Vanity"	20 - 25	25 - 30
1004 "Maid to Worship"	20 - 25	25 - 30
1005 "And Yet Her Eyes Can ..."	20 - 25	25 - 30

2000 Series
English Reprints

2040 "Love Lyrics"	15 - 20	20 - 25
2041 "A Fair Exhibitor"	18 - 22	22 - 28
2042 "Can't You Speak"	15 - 20	22 - 28
2043 "Serenade"	15 - 20	20 - 25
2044 "Undecided"	15 - 20	20 - 25
2045 "Behave!"	15 - 20	20 - 25
2046 "Princess Pat"	20 - 25	25 - 30
2047 "Good Little Indian"	15 - 20	20 - 25
2048 "Chocolate"	15 - 20	20 - 25
2049 "Beauty and Value"	15 - 20	20 - 25
2050 "Contentment"	15 - 20	20 - 25
2051 "Preparing to Conquer"	15 - 20	20 - 25
2053 "The Kiss"	15 - 20	20 - 25
2054 "What to See in America"	15 - 20	20 - 25
2069 "Paddling their own Canoe"	15 - 20	20 - 25
2076 "Good Morning, Mama"	15 - 20	20 - 25

2086 "The Pink of Perfection"	15 - 20	20 - 25
2087 "He Won't Bite"	18 - 22	22 - 28
2088 "Following the Race"	15 - 20	20 - 25
2089 "The Rose"	15 - 20	20 - 25
2090 "Well Protected"	15 - 20	20 - 25
2091 "Sketching"	15 - 20	20 - 25
2092 "Ready and Waiting"	15 - 20	20 - 25
2093 "The Parasol"	15 - 20	20 - 25
2094 "Courting Attention"	15 - 20	20 - 25
2095 "Mary"	15 - 20	20 - 25
2096 "Refreshments"	15 - 20	20 - 25
2097 "Isn't He Sweet?"	18 - 22	22 - 28
2098 "The Old Miniature"	15 - 20	20 - 25
2100 "Odd Moments"	15 - 20	20 - 25
2101 "Tea Time"	15 - 20	20 - 25
2102 "Good Night!"	15 - 20	20 - 25
2103 "A Prairie Belle"	15 - 20	20 - 25

FOREIGN ISSUES

FINLAND

All Finnish cards are very rare and extremely elusive. None have the R&N Copyright and all are untitled. Cards are titled using names from similar R&N images. Several have not appeared as postcards and are named if a title is known. Three have been entitled by the author until the true title surfaces.

30/25 Series

"Snowbird" *	150 - 175	175 - 225
"Merry Christmas" by author *	150 - 175	175 - 225
"Welcome Home," variety *	150 - 175	175 - 225
"A Midsummer Reverie"	140 - 165	165 - 220
"Close to Shore"	140 - 165	165 - 220
"Winners"	140 - 165	165 - 220
"My Hero"	140 - 165	165 - 220
"Winifred" *	140 - 165	165 - 220
"When the Leaves Turn"	125 - 150	150 - 175
"My Man"	125 - 150	150 - 175
"King of Hearts"	125 - 150	150 - 175
"Not Yet, But Soon"	125 - 150	150 - 175
"Autumn's Beauty"	125 - 150	150 - 175
"On Summer Seas"	125 - 150	150 - 175
"Baby Mine"	125 - 150	150 - 175

"Muriel"	120 - 140	140 - 165
"Caught Napping"	120 - 140	140 - 165
"Beauty and Value"	120 - 140	140 - 165
"Day Dreams"	120 - 140	140 - 165
"Stringing Them" * **	120 - 140	140 - 165
"All Mine"	120 - 140	140 - 165
"Two Roses"	120 - 140	140 - 165
"Reflections"	120 - 140	140 - 165
"Love Lyrics"	120 - 145	140 - 165
"An Idle Hour"	120 - 145	140 - 165

Note: For unsigned cards add $20 - 25 each.
* Image has not appeared on any R&N postcard.
** From Bowers Budd-Budd Book "Harrison Fisher"

The N:O Numbered Series

N:O 5 "Playing the Game" *	175 - 200	200 - 250
Unsigned		
N:O 10 "Midsummer Reverie"	175 - 200	200 - 250
Untitled		
N:O 4 "Close to Shore"	165 - 190	190 - 240

Harrison Fisher
30/25, "Snowbird"

Harrison Fisher
30/25, "Merry Christmas"

N:O 7 "A Novice"   165 - 225   190 - 225
N:O 11 "At the Toilet"   165 - 190   190 - 225
N:O 13 "Welcome Home"   165 - 190   190 - 225
W. & G. American Series No. 7001/1-35
Unsigned, no Numbers, no Captions
"Following the Race," No. 184   165 - 190   190 - 250
"American Beauties,"   No. 101   165 - 190   190 - 250
"Alert," No. 763   165 - 190   190 - 250
"Yet Some Prefer Mtns.," No. 571   165 - 190   190 - 250
"At the Toilet," No. 767   165 - 195   190 - 250
  W. & G. American Series No. 7001/36-50
Unsigned, no Numbers, no Captions
"A Sprig of Holly," No. 603   165 - 190   190 - 250
"The Favorite Pillow," No. 613   165 - 190   190 - 250
"Girlie," No. 261   165 - 190   190 - 250
W. & G. American Series No. 7031/1-7
Unsigned, no Numbers, no Captions
"Eavesdropping" *   200 - 225   225 - 250
* Has never appeared on an R&N postcard.
Titled by Author.
Pain. Karjalan Kirjap. Oy., Viipuri Series
Numbered, Unsigned, no Captions
N:O 5 "Playing the Game" *   175 - 200   200 - 250
N:O 10 "A Midsummer Reverie," No. 865   175 - 200   200 - 250
N:O 4 "Close to Shore," No. 764   160 - 190   190 - 235
N:O 7 "A Novice," No. 863   160 - 190   190 - 235
* Has never appeared on an R&N postcard.
K.K. Oy N:O 1-20 Series
Signed, no Numbers, no Captions
"Mistletoe" *   200 - 225   225 - 275
"Thoroughbreds," No. 304   160 - 190   190 - 235
* Has never appeared on an R&N postcard.
Titled by Author.
The Publisher at Polyphot Series
Unsigned, no Numbers, no Captions
"Eavesdropping" *   200 - 225   225 - 275
"A Sprig of Holly," No. 603   150 - 175   175 - 225
"Don't Worry," No. 614   150 - 175   175 - 225
"Following the Race," No. 184   150 - 175   175 - 225
* Has never appeared on an R&N postcard.
Titled by the Author.
The "No Identification Series"
Unsigned, no Numbers, no Captions.
"Autumn's Beauty," No. 837   175 - 200   200 - 250

Harrison Fisher
N:O Number "Playing the Game"

Harrison Fisher
KKOY N:O 1/20, "Mistletoe"

"Following the Race," No. 184	175 - 200	200 - 250
"Contentment," No. 383	175 - 200	200 - 250
"The Only Pebble," No. 838	175 - 200	200 - 250
The S & K Kouvola Reversed Image Series		
Unsigned, no Numbers, no Captions		
"Snowbird" *	225 - 250	250 - 300
"Winners," No. 864	225 - 250	250 - 300
"Study in Contentment," No. 875	225 - 250	250 - 300
The Real Photo Card Series		
Signed, no numbers, no Captions		
"American Beauties," Ser. 101	75 - 85	85 - 100
"Daydreams," No. 848	75 - 85	85 - 100
"Drifting," No. 768	75 - 85	85 - 100
"A Novice," No. 863	75 - 85	85 - 100
The Otto Andersin, Pori Series		
Unsigned, no Numbers, no Captions		
"Close To Shore," No. 765	225 - 250	250 - 300
"Drifting," No. 768	225 - 250	250 - 300

A 72-PAGE BOOK, "THE SUPER RARE POSTCARDS OF HARRISON FISHER," PUBLISHED IN MARCH, 1992, ILLUSTRATES WITH PHOTOS ALL THE FINNISH POSTCARDS LISTED ABOVE. THE BOOK IS AVAILABLE FROM: COLONIAL HOUSE, P.O. BOX 609, ENKA, NC 28728. PRICE IS $11.95, PLUS $2 POSTAGE IN U.S.A. AND $4 OVERSEAS. THE BOOK WAS WRITTEN BY JOSEPH L. MASHBURN AND IS A MUST FOR ALL FISHER COLLECTORS.

RUSSIAN CARDS BY FISHER

"Richard Phillips" Backs

No. 117 "Hexenaugen"	75 - 100	100 - 150
No. 83 "A Taste of Paradise"	75 - 100	100 - 150
No. 834 "Vanity"	75 - 100	100 - 150
Other	75 - 100	100 - 150

Russian-Polish Real Photo Types
AWE W/Russian/Polish Back

"Miss Knickerbocker"	75 - 100	100 - 150
"Miss Santa Clause" No. 182	75 - 100	100 - 125
Others	75 - 100	100 - 125

Russian-English Backs

No. 24 "Sport" (Following the Race)	75 - 100	100 - 150
Others	75 - 100	100 - 150

Apollon Sophia

No. 21 "La Musique" (The Artist)	75 - 90	90 - 125
Others	75 - 90	90 - 125
Other Russian Printed	75 - 100	100 - 125

GERMAN-AUSTRIAN FISHER CARDS
MEU

"In the Country" (R&N 131)	70 - 75	75 - 80

MEU/Alfred Schweizer

Either or Both, No Captions	75 - 100	100 - 125
"Vienne" Series 806	60 - 75	75 - 80
JTK "Kron-Trier" Series	60 - 75	75 - 80

M.J.S.

"The Kiss" (no Caption)	40 - 50	50 - 60

Utig de Muick, Amsterdam

"The Honeymoon"	50 - 60	60 - 75

Friedrich O. Wolter

"Peggy"	40 - 50	50 - 60

FLAGG, JAMES MONTGOMERY (U.S.A.)
  Detroit Publishing Co.

B&W 14000 Ser.	8 - 10	10 - 15
14011 "The Sweet Magic of Smoke"		
14149 "Sir Charles"		
14150 "It Certainly Wasn't"		
14151 "For Heavens Sake"		
14152 "So Sensible"		
14153 "Not Bad to Take"		
14154 "Beyond More Conjecture"		
14155 "A Cold Proposition"		
14156 "If You Get Gay"		
14157 "If You're a Perfect Gent"		
14158 "Make it Pleasant for Him"		

  Henderson Litho

501 "Engaged - His Attitude"	6 - 8	8 - 10
2503 "Something on Account"	6 - 8	8 - 10

  Reinthal & Newman
  "Miss Behaving" Series

288 "A Club Sandwich"	10 - 12	12 - 14
289 "Putting Out the Flames"	10 - 12	12 - 14
290 "Miss Behaving!"	10 - 12	12 - 14
291 "The Most Exciting Moment"	10 - 12	12 - 14
292 "The Real Love Game"	10 - 12	12 - 14
293 "Dry Goods"	12 - 15	15 - 18

  TP & Co., N.Y.
  Series 738 Sepia

"Trouble Somewhere"	8 - 9	9 - 10
Series 751		
"The Hypnotist"	10 - 12	12 - 14
"The Only Way to Eat an Orange"	10 - 12	12 - 14
"Say When"	10 - 12	12 - 14
Series 818-8 "Holding Hands"	10 - 12	12 - 14
Series 818-10		
"In The Hands of the Receiver"	10 - 12	12 - 14

FONTAN, LEO (France) See French Glamour

FOSTER, F.D. (U.S.A.)	4 - 5	5 - 6

FRANZONI (Italy) See Art Deco
FREIXAS, J. (U.S.A.)

Winsch, Copyright	20 - 25	30 - 40

GALLAIS, P. (France) See French Glamour
GAYAC (France) See French Glamour
GERBAULT (France) See French Glamour

Charles Dana Gibson
Gibson Heads 6

Charles Dana Gibson
Gibson Heads 4

Charles Dana Gibson
Gibson Heads 5

Charles Dana Gibson
Gibson Heads 3

GIBSON, CHARLES DANA (U.S.A.)
  Detroit Publishing Co.
  B & W 14000 Ser.

14000 "Has She a Heart?"	8 - 10	10 - 12
14003 "Their Presence of Mind"	8 - 10	10 - 12
14004 "Melting"	8 - 10	10 - 12
14005 "When Hunting ..."	8 - 10	10 - 12
14006 "Last Days of Summer"	8 - 10	10 - 12
14008 "The Dog"	8 - 10	10 - 12
14009 "Who Cares"	8 - 10	10 - 12
14017 "Good Game for Two"	10 - 12	12 - 14
14019 "Here it is Christmas"	8 - 10	10 - 12
14029 "The Half Orphan"	8 - 10	10 - 12
14046 "Bathing Suits"	8 - 10	10 - 12
14048 "The Half Orphan"	8 - 10	10 - 12
14050 "America Picturesque"	8 - 10	10 - 12
14051 "The Stout Gentleman"	8 - 10	10 - 12
14052 "No Wonder the Sea Serpent ..."	8 - 10	10 - 12
14054 "Stepped On"	8 - 10	10 - 12
14055 "Mr. A Merger Hogg ..."	8 - 10	10 - 12
14057 "Ill Blows the Wind ..."	8 - 10	10 - 12
14059 "Rival Beauties"	8 - 10	10 - 12
14065 "The Gibson Girl"	12 - 15	15 - 18
14066 "Jane"	10 - 12	12 - 15
14067 "Mabel"	10 - 12	12 - 15
14068 "Amy"	10 - 12	12 - 15
14069 "Eleanor"	10 - 12	12 - 15
14070 "Margaret"	10 - 12	12 - 15
14071 "Molly"	10 - 12	12 - 15
14072 "Helen"	10 - 12	12 - 15
14074 "The Sporting Girl"	12 - 15	15 - 18

  James Henderson & Sons

Sepia Heads	8 - 10	10 - 12
"Annie"		
"Clorinda"		
"Gladys"		
"Maude"		
"Nina"		
"Peggy"		
"Beatrice"		
"Bertha"		
"Eileen"		
Comics (36)	5 - 6	6 - 8

GILBERT, C. ALLEN (U.S.A.)

J. Henderson Co. - Heads Series	10 - 12	12 - 15
Schweizer & Co. - Emb., Sepia	12 - 15	15 - 18
GILSON, T. (U.S.A.)	6 - 8	8 - 10
GNISCHAF, RUAB (German)	6 - 8	8 - 10
GODELA, D. (Italy)		
Series 272 Head Studies	12 - 15	15 - 20
Series 296 Head Studies	12 - 15	15 - 18
GOBBI, D. (Italy) See Art Deco		
GRAF, MARTE See Art Deco & Silhouettes		
GREENE, FREDERICK (U.S.A.)	5 - 6	6 - 7
GREFE, WILL (U.S.A.)		
Moffat, Yard Co.		
"Playing Card Queens"	15 - 18	18 - 22
"Club"		
"Diamond"		
"Heart"		
"Spade"		
Moffat, Yard Co. Series 3	10 - 12	12 - 15
GRILLI, S. (Italy) See Art Deco		
GROSZE, MANNI (Italy) See Art Deco Silhouettes		
GUARNERI (Italy) See Art Deco		
GUERZONI (Italy) See Art Deco		
GUNN, ARCHIE (British)		

Archie Gunn was born in England and began painting portraits at an early age. His first works were very impressive, and he was commissioned to do portraits of some important Earls and Prime Ministers. Upon graduation from college and from the Art Academy in London, he began designing posters for some of London's principal theaters.

Archie migrated to New Rochelle, New York in 1888 at the age of 25. Here he made his home and began illustrating magazines, did some portrait painting and magazine covers, as well as posters for some of the New York play productions. Later, during the postcard era, he painted beautiful ladies that were adapted for postcards. His postcards were published by National Art, Philip Sander, Novelty Mfg. & Art Co., and the Illustrated Postal Card Co.

Archie Gunn was not as well know as Boileau, Fisher, the Christys and Underwood, but today's collectors are finding that his work was very beautiful and they have now begun collecting his cards in earnest.

J.Bergman B&W (6)	5 - 6	6 - 7
National Art Co.		

15 "Skating Girl"		8 - 10	10 - 12
16 "College Mascot"		7 - 9	8 - 9
"City Belles" Series			
33 "Miss New York"		8 - 10	10 - 12
34 "Miss Philadelphia"		8 - 10	10 - 12
35 "Miss Boston"		8 - 10	10 - 12
36 "Miss Chicago"		8 - 10	10 - 12
37 "Miss Pittsburg"		8 - 10	10 - 12
39 "Miss Toronto"		8 - 10	10 - 12
40 "Miss Washington"		8 - 10	10 - 12
41 "Miss Seashore"		8 - 10	10 - 12
71 "Miss Milwaukee"		8 - 10	10 - 12
72 "Miss Detroit"		8 - 10	10 - 12
77 "Miss Cleveland"		8 - 10	10 - 12
87 "Miss San Francisco"		8 - 10	10 - 12
90 Untitled		6 - 8	8 - 9
"Clans"		7 - 8	8 - 10
"College Belles"		8 - 10	10 - 12
"National Belles"		8 - 10	10 - 12
217 "Devotion"		8 - 10	10 - 12
219 "Yuletide"		8 - 10	10 - 12
220 "Sables"		8 - 10	10 - 12
221 "Ermine"		8 - 10	10 - 12
223 "Automobiling"		8 - 10	10 - 12
276 "The Fencer"		8 - 10	10 - 12
277 "On Guard"		8 - 10	10 - 12

Illustrated Postal Card & Novelty Co.

WWI Army Series 1368 (12)		6 - 8	8 - 10

"The American Spirit"
"Army, Navy, and Reserves"
"Don't Worry About Me"
"If Wishes Came True"
"Lest We Forget"
"None but the Brave Deserve ..."
"Pals"
"Parting is Such Sweet Sorrow"
"Repairing a Man of War"
"Rosemary! That's for Remembrance"
"Shoulder Arms"
"When the Last Goodbyes are Whispered"

WWI Army Series 1371 (12)		6 - 8	8 - 10

"A Parting Message"
"Hello! I Haven't Heard from You"
"Don't Worry, We're Alright"

"Guardian Spirits"
"Letters are Always Welcome"
"Liberty and Union Now and Forever"
"Pleasant Memories"
"The Rose for Remembrance"
"Sentry Moon"
"Warmth in the Camp and ..."
"We Won't Come Back Till it's Over ..."
"Worthwhile Fighting For ..."

Statler Calendar Cards, 1912 (12)	6 - 8	8 - 10
Anonymous B&W No Captions		
Girl Holding Basketball	6 - 8	8 - 10
Girl Wading in Water	5 - 6	6 - 7
Girl at Wheel of Sail Boat	5 - 6	6 - 7
Girl Holding Golf Club	8 - 10	10 - 12
Girl Holding Golf Club, but in Color	10 - 12	12 - 14
Beautiful Woman, Red Bow, Red Dress	6 - 8	8 - 10
Beautiful Woman, Pink, Bow, Pink Dress	6 - 8	8 - 10
Beautiful Woman, Waist up, Flowing Red Ribbon, Holding 3 Roses	6 - 8	8 - 10

A.L. Fidler
E. Gross, American Girl No. 14

J. Knowles Hare
Heckscher 1009-2, "Rosamond"

3 cards, B&W/Sepia, Women - No Captions	5 - 6	6 - 7
A.C. 2 Cards w/women and 4-line verse	5 - 6	6 - 7
HAMMICK, J.W. (GB)		
Photocom "Celesque" Series		
531 "The Motor Girl"	10 - 12	12 - 15
532 "The Society Girl"	10 - 12	12 - 1
533 "The Ball Room Girl"	10 - 12	12 - 15
534 "The Sporting Girl"	12 - 15	15 - 18
535 "The Sea Side Girl"	10 - 12	12 - 15
HARDY (British) See Art Deco		
HARE, J. KNOWLES (U.S.A.)	8 - 10	10 - 12
P. Heckscher Series 1009		
2 of "Rosamond"	8 - 10	10 - 12
Series 1026 (6)	8 - 10	10 - 12
Statler Adv. Cards, 1912 (13)	12 - 14	14 - 16
HARPER, R. FORD		
Reinthal & Newman Water color Series		
350 "Peg O' My Heart"	8 - 12	12 - 16
351 "My Summer Girl"	8 - 12	12 - 16
352 "Love's Locket"	8 - 12	12 - 16
353 "True Blue"	12 - 14	14 - 18
354 "The Favorite Flower"	12 - 14	14 - 18
355 "Miss Innocence"	8 - 12	12 - 16
Gibson Art Co.	8 - 10	10 - 12
P. Herkscher		
Series 1010	10 - 15	15 - 18
Series 1013	10 - 15	15 - 18
Series 1025	10 - 15	15 - 18
P. Sander		
Lady Santa Claus (4)	25 - 30	35 - 40
HARRISON (U.S.A.)	6 - 7	7 - 8
HEINZE, A.	5 - 6	6 - 8
HELLI (ICART) (France) See French Glamour		
Series 153 (6)	60 - 70	70 - 80
HEROUARD (France) See French Glamour		
HIDLER, G. HOWARD		
National Girl Series	6 - 8	8 - 9
HOROWITZ, H.		
R. Tuck		
Series 1 "A Dream of Fair Women" (6)	8 - 9	9 - 10
HORSFALL, MARY (British)	6 - 8	8 - 10
HUNTER, LILLIAN W. (U.S.A.)	6 - 8	8 - 9
HUTT, HENRY (U.S.A.)		
Detroit Publishing Co.	8 - 10	10 - 12
B&W 14000 Series		

14202 "Sincerity"		
14203 "Curiosity"		
14204 "Tired of Life"		
14205 "Expectancy"		
14207 "Frivolity"		
14208 "Courageous"		
14209 "Shy"		
14210 "Disappointment"		
14211 "Pleasure"		
14212 "Joy"		
14213 "Whimsical"		
H & S, Germany	10 - 12	12 - 15
ICART (France) See French Glamour		
JARACH, A. (France) See French Glamour		
JONES, J. (U.S.A.)	5 - 6	6 - 7
JOZSA, KARL (Austria) See Art Nouveau		
KEMPF, TH. (Austria) See Art Nouveau		
KENYON, ZULA	6 - 8	8 - 12
KIEFER, E.H. (GB)		
Bamforth & Co.		
"Could You Be True"	6 - 8	8 - 12
"Dear Heart"	6 - 8	8 - 12
"Good Bye"	6 - 8	8 - 12
"I'm Growing Fond of You"	6 - 8	8 - 12
"My Chum"	6 - 8	8 - 12
"There's Nobody Like You"	6 - 8	8 - 12
"You Know You're Not Forgotten"	6 - 8	8 - 12
"Waiting For You"	6 - 8	8 - 12
"When You Feel Naughty ..."	6 - 8	8 - 12
"When You're Traveling ..."	6 - 8	8 - 12
"When Your Heart Aches ..."	6 - 8	8 - 12
"Would You Learn to Love Me"	6 - 8	8 - 12
KIMBALL, ALONZO (U.S.A.)		
Reinthal & Newman		
Series 122, Lovers	6 - 8	8 - 9
KING, HAMILTON (U.S.A.)		
Advertising Card		
Coca Cola Girl	300 - 325	325 - 350
Bathing Beauties (12)	10 - 12	12 - 15
"Asbury Park Girl"		
"Atlantic City Girl"		
"Bar Harbor Girl"		
"Cape May Girl"		
"Coney Island Girl"		

"Long Beach Girl"
"Larchmont Girl"
"Manhattan Beach Girl"
"Narragansett Girl"
"Newport Girl"
"Palm Beach Girl"
"Ocean Grove Girl"

KINNYS, THE (U.S.A.)	6 - 8	8 - 10

KIRCHNER, RAPHAEL (Austria) See Deco,
  Nouveau, and French Glamour.
KLAVITCH, RUDOLF   See Art Nouveau
KNOEFEL

Novitas Illumination Series		
Series 668 Nudes (4)	15 - 20	20 - 25
Series 20888 Mother/Baby	10 - 12	12 - 15
Series 15662 Jap. Lantern	15 - 18	18 - 22
Other Illuminated	12 - 15	15 - 18
M. Munk Illumination		
Series 1992 Jap. Lantern	15 - 18	18 - 22

KOEHLER, MELA (Austria) See Art Nouveau/Deco

Early works	40 - 50	50 - 60
After 1915	20 - 25	25 - 30

KOISTER (France) See French Glamour
KOSEL, H.C.

B.K.W.I. Series 181		
"The Slave"	10 - 12	12 - 15
Semi-Nudes	12 - 15	15 - 20
Nudes	12 - 15	15 - 22

KUDERNY

M. Munk, Vienna		
Series 606	10 - 12	12 - 18
Series 634	8 - 10	10 - 15
Series 841, Semi-Nudes	12 - 15	15 - 18
Series 835, Tiny Men	12 - 15	15 - 18

KURT, E. MAISON

Fantasy Deco	15 - 20	20 - 25

LAUTREC, TOULOUSE (France)

Cabaret Bruant	600 - 700	700 - 900

LENOLEM (France)

Meissner & Buch Series 219	12 - 15	15 - 20
See French Glamour		

LONGLEY, CHILTON (U.S.A.) See Art Deco
MSM

Meissner & Buch	10 - 12	12 - 15
MANNING, FRED S. (U.S.A.)	8 - 9	9 - 10

MANNING, REG (U.S.A.)	7 - 8	8 - 9
MANUEL, HENRI (France) See French Glamour		
MANSELL, VIVIAN (GB)		
"National Ladies" Series	8 - 10	10 - 12
MARCOS. J. (Italy)		
Lady/Bubbles Fantasy	10 - 12	12 - 15
MARCO, M.		
Raphael Tuck		
Series 2763 (Asti-type)	6 - 8	8 - 10
MARTIN-KAVEL		
Head Studies		
Series 5027-5036	10 - 12	12 - 15
Lapina Nudes	12 - 15	15 - 18
MAUZAN (Italy) See Art Deco		
MAYER, LOU (U.S.A.)		
Reinthal & Newman		
400 Series	7 - 8	8 - 10
500 Series	8 - 10	10 - 12
Fantasy Series 878-883	12 - 15	15 - 18
Ullman Mfg. Co.		
Pretty Girl Series	5 - 8	8 - 10
McMEIN, A. (U.S.A.)		
Novitas Series 15672		
Head Studies	10 - 12	12 - 15
Osh Kosh Pennant Girls (6)	10 - 12	12 - 15
MESCHINI (Italy) See Art Deco		
METLOKOVITZ (Italy) See Art Deco		
MEUNIER, SUSAN See French Glamour		
MILLIERE, M. (France) See French Glamour		
MOLINA, ROBERTO		
"Diabolo" Series	8 - 10	10 - 12
MONESTIER, C. (Italy) See Art Deco		
MONTEDORO (Italy) See Art Deco		
MORAN, LEON (U.S.A.)	5 - 6	6 - 7
MOSTYN, MARJORIE (GB)		
Raphael Tuck		
Series 108 Jewel Girls	10 - 12	12 - 15
Series 11 "Fair of Feature"	10 - 12	12 - 15
MUSSINO (Italy) See Art Deco		
MUTTICH, C.V. (Czech.)		
Head Studies	5 - 8	8 - 10
Others	5 - 8	8 - 10
NANNI, G. (Italy) See Art Deco,		
Horses/Dogs W/Ladies.		

NAST, THOMAS, JR.
    Tennis "Love Game"   15 - 18   18 - 20
    Others   6 - 8   8 - 10
NEY (France) See French Glamour
NIKOLAKI, Z.P.
    Reinthal & Newman Ladies Series   6 - 8   8 - 10
NYSTROM, JENNY   10 - 12   12 - 15
PALANTI, G. (Italy) See Art Deco
PATELLA (Italy) See Art Deco
PELTIER, L. (France) See French Glamour
PENNELL
    M. Munk Series
    913 Sporting Girls   6 - 8   8 - 10
    1114 Sporting Girls   5 - 7   7 - 8
PAGONI (Italy) See Art Deco
PENOT, A. (France) See French Glamour
PERAS (France) See French Glamour
PEW, C.L.
    Aquarelle Series 2239   6 - 8   8 - 10
    Others   6 - 8   8 - 10
PAGONI (Italy) See Art Deco
PHILLIPS, COLES (U.S.A.)

The creator of The Fadeaway Girl was born in Springfield, Ohio in 1881. There was little of the artistic temperament in his early years; rather more of the healthy, fun-loving boy's capacity to fall into deviltry, and it was not until his college days that he realized his natural ability to draw might be of use to him. In an effort to work his way through Kenyon College at Gambier, Ohio, he earned his first money as an artist illustrating and decorating the college monthly magazine.

After graduation, he went to New York and for some time picked up varied experience in clerking and working at odd jobs. He became a solicitor in one of the city's biggest advertising and designing houses. In this position he represented his chosen field, and cultivated a keen business sense and a practical knowledge of commercial art.

He soon used this knowledge to good advantage in forming a dozen artists into an advertising organization of his own. This new venture caused his painting to suffer from neglect and he finally retired from it and rented a studio. He enhanced his technical training by attending the Chase School in the afternoons and the Free Art School in the evenings.

Phillips worked a month on his first drawing. Life Publishing Co.

accepted it as a double-page cartoon and he immediately became a regular contributor. His Fadeaway Girls, placed on *Life* covers, were an immediate success. So original was the conception that the Fadeaway Girl will always stand for Coles Phillips, and Coles Phillips will always stand for the Fadeaway Girl.

Coles lived in New Rochelle, a New York suburb just 45 minutes from Broadway, where his studio overlooked Long Island Sound. His model for most of his works was his beautiful and slender wife, Tess.

The Coles Phillips Girl typifies the subtle charm of American womanhood. In the drawing room or in the kitchen, breaking hearts or baking pies, or enjoying the stillness of the great outdoors, a real woman from the tip of her dainty boot to the soft glory of her head, she stands out from her flat background and answers completely to a young man's fancy at its highest and best.

COLES PHILLIPS
   * **Cards Listed With an asterisk**
         are Fadeaway Girls.

Life Pub. Co., 1907		
Life Series 1		
"Her Choice"	22 - 25	25 - 30
Life Pub. Co., 1909		
© **Coles Phillips Series**		
"Arms and the Man" *	25 - 28	28 - 35
"Between You and Me ..." *	25 - 28	28 - 35
"Home Ties" *	25 - 28	28 - 35
"Illusion" *	25 - 28	28 - 35
"Inclined to Meet" Ser. 2 *	28 - 30	32 - 38
"The Sand Witch"	22 - 25	25 - 30
"Such Stuff as Dreams are Made Of"	22 - 25	25 - 30
"What Next?" Ser. 2	25 - 28	28 - 35
"Which?" Ser. 2 *	28 - 30	32 - 38
Life Pub. Co., 1910		
"All Wool and Face Value" Ser. 2	25 - 28	28 - 35
"And Out of Mind as ..." Ser. 2	25 - 28	28 - 35
"Discarding from Strength" Ser. 2 *	28 - 30	32 - 38
"Hers"	22 - 25	25 - 30
P.F. Volland & Co., Chicago		
© **by Life Pub. Co.**		
"The Latest in Gowns ..." *	22 - 25	25 - 30

Unsigned Coles Phillips
SB 973, No Caption

Cecil Quinnell
BKWI 258-1, "Pearl"

"Long Distancc Makes ..." *	22 - 25	25 - 30
"Memories" *	22 - 25	25 - 30
"My Christmas Thoughts ..." *	22 - 25	25 - 28
"The Survival of the Fittest" *	22 - 25	25 - 28
C.P. Co., Inc., N.Y.		
Painting of Alice Joyce *	28 - 30	30 - 35
ADVERTISING		
R. Stafford Collins, N.Y.		
Comm. Silver Plate,		
Ad for Brunner Fl. Jeweler	28 - 30	30 - 35
Community Silver Plate		
"A Case of Love at First Sight"	28 - 30	30 - 35
Book Advertisement		
"The Dim Lantern," by Temple Bailey	30 - 35	35 - 40
Calendar Cards, W/Verse	28 - 30	30 - 35
Unsigned—Ten unsigned Fadeaway Girls		
have been attributed to Coles Phillips.		
Prices of these are:	15 - 18	18 - 20

PINOCHI   (Italy) See Art Deco
POWELL, LYMAN (U.S.A.)
  "Eventful Days" Series

"Graduation Day"	6 - 8	8 - 10
"Engagement Day"	6 - 8	8 - 10
"Wedding Day"	6 - 8	8 - 10
"Birthday"	6 - 8	8 - 10
Series 783 Flower Series	6 - 8	8 - 10

PUTTKAMER

Erotic Lovers Ser. 8027 (6)	15 - 18	18 - 22

QUINNELL, CECIL W.

B.K.W.I. 251 "The Jewel Girls"	8 - 10	10 - 12

  "Pearl"
  "Ruby"
  "Emerald"
  "Topaz"
  "Turquoise"
  "Sapphire"

"Glad Eye" Series	8 - 10	10 - 12

RALPH, LESTER (U.S.A.)
  Reinthal & Newman
  "Dancing" Series 801-806

"The La Furlana"	10 - 12	12 - 14
"The Cortez"	10 - 12	12 - 14
"The Half and Half"	10 - 12	12 - 14
"The Tango"	10 - 12	12 - 14
"The One Step"	10 - 12	12 - 14
"The Maxie"	10 - 12	12 - 14

  813-818 Series *

813 "The Awakening of Love"	8 - 10	10 - 12
814 "The Stage of Life"	8 - 10	10 - 12
815 "Up in the Clouds"	8 - 10	10 - 12
816 "For All Eternity"	8 - 10	10 - 12
817 "In Proud Possession"	8 - 10	10 - 12
818 "The Home Guard"	8 - 10	10 - 12

* With German Caption add $2.
The Knapp Co., N.Y.
Series 302, **Paul Heckscher**

1		
2 "An Offer of Affection"	8 - 10	10 - 12
3 "Weathering it Together"	8 - 10	10 - 12
4		
5 "Four-In-Hand"	8 - 10	10 - 12
6 "Her First Mate"	8 - 10	10 - 12

Lester Ralph
R&N 801, "La Furlana"

Lester Ralph
R&N 816, "For All Eternity"

7 "Two is Company Enough"	8 - 10	10 - 12
8 "Weathering Together"	8 - 10	10 - 12
9 "Fellow Sports"	8 - 10	10 - 12
10 "Diana of the Shore"	8 - 10	10 - 12
Series 307 **H. Import**		
1 "Take Me Along"	8 - 10	10 - 12
4 "A Stroll Together"	8 - 10	10 - 12
7 "Two is Company Enough"	8 - 10	10 - 12
Others	8 - 10	10 - 12
Series 308		
1 "Confidential Chatter"	8 - 10	10 - 12
3 "A Social Call"	8 - 10	10 - 12
5 "The Wings of the Wind"	8 - 10	10 - 12
6 "A Surprise Party"	8 - 10	10 - 12
9 "Fellow Sports"	10 - 12	12 - 14
Others	10 - 12	12 - 14
Series 1026		
2 "Feathered Friends"	8 - 10	10 - 12
Others	8 - 10	10 - 12
Series 7 *		
9523 "Fellow Sports"	10 - 12	12 - 14

9543 "Favored by Fortune"	10 - 12	12 - 14
9563 "Two is Company Enough"	10 - 12	12 - 14
9573 "Her First Date"	10 - 12	12 - 14
9583 "A Challenge from the Sea"	10 - 12	12 - 14
9593 "A Game in the Surf"	10 - 12	12 - 14
9603 "Diana of the Shore"	10 - 12	12 - 14
9613 "Four-in-Hand"	10 - 12	12 - 14
9623 "Fellow Sports"	10 - 12	12 - 14
9633 "An Offer of Affection"	10 - 12	12 - 14
Others	10 - 12	12 - 14

* This series also adapted as Knapp Calendars.
Add $3-5 to prices for Knapp Calendars.
C.W.Faulkner

Ser. 1314B "Fast Companions"	10 - 12	12 - 14
Ser. 1315D "Her Proudest Moment"	10 - 12	12 - 14
Others	10 - 12	12 - 14

RAPPINI (Italy) See Art Deco
REYNOLDS (U.S.A.)

Cowgirls Series	5 - 6	6 - 7

REZSO, KISS

"Siren Lady" Series 68-73	10 - 12	12 - 14

RICCO, LORIS (Italy) See Art Deco
ROBERTY, L.
M. Munk, Vienna

Bather Series 1124	10 - 12	12 - 15
RUSSELL, MARY LA F.	6 - 7	7 - 8

RYAN, E. (U.S.A.) See Art Nouveau

Non-Art Nouveau, Ladies	5 - 6	6 - 8

SLS (SAMUEL L. SCHMUCKER) (U.S.A.)
Detroit Publishing Co.

Butterfly Series	100 - 110	110 - 120
Childhood Days Series	150 - 160	160 - 170
Mermaid Series	125 - 135	135 - 145
Fairy Queens Series	150 - 160	160 - 170
Drinks Series	125 - 135	135 - 145
Smokers Series, uns.	125 - 135	135 - 145
National Girl Series	125 - 135	135 - 145
Winsch, Copyright Cards		
Halloween	35 - 100	40 - 110
Tuck's Halloween	35 - 100	40 - 110

SAGER, XAVIER (France)
See French Glamour, Fantasy
ST. JOHN
National Art

"National Girls" Series	8 - 10	10 - 12
"Foreign Girls" Series	6 - 8	8 - 10
"The Four Seasons"	10 - 12	12 - 14
SALMONI (Italy) See Art Deco		
SANTINO (Italy) See Art Deco		
SCATTINI (Italy) See Art Deco		
SCHMUTZLER, L.	6 - 8	8 - 9
SHARPE	8 - 9	9 - 10
SGALLI, S. (Italy) See Art Deco		
SIMONETTI (Italy) See Art Deco		
SOLOMKO S. (Russia)		
Lapina, Paris		
Russian Princess Series *		
"Queen Aeviakovna"	15 - 18	18 - 22
"Wassillisa Mikouichuna"	15 - 18	18 - 22
"Princess Apaaksia"	15 - 18	18 - 22
"Princess Warrior Nastasia"	20 - 22	22 - 25
"Princess Mary, The White Swan"	20 - 22	22 - 25
"Princess Zabava Poutiatichna"	15 - 18	18 - 22
* Russian Backs - Add $4-5 each.		
T.S.N. (Theo Strofer, Nurnberg) *		
15 "Parisiene"	14 - 16	16 - 18
175 "Phantasy"	16 - 18	18 - 22
"Dream of Icarius"	14 - 15	15 - 18
"Pearl of Creation"	15 - 18	18 - 20
"Vanity" Semi-nude	15 - 20	20 - 25
"Circe" Semi-nude	15 - 20	20 - 25
"The Tale" Fantasy	15 - 17	17 - 18
"The Blue Bird" Fantasy	18 - 20	20 - 22
"Magician Circle" Semi-nude	15 - 20	20 - 25
154 "Temptations" Semi-nude	15 - 20	20 - 25
"Glow Worm" Fantasy	15 - 18	18 - 20
"Fortune Telling" Fantasy	15 - 18	18 - 20
Other **T.S.N.** (Many)	8 - 10	10 - 12
* Russian Backs - Add $4-5 to prices.		
STANLAWS, P. (U.S.A.)		
Edward Gross		
Stanlaws 1-12 No Captions	14 - 16	16 - 20
Knapp Co., N.Y.		
900 Series		
"A Midsummer Maid"	14 - 15	15 - 18
"After the Matinee"	14 - 15	15 - 18
"Daisies Won't Tell"	14 - 15	15 - 18
"Fair as the Lily"	15 - 18	18 - 20

P. Stanlaws
AR & CiB 551, "After the Matinee"

P. Stanlaws
AR & CiB 551, "School Days"

"Fresh as the Morn"	15 - 18	18 - 20
"Girl of the Golden West"	14 - 15	15 - 18
"Kissed by the Snow"	15 - 18	18 - 20
"The Pink Lady"	15 - 18	18 - 22
"School Days"	15 - 18	18 - 22

K. Co. Distr. by A.R. & C.i.B (Reprints of 900 Ser.)
Series 550

"A Midsummer Maid"	15 - 18	18 - 20
"Daisies Wont Tell"	15 - 18	18 - 20
"Girl of the Golden West"	15 - 18	18 - 20
"The Pink Lady"	15 - 18	18 - 20

Series 551

"After the Matinee"	15 - 18	18 - 20
"Kissed by the Snow"	15 - 18	18 - 20
"School Days"	15 - 18	18 - 20
"Fair as the Lily"	15 - 18	18 - 20

Reinthal & Newman
Military Ladies Series

981 U.S.A.	15 - 18	18 - 22
982 Serbia	12 - 14	14 - 16
983 Belgium	12 - 14	14 - 16

984 France	12 - 14	14 - 16
985 Italy	12 - 14	14 - 16
986 Greece	12 - 14	14 - 16
987 Great Britain	12 - 14	14 - 16
988 Russia	12 - 14	14 - 16

TAM, JEAN (France) See French Glamour
TERZI, A. (Italy) See Art Deco
TORNROSE, ALEX

Wells Head Series	6 - 8	8 - 9
Others	6 - 7	7 - 8

TRAVER, C. WARD (U.S.A.)
H & S Art Co.

"The Beauty of the Season"	8 - 10	10 - 12
"Sweet Seventeen"	8 - 10	10 - 12
Others	8 - 10	10 - 12

UNDERWOOD, CLARENCE

Clarence Underwood was another of the more important illustrators of magazine covers and magazine fiction who benefitted from the great postcard era. This painter of beautiful ladies did work for Reinthal & Newman of New York, but his most beautiful images were published by the R. Chapman Co. (better known as the R.C. Co., N.Y.). They did the 1400 Series Water Colors of his ladies wearing big, beautiful, and colorful hats. These will always be some of the most beautiful renderings of the era.

Marcus Munk, the famous postcard publisher of Vienna, also did many of his images on postcards. These were mainly of loving couples with colorful backgrounds, and many were sport oriented. Other foreign publishers produced some of his works, but Underwood was unable to gain the great popularity attained by his fellow American artists—Fisher, Boileau and Christy.

CLARENCE UNDERWOOD (U.S.A.)

C.W. Faulkner

Series 5	10 - 12	12 - 14
Series 1010	10 - 12	12 - 14
1278 "A Symphony of Hearts"	8 - 10	10 - 12
"Their Search for Old China"	8 - 10	10 - 12
National Art		
"Playing Card" Series		
78 "Hearts" Two Men, Two Women	8 - 10	10 - 12

79 "Poker" Five Men	8 - 10	10 - 12
80 "Bridge" Four Women	8 - 10	10 - 12
81 "Euchre" Five Men	8 - 10	10 - 12

Reinthal & Newman
300 Series Water Colors

345 "The Flirt"	10 - 12	12 - 15
346 "Pretty Cold"	10 - 12	12 - 15
347 "Her First Vote"	25 - 30	30 - 35
348 "It's Always Fair Weather"	10 - 12	12 - 15
349 "Rain or Shine"	10 - 12	12 - 15
350 "Pleasant Reflections"	10 - 12	12 - 15

R.C. CO., N.Y.
1400 Water Color Series

1436 "Constance"	10 - 15	15 - 20
1437 "Diana"	10 - 15	15 - 20
1438 "Vivian"	10 - 15	15 - 20
1439 "Phyllis"	10 - 15	15 - 20
1440 "Celestine"	10 - 15	15 - 20
1441 "Rosabella"	10 - 15	15 - 20
1442 "Juliana"	10 - 15	15 - 20
1443 "Victoria"	15 - 20	20 - 25
1444 "Aurora"	10 - 15	15 - 20
1445 "Sylvia"	10 - 15	15 - 25
1446 "Virginia"	10 - 15	15 - 20
1447 "Doris"	10 - 15	15 - 20

Frederick A. Stokes Co.
Series 1

"A Problem of Income"	7 - 8	8 - 10
"Castles in the Smoke"	7 - 8	8 - 10
"For Fear of Sunburn"	8 - 9	9 - 12
"Knight Takes Queen"	7 - 8	8 - 10

Series 2

"Love Me, Love My Cat"	8 - 9	9 - 12
"Love Me, Love My Dog"	8 - 9	9 - 12
"Love Me, Love My Donkey"	8 - 9	9 - 10
"Love Me, Love My Horse"	8 - 9	9 - 12

Series 3

"When We're Together Fishing"	8 - 9	9 - 12
"When We're Together at Luncheon"	7 - 8	8 - 10
"When We're Together Shooting"	8 - 9	9 - 12
"When We're Together in a Storm"	7 - 8	8 - 10

Series 4

"Beauty and the Beast"	8 - 9	9 - 12
"The Best of Friends"	8 - 9	9 - 12

"Expectation"	8 - 9	9 - 12
"The Promenade"	8 - 9	9 - 12
Series 5		
"A Lump of Sugar"	8 - 9	9 - 12
"After the Hunt"	8 - 9	9 - 12
"The Red Haired Girl ..."	10 - 12	12 - 14
"Three American Beauties"	10 - 12	12 - 14
Series 6		
"Feeding the Swans"	7 - 8	8 - 10
"A Pet in the Park"	7 - 8	8 - 10
"Posing"	7 - 8	8 - 10
"A Witch"	8 - 10	10 - 12
Series 7		
"An Old Melody"	7 - 8	8 - 10
"Over the Teacups"	7 - 8	8 - 10
"The Opera Girl"	7 - 8	8 - 10
"The Violin Girl"	7 - 8	8 - 10
Series 8		
"At the Races"	8 - 10	10 - 12
"Embroidery for Two"	7 - 8	8 - 10
"Out for a Stroll"	7 - 8	8 - 10
"Two Cooks"	7 - 8	8 - 10
Series 14		
"Their First Wedding Gift"	7 - 8	8 - 10
"Their Love of Old Silver"	7 - 8	8 - 10
"Two and an Old Flirt"	7 - 8	8 - 10
"Vain Regrets"	7 - 8	8 - 10
Series 15		
"A Lesson in Motoring"	8 - 10	10 - 12
"A Skipper and Mate"	7 - 8	8 - 10
Series 19		
"The Only Two at Dinner"	7 - 8	8 - 10
"The Only Two at the Game"	8 - 10	10 - 12
"The Only Two at the House Party"	7 - 8	8 - 10
"The Only Two at the Opera"	7 - 8	8 - 10
Series 22		
"The Greatest Thing in the World"	7 - 8	8 - 10
"The Last Waltz"	7 - 8	8 - 10
"Lost?"	7 - 8	8 - 10
"Love on Six Cylinders"	8 - 10	10 - 12
Series 377 Untitled (4) B&W	5 - 6	6 - 8
Taylor, Platt & Co.		
Series 782		
"A Fisherman's Luck"	10 - 12	12 - 15

"A Heart of Diamonds"	10 - 12	12 - 15
"A Modern Siren"	10 - 12	12 - 15
"Daisies Won't Tell"	10 - 12	12 - 15
"The Glories of March"	10 - 12	12 - 15
"His Latest Chauffeur"	10 - 12	12 - 15
"Indicating a Thaw"	10 - 12	12 - 15
"The Magnet"	10 - 12	12 - 15
"Let's Paddle Forever"	10 - 12	12 - 15
"Love Has It's Clouds"	10 - 12	12 - 15
"Stolen Sweets"	10 - 12	12 - 15
"True Love Never Runs Smooth"	10 - 12	12 - 15
Osborne Calendar Co. Adv. Cards	12 - 15	15 - 18
1521 "Fancy Work"		
1561 "Mary had a Little Lamb"		
1571 "The Tongue is Mightier ..."		
1601 "The Favorite's Day"		
1621 "Music Hath Charm"		
Others		
A.R. & C.		
1283 "Des Meeres und der Liebe Wellen"	8 - 10	10 - 11
M. Munk, Vienna		
Series 303 (8)		
Beautiful Ladies W/Pets No Captions	8 - 10	10 - 12
Series 377, 385, 387, & 388	10 - 11	11 - 13
Series 742 *		
"Love Laughs at Winter"	8 - 10	10 - 12
"Love on Wings"	12 - 15	15 - 18
"Under the Mistletoe"	8 - 10	10 - 12
"The Sender of Orchids"	8 - 10	10 - 12
"The Last Waltz"	8 - 10	10 - 12
"The Greatest Thing"	8 - 10	10 - 12
"The Sender of Orchids"	8 - 10	10 - 12
* Series 742 A,B,C,D,E,F,G & H		
All Same as Ser. 742		
But W/German Captions		
* Add $3 per card to prices.		
Series 832, 834, 837 & 860 *		
"A Penny for Thought"	8 - 10	10 - 12
"A Problem of Income"	8 - 10	10 - 12
"Cherry Ripe"	8 - 10	10 - 12
"He Loves Me ..."	8 - 10	10 - 12
"How to Know Wildflowers"	12 - 15	15 - 18
"Only a Question of Time"	8 - 10	10 - 12
"The Sweetest Flower that ..."	8 - 10	10 - 12

"Skipper and Mate"	10 - 12	12 - 15
"Love and Six Cylinders"	12 - 15	15 - 18

* Series 832, 834, 837, 860
W/German Captions
Add - $3 per card to prices.

Novitas, Germany
400 Series
Series 445-453 With German Captions

445 "Gestand nis"	8 - 10	10 - 12
447 "Einig"	10 - 12	12 - 14
449 "Zukunftplane"	10 - 12	12 - 14
Others	10 - 12	12 - 14
Others, W/O Captions	8 - 10	10 - 12

20,000 Series

20391 No Caption	8 - 10	10 - 12
20392 No Caption	8 - 10	10 - 12
20451 "Wer Wird Siegen"	8 - 10	10 - 12
20452 "Dem Fluck Entgegen"	8 - 10	10 - 12
20453 No Caption (Lovers of Beauty)	8 - 10	10 - 12
20454 "Liebe Auf Eis"	8 - 10	10 - 12
20455 "Abwesend, Aber Nicht Vergessen"	8 - 10	10 - 12
20456 No Caption	8 - 10	10 - 12
20457 "Zwei Seelen und ein Genankt"	8 - 10	10 - 12
20458 "Zukunpt Straune"	8 - 10	10 - 12
20459 No Caption	8 - 10	10 - 12
20460 "Glucklicht Tagt"	8 - 10	10 - 12

FINLAND
W. & G. (Weilin & Goos)

American Ser. N:0 7001 1-35 (6)	20 - 22	22 - 25

RUSSIAN

Phillips "The Last Waltz Together"	15 - 20	20 - 25

USABAL   (Italy) See Art Deco

P.F.B. Series 3796 (6)	12 - 14	14 - 16
Erkal Series 336 "Tennis" (6)	15 - 18	18 - 20
Ser. 303 "Smoking Ladies" (6)	10 - 12	12 - 14

VALLET, L. (France) See French Glamour
VINNOY (France) See Art Deco
VOGLIO, BENITO   (France)
WICHERA, R.R.
  M. Munk, Vienna Color

Series 112, 322, 411 (6)	8 - 10	10 - 12
Series 450, 530, 683 (6)	10 - 12	12 - 15
Series 559, 5590 Big Hats (6)	12 - 14	14 - 18
Series 684 Semi-Nudes (6)	12 - 15	15 - 20

ZANDRINO   (Italy) See Art Deco

ART DECO

Beautiful **Colors!** Beautiful strong, deep, vibrant **Colors!** This wording only partially describes the new Art Deco movement that began around 1910—just as the Art Nouveau era was ebbing—and continued into the early 1930's. Due to the great influx of Art Deco postcards to the U.S., there has been a great demand for them in recent years as more and more American collectors discover their beauty.

Basically, for the postcard collector there are two types of Art Deco. The first, and most sought-after, were the earlier works of Brunelleschi, Chiostri, Montedoro, Bentivoglio, Meschini and Scattina, and a small number of the works of Adolfo Busi, Colombo and T. Corbella. Most of these artists did paintings of beautiful women in their mode of dress of the era, along with beautiful scenic backgrounds, etc.

The second type was predominantly of ladies in fashionable attire starting around 1915 and continuing into the 1920's. The Italian artists were the most prolific as they produced many cards, usually in sets of six, depicting a particular theme. Beautiful ladies, smartly dressed, pictured with wild animals, sleek dogs or colorful horses played a dominant role, while those engaged in tennis and golf and other sports were a close second. Corbella, Nanni, Mauzan and Colombo seem to generate the most interest.

The principal publishers of the artists were **Dell Anna & Gasparini, Milano, Uff. Rev. Stampa, Milano, Ballerini & Fratini, Florence, Degami, Majestic and "Ultra."**

Unfortunately, very few minor works by American artists have become highly collectible. At the present time, Art Deco cards hold the distinction of being the most pursued artist-signed cards in the hobby.

ART DECO LADIES

ANICHINI, E. (Italy)

"Fairies" Series	15 - 20	20 - 25
Dancer Series	15 - 20	20 - 25
Others	12 - 15	15 - 18

AZZONI, N. (Italy)

Series 517 (6)	15 - 20	20 - 25
Others	12 - 15	15 - 18

BACHRICH, M.
Ladies/Fashion	10 - 12	12 - 15
Ladies/Sports	12 - 15	15 - 18
Ser. 102 (Dance Series)	12 - 15	15 - 18

BALONTI (Italy)
Ladies/Fashion	12 - 15	15 - 18

BERTIGLIA (Italy)
Ladies/Heads	12 - 15	15 - 18
Ladies/Fashion	12 - 15	15 - 18
Ladies/Animals	15 - 18	18 - 22
Ladies/Tennis-Golf	15 - 18	18 - 22
Harlequins	18 - 22	22 - 25
Ladies/Harlequins	15 - 18	18 - 22
Children	10 - 12	12 - 15
Ethnic/Blacks	18 - 22	22 - 25

BETTINELLI (Italy)
	10 - 12	12 - 15

BIANCHI (Italy)
Ladies/Heads	10 - 12	12 - 15
Ladies/Fashion	10 - 12	12 - 15
Ladies/Animals	12 - 15	15 - 18
Ladies/Tennis-Golf	15 - 18	18 - 22

BIRI, S. (Italy)
Ladies/Harlequins	18 - 22	22 - 25
Others	12 - 15	15 - 18

BOMPARD, S. (Italy)
Ladies/Heads	10 - 12	12 - 15
Ladies/Fashion	12 - 15	15 - 18
Ladies/Animals	12 - 15	15 - 18
Ladies/Tennis-Golf	15 - 18	18 - 22
Harlequins	18 - 22	22 - 25
Erotic/Semi-Nude	18 - 22	22 - 25

BONORA (Italy)
Ladies	15 - 18	18 - 22
Harlequins	20 - 25	25 - 28

BOTTARO (Italy)
Series 123 Bathing	18 - 22	22 - 25
Series 135 Illuminated	15 - 18	18 - 22
Others	12 - 15	15 - 18

BRUNELLESCHI, UMBERTO (Italy)
Series of 6	150 - 175	175 - 200
Advertising	50 - 60	60 - 75

BUHNE, BUNTE
Deco Silhouette Ser. 225-228	12 - 15	15 - 18

BUSI, ADOLFO (Italy)

Series 110 (6)	15 - 18	18 - 22
Series 112 - Diabolo (6)	18 - 22	22 - 25
Series 153 - Pajamas	15 - 18	18 - 22
Series 126 - Girl/Fruits	15 - 18	18 - 22
Series 100 - Fantasy	20 - 25	25 - 30
Heads/Ladies	12 - 15	15 - 18
Ladies/Fashion	15 - 18	18 - 22
Ladies/Sports	20 - 25	25 - 30
Harlequins	15 - 18	18 - 22
CALDONA (Italy)		
Ladies/Fashion	10 - 12	12 - 15
CASTELLI (Italy)		
Children/Comics	8 - 10	10 - 12
CHERUBINI (Italy)		
Ladies/Heads/Fashion	12 - 15	15 - 18
Harlequins	15 - 18	18 - 22
CHIOSTRI, SOFIA (Italy)		
Series 320 Deco Lady/Animal	35 - 45	45 - 60
Series 220 Deco Santas (6)	20 - 25	25 - 35
220 Black Robe	35 - 40	40 - 50
Series 181 Bathers	25 - 30	30 - 40
Series 243 Witches	25 - 30	30 - 40
Series 316 W/Animals	25 - 28	28 - 32
Series 317 Mermaids (6)	35 - 40	40 - 45
Mermaid Series	30 - 35	35 - 45
Harlequins	25 - 30	30 - 35
Others, Color Background	25 - 30	30 - 40
Others, Season Greetings	15 - 18	18 - 25
Signed/SOFIA	10 - 15	15 - 18
CLIRIO, L. (Italy)		
Series 29	15 - 18	18 - 22
COLOMBO (Italy)		
Series 936 (6)	12 - 15	15 - 18
Series 894 (6)	12 - 15	15 - 18
Ladies/Heads	12 - 15	15 - 18
Ladies/Fashion	12 - 15	15 - 18
Ladies/Animals	15 - 18	18 - 22
Ladies/Sports	18 - 22	22 - 25
Harlequins	20 - 22	22 - 25
Colonial-type Deco	12 - 15	15 - 20
Children	12 - 15	15 - 18
CORBELLA, T. (Italy)		
Series 236 (6)	12 - 15	15 - 18
Series 516 (6)	12 - 15	15 - 18

Chiostri
Ballerini & Fratini 317

Chiostri
Ballerini & Fratini 209

Ladies Heads/Fashion	12 - 15	15 - 20
Ladies/Animals	15 - 18	18 - 22
Ladies/Sports	18 - 22	22 - 25
Colonial-type Lovers	12 - 15	15 - 18
Erotic/Semi-Nude	18 - 22	22 - 25
CRAMER, RIE	10 - 12	12 - 15
CYRANICUS (Italy)		
Series 204 (6)	12 - 15	15 - 18
Ladies/Heads	12 - 15	15 - 18
Ladies/Fashion	12 - 15	15 - 18
Ladies/Animals	15 - 18	18 - 22
Ladies/Golf-Tennis	15 - 18	18 - 22
DEGAMI (Italy)		
Ultra 2195 W/Dogs	20 - 22	22 - 25
Ladies	18 - 22	22 - 25
DERNINI (Italy)		
Ladies	15 - 18	18 - 22
DERRANTI, D.		
"Elite" Series 2568	25 - 30	30 - 35
DOUKY	10 - 12	12 - 14
DUDOVICH (Italy)		

Busi
Dell, Anna & Gasp., 112-3, "Diabolo"

Chilton Longley
A.G. & Co. Ltd. Series 422

Degami, Unsigned
Ultra 2195, No Caption

Ladies	15 - 18	18 - 22
FRANZONI (Italy)		
Ladies/Fashion	12 - 15	15 - 18
Ladies/Animals	15 - 18	18 - 22
Erotic/Semi-Nudes	15 - 18	18 - 22
Ladies/Golf-Tennis	15 - 18	18 - 22
GOBBI, D. (Italy)		
Series 2564 Chinese Dragon	15 - 18	18 - 22
Ladies	20 - 22	22 - 25
Gondola/Lovers	15 - 18	18 - 22
GRAF, MARTE		
Deco Silhouettes		
Series 733-758	8 - 12	12 - 18
Other Deco Silhouettes	10 - 12	12 - 15
GRILLI, S. (Italy)		
Ladies	12 - 15	15 - 18
GROSZE, MANNI		
Deco Silhouettes		
Deco Series 2041, Nudes	12 - 15	15 - 18
PFB Series Nudes, 2042	12 - 15	15 - 18
PFB Series Nudes, 3339	18 - 20	20 - 22
Others	10 - 12	12 - 15
GUARNERI, E. (Italy)		
Ladies	15 - 18	18 - 22
GUERZONI (Italy)		
Ladies/Heads/Fashion	7 - 9	9 - 12
Ladies/Animals	8 - 10	10 - 15
Erotic/Semi-Nudes	10 - 12	12 - 18
GUZERONI (Italy)		
Ladies Heads/Fashion	12 - 15	15 - 18
Ladies/Golf-Tennis	15 - 18	18 - 22
Erotic/Semi-Nudes	18 - 22	22 - 25
HARDY (GB)		
Ladies	8 - 10	10 - 12
Ladies/Animals	10 - 12	12 - 15
Erotic/Semi-Nudes	15 - 18	18 - 22
ICART, LOUIS (France)		
Lady and Black Dog	40 - 50	50 - 60
Signed HELLI	35 - 40	40 - 50
KASKELINE		
Deco Silhouette Ladies	12 - 15	15 - 18
KOEHLER, MELA (Austria)		
B.K.W.I. Series 620 (6)	35 - 40	40 - 45
Early Ladies	45 - 55	55 - 75

Nanni
Uff. Rev. Stampa Series 205-6

Mauzan
Uff. Rev. Stampa Series 321-4

Ladies, after 1920	30 - 35	35 - 40
Children, after 1920	20 - 25	25 - 30
KURT, E. MAISON		
Fantasy	15 - 18	18 - 22
Japanese	12 - 15	15 - 18
LE DUC, A.		
Ladies	10 - 12	12 - 15
LENOLEM		
M & Buch Series 219	18 - 20	20 - 25
LONGLEY, CHILTON (U.S.A.)		
A. G. & Co., Ltd. Ser. 422	18 - 22	22 - 26
Others	18 - 20	20 - 25
MASTROAINI (Italy)		
Ladies	7 - 9	9 - 12
MAUZAN (Italy)		
Series 321 (6)	12 - 15	15 - 18
Ladies/Heads	12 - 15	15 - 18
Ladies/Fashion	12 - 15	15 - 18
Ladies/Animals	15 - 18	18 - 22
Ladies/Golf-Tennis	18 - 20	20 - 25
Harlequins	18 - 20	22 - 25

Erotic/Semi-Nudes	20 - 22	22 - 28
Children	8 - 10	10 - 12
MESCHINI (Italy)		
Ladies	18 - 20	22 - 25
Harlequins	22 - 25	25 - 30
Lovers	15 - 18	18 - 22
METLOKOVITZ (Italy)		
Ladies/Fashion	10 - 12	12 - 15
Bathing Beauties	10 - 12	12 - 15
MONESTIER (Italy)	8 - 10	10 - 12
MONTEDORO (Italy)		
Series A (6)	35 - 40	40 - 50
Series B (6)	40 - 50	50 - 60
MUGGIANY (Italy)		
Ladies/Heads/Fashion	12 - 15	15 - 18
Ladies/Animals	15 - 18	18 - 22
NANNI (Italy)		
Series 255, Nat. Girls	15 - 18	18 - 22
Series 529, Pajamas/Smoking	15 - 18	18 - 22
Series 205, Lady and Dog	15 - 18	18 - 22
Ladies/Heads/Fashion	15 - 18	18 - 22
Ladies/Animals	15 - 18	18 - 22
Harlequins	18 - 22	22 - 25
Soccer Series	18 - 22	22 - 25
Erotic/Semi-Nudes	22 - 25	25 - 30
PAGONI (Italy)		
Ladies	10 - 12	12 - 15
PENTSY	8 - 10	10 - 12
PINOCHI (Italy)		
Ladies	10 - 12	12 - 15
RAPPINI (Italy)		
Ladies/Heads/Fashion	12 - 15	15 - 18
Ladies/Animals	15 - 18	18 - 22
Ladies/Sports	15 - 18	18 - 22
RICCO, LORIS (Italy)		
Ladies, Lovers	18 - 20	20 - 25
SALMONI (Italy)		
Ladies	10 - 12	12 - 15
SANTINI (Italy)		
Ladies	10 - 12	12 - 15
SCATTINI (Italy)		
Ladies	15 - 18	18 - 22
Harlequins	18 - 22	22 - 28
SIMONETTI (Italy)		

Ladies	12 - 15	15 - 18
TERZI, A. (Italy)		
Ladies/Heads/Fashion	10 - 12	12 - 15
Ladies/Animals	12 - 15	15 - 18
Ladies/Golf-Tennis	15 - 18	18 - 22
TUHKA, A. (Finland)	6 - 8	8 - 10
VINNOY (Italy)		
Ladies	12 - 15	15 - 18
VOGLIO, BENITO (Italy)		
Lady & Greyhound	30 - 35	35 - 40
ZANDRINO (Italy)		
Series 18, Lady/Wild Animals	20 - 25	25 - 30
Ladies/Heads/Fashion	12 - 15	15 - 18
ZINI, M.		
Ladies	10 - 12	12 - 14

BEAUTIFUL CHILDREN

ALANEN, JOSEPH (Finland)		
Easter Witch Children	8 - 10	10 - 12
Miniature Witch Cards	15 - 18	18 - 20
ANDERSON, V.C. (U.S.A.)	5 - 6	6 - 7
ANTTILA, EVA (Finland)	6 - 8	8 - 10
ATWELL, MABEL LUCIE (British)		
Early Period	10 - 12	12 - 15
Middle Period	6 - 8	8 - 12
1930's	5 - 6	6 - 8
BARHAM, S. (British)		
BAUMGARTEN, F. FB		
Meissner & Buch	5 - 6	6 - 8
Other Publishers	5 - 6	6 - 8
BEM (Russian)		
Russian Alphabet W/Children	12 - 15	15 - 18
Russian Children	10 - 12	12 - 15
BERTIGLIA, A. (Italy) See Art Deco Children		
BLODGETT, BERTHA		
AMP Co. Series 209, Easter	6 - 7	7 - 8
Series 410, Christmas	5 - 6	6 - 7
Little Girls/Huge Hats Series	6 - 8	8 - 10
BOMPARD, S. (Italy) See Art Deco Children		
BORISS, MARGARET	6 - 8	8 - 10
BRUNDAGE, FRANCES (U.S.A.)		
Sam Gabriel		
New Year		

Mabel Lucie Atwell
Valentine 1087

Bem
Russian, No Caption

Ser. 300, 302, 316 (10)	10 - 12	12 - 14
St. Patrick's		
Ser. 140 (10) (Uns.)	8 - 10	10 - 12
Valentines Ser 413 (6)	8 - 10	10 - 12
Halloween		
Ser. 120, 121 (10)	15 - 17	17 - 20
Ser. 123 (10)	12 - 15	15 - 18
Ser. 125 (6)	15 - 18	18 - 20
Thanksgiving		
Ser. 130, 132, 133 (10)	8 - 10	10 - 12
Ser. 135 (6)	6 - 8	8 - 10
Christmas		
Ser. 200, 208, 219	10 - 12	12 - 15
Santas	15 - 18	18 - 20
Raphael Tuck		
New Year		
Ser. 601 (Uns.)	8 - 10	10 - 12
Ser. 1036	10 - 12	12 - 15
Valentine		
Ser. 11 (4) (Uns.)	8 - 10	10 - 12
Ser. 20, 26 (Uns.)	10 - 12	12 - 15

Frances Brundage
Carl Hirsch Series 12

Frances Brundage
W.H.B. Series

Ser. 100, 101 (6) (Uns.)	10 - 12	12 - 14
Blacks	15 - 18	18 - 22
Ser. 102 (6)	12 - 15	15 - 18
Blacks	22 - 25	25 - 30
Ser. 115 (4)	8 - 10	10 - 12
Blacks	22 - 25	25 - 30
Ser. 118 (4)	10 - 12	12 - 14
Blacks	18 - 20	20 - 22
Easter Ser. 1049 (3)	8 - 10	10 - 12
Decoration Day Ser. 173 (12) (Uns.)	8 - 10	10 - 12
Halloween		
Ser. 174 (12) (Uns.)	12 - 14	14 - 16
Christmas		
Ser. 4 (12)	12 - 15	15 - 20
Ser. 165 (2)	10 - 12	12 - 15
Blacks	18 - 20	20 - 25
Ser. 1035 (2)	10 - 12	12 - 15
Blacks		
Oilette Ser. 2723 "Colored Folks" (6)	50 - 60	60 - 70
Ser. 4096 "Funny Folks" (4)	25 - 30	30 - 35
Early Foreign Publishers		

Large Images	25 - 30	30 - 35
Small Images	15 - 20	20 - 25
BURD, C.M. (U.S.A.)		
Rally Day Series	5 - 6	6 - 8
Birthday Series	4 - 5	5 - 6
CHIOSTRI, S. (Italy) See Art Deco Children		
CLAPSADDLE, ELLEN H. (U.S.A.)		
International Art. Pub. Co.		
Angels, Cherubs	4 - 6	6 - 8
Animals	4 - 5	5 - 6
Ladies, Women	5 - 6	6 - 8
Bells, Florals	2 - 3	3 - 4
Good Luck, Thanksgiving	2 - 3	3 - 4
Thanksgiving Children	5 - 6	6 - 9
Indians	6 - 7	7 - 9
Transportation	2 - 3	3 - 4
Christmas Children	7 - 9	9 - 12
Santas	10 - 12	12 - 18
Easter Children	7 - 9	9 - 14

Helen Clapsaddle
Int. Art Pub. Co. Series 952

Helen Clapsaddle
Wolfe & Co., "A Day of Joy"

Valentine Greetings	5 - 7	7 - 10
Valentine Children	6 - 8	12 - 18
Valentine Mechanicals	25 - 35	35 - 50
Lincoln's Birthday	5 - 8	8 - 12
Washington's Birthday	5 - 8	8 - 12
St. Patrick's Day	6 - 9	9 - 12
Independence Day	8 - 9	9 - 15
Halloween	15 - 20	20 - 35
Halloween Mechanicals (4)		
Series 1236 - Black Child	80- 90	90 - 100
Others	50 - 55	55 - 60
Wolfe & Co.		
Add $2-4 to above prices.		
Add $8-10 above Halloween prices.		
Suffragettes		
"Love Me, Love My Vote"	60 - 70	70 - 80
"Woman's Sphere is in the Home"	80 - 90	90 - 100
Foreign Publishers		
Add $3-4 to above prices.		
CORBETT, BERTHA (U.S.A.)		
J.I. Austin		
Sunbonnet Children	8 - 10	10 - 15
CURTIS, E. (U.S.A.)		
R. Tuck Garden Patch 2	8 - 10	10 - 12
"Apple"		
"Beet"		
"Cantelope"		
"Carrot"		
"Peach"		
"Radish"		
"Red Pepper"		
"Watermelon"		
R. Tuck "Valentine Maids" Series D12		
PC 1 "School Slates" (12)	6 - 7	7 - 8
PC 3 "Love's Labors" (12)	6 - 7	7 - 8
PC 4 "From Many Lands" (12)	6 - 7	7 - 8
CZEGKA, B. (Polish)		
W.R.B. & Co. Series 22 (6)	8 - 10	10 - 12
DEWEES, ETHEL, E.D., EHD (U.S.A.)		
AMP Co.	6 - 8	8 - 9
Nister Series 2543	8 - 10	10 - 12
DIXON, DOROTHY		
Ullman Mfg. Co.		
Sunbonnet Babies	8 - 10	10 - 12

DRAYTON, GRACE - **(Wiederseim)** (U.S.A.)
  Reinthal & Newman

489	"Oh Dear Me"	15 - 20	20 - 25
492	"Gee up Dobin" (uns.)	15 - 20	20 - 25
493	Skipping Rope	15 - 20	20 - 25
488	"Lambey Dear"	15 - 20	20 - 25
489	"Oh Dear Me ..."	15 - 20	20 - 25
495	Teacher & Children	15 - 20	20 - 25
496	"Do you, or don't you?"	15 - 20	20 - 25
497	"I should worry"	15 - 20	20 - 25
500	"More of All"	15 - 20	20 - 25
502	"Love at first sight"	20 - 25	25 - 30
503	"The Trousseau"	20 - 25	25 - 30
504	"The Wedding"	20 - 25	25 - 30
505	"The Honeymoon"	20 - 25	25 - 30
506		20 - 25	25 - 30
507	"Their New Love"	20 - 25	25 - 30

  R. Tuck

Ser. 241 "Bright Eyes" (Uns.) (6)	20 - 25	25 - 30
"I'se Awful Sweet ..."	20 - 25	25 - 30

Grace Drayton
R&N 503, "The Trousseau"

Grace Drayton
R&N 306, "A Button..."

"I'm Your Little Darling Boy ..."	20 - 25	25 - 30
"The Boys About Me Rant ..."	20 - 25	25 - 30
Others	20 - 25	25 - 30
Ser. 243 "Love Message" (Uns.) (6)	20 - 25	25 - 30
Oilette Series 2723 (4)		
"Colored Folks"		
"Church Parade"	30 - 35	35 - 40
"Don't Took the Last Piece"	30 - 35	35 - 40
"The Christening"	30 - 35	35 - 40
"De Proof of de Puddin"	30 - 35	35 - 40

DULK, M.
  Gibson Art Series 252

Fantasy Flower Girls, Birthday	10 - 12	12 - 16

"Daffodil"   "Pansy"
"Forget me Not"   "Poppy"
"Pussy Willow"   "Rose"
"Sweet Pea"   "Violet"
"Red Rose"   "Tulip"

Valentine Series - Girls (6)	8 - 10	10 - 12

EBNER, PAULI (German)

Pauli Ebner
AR 1448

Early Pauli Ebner (PE)
PE Series

Early - Signed PE	15 - 18	18 - 22
Santas	15 - 18	18 - 22
Children Series by M. Munk	10 - 12	12 - 15
Children by other Publishers	10 - 12	12 - 15
"Puppet Marriage Series"	15 - 18	18 - 22
ELLAM, WILLIAM (British)		
ELLIOTT, KATHRYN (U.S.A.)	4 - 5	5 - 6
F.S.M.		
Heininger "Courtship/Marriage" Ser.	8 - 9	9 - 10
FEDERLEY, ALEXANDER (Finland)	5 - 6	6 - 8
FIALKOWSKI, WALLY		
Large Children, Comical	8 - 10	10 - 12
Small Children & Babies	6 - 8	8 - 10
Black Children	12 - 13	13 - 15
FLOWERS, CHARLES (U.S.A)	5 - 6	6 - 7
FRANK, E.	5 - 6	6 - 7
GASSAWAY, KATHERINE (U.S.A)		
R. Tuck & Sons		
Series 113 Bridal Series Val. (6)	6 - 8	8 - 10
Series 130 Easter Series (12)	6 - 7	7 - 8
Series 22495 "The New Baby" (6)	6 - 8	8 - 10
Rotograph Co.		
National Girls		
220 "America"	8 - 10	10 - 12
221 "Ireland"	7 - 8	8 - 10
222 "England"	7 - 8	8 - 10
223 "Germany"	7 - 8	8 - 10
224 "France"	7 - 8	8 - 10
225	7 - 8	8 - 10
226 "Italy"	7 - 8	8 - 10
227 "Sweden"	7 - 8	8 - 10
American Kid Series (6)	5 - 6	6 - 8
Black Children	8 - 10	10 - 12
Others	5 - 6	6 - 8
GEORGE, MARY ELEANOR		
Ernest Nister Issues	15 - 18	18 - 22
GILSON, T. (U.S.A.)		
Black Children Comics	8 - 10	10 - 12
GOODMAN, MAUDE		
R. Tuck Series 824-833	8 - 10	10 - 12
GREENAWAY, KATE (KG) (British)		

Kate Greenaway was one of the first well-known illustrators of children. Her earliest works were of Valentines, Birthday and Christmas

non-postcards. Later came her famous children's books and almanacs.
She did many fine illustrations that were used in the "Mother Goose"
and "Old Nursery Rhymes" books printed by Rutledge and Sons.

Postcards were produced in limited quantities from these illustrations.
They are rarities, and are very hard to find in any condition. Kate died
in 1901 before the postcard-craze era of 1905-1918 began. The works
that were adapted for postcards are signed "KG" and have undivided
backs. They depict well-known children types and a verse from the
"Mother Goose" book which she illustrated.

KATE GREENAWAY		
Multilingual backs, No Pub.	60 - 70	70 - 85
GREINER, MAGNUS (U.S.A.)		
International Art Pub. Co.		
Dutch Children Ser. 491 (6)	6 - 7	7 - 8
Dutch Children Ser. 692	6 - 7	7 - 8
"Molly & the Bear" Ser. 791	10 - 12	12 - 15
Black Series 701-710		
701 "A Darktown Trip"	10 - 12	12 - 16
702 "The Serenade"	10 - 12	12 - 16
704 "A Lad & a Ladder"	10 - 12	12 - 16
707 "A Darktown Idyl"	10 - 12	12 - 16
708 "A Feast"	10 - 12	12 - 16
709 "A Darktown Lover"	10 - 12	12 - 16
710 "A Darktown Philosopher"	10 - 12	12 - 16
GRIGGS, H.B.		
L & E		
Children - Easter, Thanksgiving,		
and others	7 - 8	8 - 9
Halloween		
Series 2214, 2231, 2262	10 - 11	11 - 12
Series 2272	12 - 13	13 - 15
Anon Ser. 2215, 7010	12 - 13	13 - 15
GRIMBALL, M.		
Gutmann & Gutmann	12 - 15	15 - 18
R & N	10 - 12	12 - 15
FOREIGN ISSUES		
Novitas 20607-1 Uns.	22 - 25	25 - 30
10726 "Puppen Mutterchen's Einkauf"	22 - 25	25 - 30
"Storenfried"	22 - 25	25 - 30
10930 "Say Das Nicht Noch Mal!"	22 - 25	25 - 30

Meta Grimball
Novitas 20607-1, German Caption

Hoppa Hoppa Reiter!

Bessie Pease Gutmann
Novitas 10930, German Caption

Bessie Pease Gutmann
Russian 1155

"Kinderdieb"	22 - 25	25 - 30
Others	22 - 25	25 - 30

GUTMANN, BESSIE PEASE (U.S.A.)

Gutmann & Gutmann

No Number - "Sweet Sixteen"		15 - 20	20 - 25
501	"Senorita"	15 - 20	20 - 25
502	"Waiting"	15 - 20	20 - 25
505	"I Wish You Were Here"	15 - 20	20 - 25
803	"Alice"	20 - 25	25 - 28

Novitas, German

10726	"Naschkatzchen"	40 - 45	45 - 50
10930	"Zwietracht"	40 - 45	45 - 50
10966	"Delighted"	35 - 40	40 - 45
Series 20360	"The Bride"	35 - 40	40 - 45
"The Debutante"		35 - 40	40 - 45
"The Baby"		35 - 40	40 - 45
"Off to School"		35 - 40	40 - 45
"The Mother"		35 - 40	40 - 45
Series 20361	"Sunshine"	35 - 40	40 - 45
20556	Images in Water	35 - 40	40 - 45
20607-4	"The First Lesson"	35 - 40	40 - 45
20607-6	"The New Love"	35 - 40	40 - 45
20608	"Music Hath Charm"	35 - 40	40 - 45
"Love is Blind"		35 - 40	40 - 45
"Margaret"		35 - 40	40 - 45
Russian Card 155, Uns.			
(W/Many Dolls)		40 - 50	50 - 60
Others		35 - 40	40 - 45

HARDY, FLORENCE (British)

C.W. Faulkner & Co.	8 - 9	9 - 10
M. Munk Series 352 (6)	8 - 10	10 - 12
Others	6 - 8	8 - 10

HAYS, MARGARET G. (U.S.A.)

Margaret G. Hays, born in Philadelphia, was the sister of the more famous children's artist, Grace Wiederseim. They worked together on many projects, with Margaret writing poems and stories that were to be illustrated by Grace.

Margaret also produced many beautiful works of children. Her cards by the publisher Nister were very exceptional and of the highest quality. Other cards were published by the Rose Company, as well as some anonymous firms. Works by this fine artist are relatively elusive and are highly desirable.

MARGARET G. HAYS
    Ernest Nister

"Miss Polly Pigtail" Series (6)	25 - 30	30 - 35
2748 Dressed in Pink		
2749 Dressed in Green		
2750 Dressed in Purple		
2751 Dressed in Red		
2752 Dressed in Yellow		
2753 Dressed in Blue		
Nister Ser. 3061 (6) Large Images	15 - 17	17 - 20

    The Rose Co.

Christmas Series (6)	15 - 17	17 - 20

    Anonymous

Paper Doll Series 3 (6)	60 - 70	70 - 85
Paper Doll Series 6 (6)	60 - 70	70 - 85

HEINMULLER, A.
    International Art Pub. Co.

Series 1002, Halloween (6)	8 - 10	10 - 12

M.G. Hays
Nister 3061

H.G. Marsh
BD 410

Series 1003, St. Pats. (6)	4 - 6	6 - 7
Series 1004, Thanks. (6)	4 - 5	5 - 6
Series 1620, Valentines (6)	5 - 6	6 - 7
HUMPHREY, MAUDE (U.S.A.)		
R.L. Conwell Co., N.Y. unsigned	8 - 10	10 - 12
HUTAF, AUGUST (U.S.A.)		
Ullman Mfg. Co. Comical	4 - 5	5 - 8
I.M.J.		
M. Munk Children Series	6 - 8	8 - 10
K.V.		
LP Kewpie Series		
White Children	8 - 10	10 - 12
Black Children, or Mixed	10 - 12	12 - 15
KASKELINE, F.		
Silhouette Series 9033 (6)	6 - 8	8 - 9
Others	6 - 7	7 - 8
KNOEFEL		
Illuminated Cards		
Novitas Series 664 (6)	6 - 8	8 - 10
Novitas Series 656 W/Phones (6)	10 - 12	12 - 14
Novitas Series 15834, 20887		
Mother/Child Series (6)	8 - 10	10 - 12
LeMAIR, H. WILLEBEEK (British)		
Augener Ltd.		
Children's" Pieces of Schumann"	12 - 15	15 - 18

"Catch Me if You Can"   "Dreaming"
"Perfect Happiness"   "Melody"
"The Merry Peasant"   "First Loss"
"The Poor Orphan"   "Romance"
"Roundelay"   "Sicilienne"
"Soldier's March"   "Vintage"

Old Dutch Nursery Rhymes (12)	10 - 12	12 - 15
Old Rhymes W\New Pictures (12)	10 - 12	12 - 15

"Humpty Dumpty"   "Little Boy Blue"
"Little Miss Muffet"   "Lucy Locket"
"Polly Put the Ket ..."   "Twinkle Twinkle"
"Jack & Jill"   "Little Jack Horner"
"Little Mother"   "Mary, Mary ..."
"Three Blind Mice"   "Yankee Doodle"

Our Old Nursery Rhymes (12)	10 - 12	12 - 15
Small Rhymes/Small People (12)	10 - 12	12 - 15
The Children's Corner (12)	6 - 7	7 - 8
LEWIN, F.G.		
Bamforth "Black Kids" Comics	8 - 10	10 - 12

LINDEBERG		
Children Head Studies	6 - 8	8 - 10
KINSELLA, E.P.	6 - 8	8 - 10
KNOEFEL (Illuminated)	7 - 9	9 - 12
LD		
Meissner & Buch	6 - 8	8 - 9
LANDSTROM, B. (Finland)		
Fairy Tales	6 - 8	8 - 9
MAILICK, R. (German)		
Angels, Children	8 - 10	10 - 15
MALLET, BEATRICE (British)		
R. Tuck Oilettes		
"Cute Kiddies " Series		
3567, 3568, 3628, 3629 (6)	8 - 9	9 - 10
MARCELLUS, IRENE		
P. Nister		
Child in Glove, Child in Pie, etc.	10 - 12	12 - 15
MARSH, H.G.C. (British)		
"Wee Willie Winkle"	8 - 10	10 - 12
"Curly Locks"	7 - 8	8 - 10
M.E.P., MARGARET EVANS PRICE, MP		
Children	6 - 8	8 - 10
Halloween	8 - 10	10 - 12
Girl Scouts (See Topical Listing)		
M.D.S.		
Black Children	8 - 10	10 - 12
Others	6 - 7	7 - 8
NASH, A. (U.S.A.)	8 - 10	10 - 12
NOSWORTHY, FLORENCE (British)	6 - 8	8 - 10
NYSTROM, JENNY (Sweden)	10 - 12	12 - 15
See Fairy Tales		
NYSTROM, KURT (Sweden)	6 - 8	8 - 12
O'NEILL, ROSE (U.S.A.)		

One of the most popular of all the signed artists is Rose O'Neill, who created and drew the lovable Kewpies doll. The Kewpies delighted children and adults during the period after World War 1 through the Depression of the thirties.

Her first works were for advertising, covers and inside illustrations for some of the leading magazines. All showed the adorable Kewpies in various activities. The Gibson Art Company published many of O'Neill's designs on postcards for most of the holiday seasons. Her best and most popular were probably those of Christmas.

The Edward Gross Co. did a great set of six large image Kewpies, while Campbell Art and National Woman Suffrage each issued a card on Women's Suffrage that have become the most famous of all her works. She also did two series of blacks that were published by Raphael Tuck. These are very scarce and would be prizes for any collection. Rose O'Neill's Kewpie cards continue to be among the favorites in the deltiological field, and are avidly pursued by many collectors.

ROSE O'NEILL

Gibson Art Kewpies	30 - 35	35 - 40
Large Kewpie Series **(Gross)**	40 - 45	50 - 60
Unsigned Kewpies	12 - 15	15 - 18
Campbell Art Klever Kards	30 - 35	35 - 40
Dated 1914 (26)		
Dated 1915 (20)	30 - 35	35 - 40
228 "Votes for Women ..."	110 - 125	125 - 150
National Woman Suffrage		
"Votes for our Mothers"	225 - 250	250 - 275
R. Tuck		
Blacks, Ser. 2482 Oilettes		

Rose O'Neill
Gibson Art 66058

"High Society in Coontown"	100 - 110	110 - 120
Blacks, "Coontown Kids"	80 - 90	90 - 100
Rock Island Line, Adv.	45 - 50	50 - 60
Parker-Bruaner Co. Ice Cream ad	40 - 45	45 - 50
OUTCAULT, R. (U.S.A.) **See Artist-Signed Comics**		
Ullman Mfg. Co.		
Darktown Series 76 (Blacks)	10 - 12	12 - 15
PARKINSON, ETHEL	8 - 10	10 - 15
BC Series 745 (6)	8 - 10	10 - 12
M. Munk Series 531 (6)	8 - 10	10 - 12
PEASE, BESSIE COLLINS		
See Bessie P. Gutmann		
PEARSE, S.B. (Susan)		
M. Munk, Vienna		
Series 563 (6)	8 - 10	10 - 12
635 (6)	8 - 10	10 - 12
679 (6)	8 - 10	10 - 12
712 (6)	8 - 10	10 - 12

Millicent Sowerby
R&N 2001, "Peggy"

Uns. S.P. Pearse
M. Munk 635

713 (6)	10 - 12	12 - 15
727 (6)	8 - 10	10 - 12
Dancing 758 (6)	12 - 15	15 - 16
844 (6)	10 - 12	12 - 15
W/Toys 856 (6)	12 - 15	15 - 18
862 (6)	8 - 10	10 - 12
922 (6)	10 - 12	12 - 15
925 (6)	10 - 12	12 - 15
Dancing 958 (6)	12 - 15	15 - 18
Others	8 - 10	10 - 12
PETERSEN, HANNES	5 - 6	6 - 8
PITTS, JOHN E. J.E.P. (U.S.A.)	5 - 6	6 - 10
PRESTON, CHLOE (British) See Art Deco Children		
PRICE, MARGARET EVANS M.E.P		
Stecher Litho Co.		
Series 417 Christmas (6)	6 - 7	7 - 8
Series 749 Christmas (6)	6 - 8	8 - 10
Series 821 Valentines (6)	6 - 8	8 - 10
RICHARDSON, A. (British)		
M. Munk Series 706 (6)	8 - 10	10 - 12
Int. Art Co.		
1958 "My Love is Like ..."	6 - 8	8 - 10
1959 "I'll Take Care of Mummy"	6 - 8	8 - 10
ROBINSON, ROBERT (U.S.A.)		
E. Gross Series 205		
Boy Ball Player	15 - 20	20 - 25
RUSSELL, MARY LA FENETRA (U.S.A.)		
Sam Gabriel Co.		
Children	4 - 6	6 - 8
Halloween	8 - 10	10 - 12
SANFORD, M. (British)		
Raphael Tuck Black Series	8 - 10	10 - 14
SAUNDERS, E.H.	5 - 6	6 - 8
SMITH, JESSIE WILCOX (U.S.A.)		
R & N "Garden" Series 100	12 - 15	15 - 18
"Among the Poppies"		
"Five O'Clock Tea"		
"The Garden Wall"		
"The Green Door"		
"In the Garden"		
"The Lily Pool"		
SOWERBY, MILLICENT (British)		

Amy Millicent Sowerby was an English artist who illustrated several wonderful children's books. Her most famous was Lewis Carroll's "Alice in Wonderland," and then Robert Lewis Stevenson's "A Child's Garden of Verse." Her illustrations also appeared on picture postcards that were intended for children.

Her cards all have precise detail. Colors are exceptionally bright and the lithography is excellent. Most of Sowerby's cards were published in England and Europe. The American Post Card Co. and Reinthal & Newman, of New York, published several series for distribution in the U.S.

MILLICENT SOWERBY

R&N Unnumbered Series	10 - 12	12 - 15
"Cold," "Fair," "Wet"		
"Dry," "Cloudy," "Dull"		
R&N Series 2001	10 - 12	12 - 15
"Peggy"		
"Phoebe"		
"Phyllis"		
"Priscilla"		
Humphrey Milford, London		
Name of Series		
"Favorite Children" (6)	10 - 12	12 - 15
"Flower Children" (6)	12 - 15	15 - 18
"Flowers & Wings" (6)	12 - 15	15 - 18
"Merry Elves" (6)	12 - 15	15 - 18
"Old Time Games" (6)	10 - 12	12 - 15
"Sky Fairies" (6)	12 - 15	15 - 18
No Publisher		
Little Jewels Series	12 - 15	15 - 18
"Amethyst"		
"Emerald"		
"Pearl"		
"Ruby"		
"Sapphire"		
"Turquoise"		
Nursery Rhymes Series (6)	12 - 15	15 - 18
"Little Bo-Peep"		
"Little Jack Horner"		
"Little Miss Muffet"		
"Mistress Mary"		
"The Piper's Son"		
"Wee Willie Winkle"		

Woodland Games (6)	10 - 12	12 - 15
See Nursery Rhymes		
SPARK, CHICKY	5 - 6	6 - 8
SPURGIN, FRED (British)		
STENBERG, AINA (Sweden)	12 - 15	15 - 18
TARRANT, MARGARET (British)	6 - 8	8 - 15
TEMPEST, D. (British)		
Bamforth Co.		
Comic Kids and Animals	3 - 5	5 - 6
Black Kid Comics	6 - 8	8 - 12
TWELVETREES, C.H. (U.S.A.)		
Ullman Mfg. Co.		
National Cupid Series 75	6 - 8	8 - 10
1877 "United States"		
1878 "England"		
1879 "Ireland"		
1880 "Scotland"		
1882 "Mexico"		
1883 "Holland"		
1884 "Spain"		
1885 "Canada"		
1887 "China"		
1888 "Italy"		
Edward Gross Comical Kids	6 - 8	8 - 10
Wedding Series	8 - 10	10 - 12
1050 "Infant Series"	6 - 7	7 - 8
"Am I crying..."		
"I'm a war baby, but..."		
"I'm the family darling..."		
"Folks all say..."		
"Our baby can't talk..."		
"Watch your step..."		
National Art		
Days of the Week (7)	6 - 7	7 - 8
Morning-Noon-Night Ser.	6 - 8	8 - 10
WALL, BERNHARD C. (U.S.A.)		
Ullman's "The Little Coon" Series 559		
1660 "You all can hab de rine"	8 - 10	10 - 12
1661 "Deed, I Didn't Steal um!"	8 - 10	10 - 12
1662 "Who's dat say Chicken"	8 - 10	10 - 12
1663 "Just Two Coons"	8 - 10	10 - 12
"Cute Coon" Series 570		
1852 "A Chip of the Ole Block"	8 - 10	10 - 12
1853 "Whose Baby is OO?"	8 - 10	10 - 12

1854 "He Lubs Me"		8 - 10	10 - 12
1855 "I'se so Happy"		8 - 10	10 - 12
Nursery Rhymes 1664-1669 (uns.)		6 - 8	8 - 10
1664 "Little Bo Peep"			
1665 "To Market, To Market"			
1666 "Rain, Rain Go Away"			
1667 "See Saw, Marjorie Daw"			
1668 "Goosey, Goosey, Gander"			
1669 "Come, let's go to bed"			
Sunbonnet Months of the Year			
Unsigned, 1634-1644		10 - 12	12 - 15
Sunbonnet Girl's Days of the Week			
Uns., 1408-1410, 1491-1494		12 - 15	15 - 18
Sunbonnet Twins			
1645 "Give us this Day ..."		10 - 12	12 - 15
1646 "The Star Spangled ..."		10 - 12	12 - 15
1647 "Should Auld Acquaintance ..."		10 - 12	12 - 15
1648 "A Good Book is ..."		10 - 12	12 - 15
1649 "Now I Lay Me Down ..."		10 - 12	12 - 15
1650 "Be It Ever So Humble ..."		10 - 12	12 - 15
Bergman Unnumbered Sunbonnet Series		8 - 10	10 - 12
Animated Fruit & Vegetable Set		7 - 8	8 - 9

No Publisher

"Apple"	"Cabbage"
"Karat"	"Ears"
"Cucumber"	"Lemon"
"Melon"	"Onion"
"Pair"	"Peach"
"Pine"	"Potato"
"Pumpkin"	"Turnip"

Black Children	8 - 10	10 - 12

WIEDERSEIM, GRACE (also Grace Drayton)
Reinthal & Newman
No Number

"A button sewed on..."		15 - 20	20 - 25
"Blow"		15 - 20	20 - 25
"I think I'd rather..."		15 - 20	20 - 25
"The more I see ..."		15 - 20	20 - 25
"You're going to get ..."		15 - 20	20 - 25
98	"Nothing doing"	15 - 20	20 - 25
99	"Where's oo hanky"	15 - 20	20 - 25
110	"What you don't know ..."	15 - 20	20 - 25
112	"No Ma'am, we ain't ..."	15 - 20	20 - 25
113	"So near & yet so far"	15 - 20	20 - 25

115	"Curfew shall not ..."	15 - 20	20 - 25
116	"I'm so discouraged ..."	15 - 20	20 - 25
117	"Courage"	15 - 20	20 - 25
120	"I hate a spanking ..."	15 - 20	20 - 25
121	"Stung!"	15 - 20	20 - 25
174	"Here's How"	15 - 20	20 - 25
175	"Don't wake me up ..."	15 - 20	20 - 25
176	"I wish somebody was ..."	15 - 20	20 - 25
177	"And what did Mamma ..."	15 - 20	20 - 25
249	"Gee! but this is ..."	15 - 20	20 - 25
250	"Wanted! Somebody ..."	15 - 20	20 - 25
308	"I'd rather say Hello ..."	15 - 20	20 - 25
493	Skipping Rope	15 - 20	20 - 25
496	"Do you or don't you"	15 - 20	20 - 25

R. Tuck
"In Arcady"   25 - 30   30 - 35
Armour & Co.
American Girl Series
"The Wiederseim Girl"   25 - 30   35 - 40
A.M. Davis, Boston
Ser. 34 Christmas Messages   15 - 20   20 - 25
Ser. 143 Birthday Messages   15 - 20   20 - 25
Ser. 357 Easter Messages   15 - 20   20 - 25
Campbell Art Co.   30 - 35   35 - 40
Campbell Soup Co.
Campbell Soup Kids
Copyrt., Large Images   70 - 80   80 - 90
Copyrt., Small Images   40 - 50   50 - 60
Swift & Co.
W/Ads on reverse (6)   30 - 35   35 - 40
Schweizer Co.
Series 10596
Boy/Girl under Mistletoe   30 - 33   33 - 38
"Beware of Dog" Sign   30 - 33   33 - 38
"Choose Me"   30 - 33   33 - 38
"Help the Poor"   30 - 33   33 - 38
"You mustn't kiss me!"   30 - 33   33 - 38
WHITE, FLORA
Salmon & Co. Fairy Tale Series   10 - 12   12 - 14
See Fairy Tales

ART DECO CHILDREN

AZZONI, N.

Series 517 (6)	8 - 10	10 - 12
BERTIGLIA, A.		
Series 2461 (6)	10 - 12	12 - 15
Series 2444 (6)	8 - 10	10 - 12
Series 2428 (6) Making Movies	12 - 15	15 - 18
BOMPARD, S.		
Series 379 (6)	8 - 9	9 - 10
Series 497 (6)	8 - 9	9 - 10
Series 523 (6)	8 - 10	10 - 11
Series 454 (6)	8 - 9	9 - 10
Series 567 (6)	8 - 10	10 - 12
Series 906 (6)	8 - 10	10 - 12
Series 993 (6)	8 - 10	10 - 12
BORISS, M.	6 - 8	8 - 10
Armag Co. "Occupation Series" (6)	6 - 8	8 - 10
BUSI, A.		
Series 500 (6)	12 - 14	14 - 16
CASTILLI, V.		

Perini
Ultra 2306

Castilli
Ultra

Series 533 (6)	8 - 10	10 - 12
COLOMBO		
Series 234 (6)	6 - 8	8 - 9
Series 454 (6)	8 - 9	9 - 10
Series 618 (6)	8 - 10	10 - 12
Series 960 (6)	8 - 10	10 - 12
Series 1764 (6)	8 - 10	10 - 12
Series 1968 (6)	10 - 12	12 - 15
Series 2007 (6)	6 - 8	8 - 10
Series 2033 (6)	8 - 10	10 - 12
Series 2044 (6)	8 - 10	10 - 12
Series 2140 (6)	6 - 8	8 - 9
Series 2181 (6)	8 - 10	10 - 12
Series 2223 (6)	10 - 12	12 - 14
Series 2252 (6)	6 - 8	8 - 9
COOPER, PHYLLIS		
R. Tuck Series 3463	8 - 10	10 - 12
CHIOSTRI, SOFIA		
Series 184 (6) Japanese	10 - 12	12 - 15
Series 188 (6)	10 - 12	12 - 15
Series 188 (6)	10 - 12	12 - 15
GRILLI, S.	6 - 8	8 - 10
MAUZAN		
Series 45	10 - 12	12 - 15
MAISON-KURT, E.		
Fantasy Bear Set (4) W/Girl	12 - 15	15 - 18
PIATTAIT	6 - 8	8 - 10
PRESTON, CHLOE	8 - 10	10 - 12
PRICE, MARGARET ELLEN, MEP	8 - 10	10 - 12
ROWLES, L.	8 - 10	10 - 11
S.K.	8 - 10	10 - 12

ART NOUVEAU

B.G.	$40 - 45	$45 - 50
ABIELLE, JACK	40 - 45	45 - 50
BASCH, ARPAD (Hungary)		
Nouveau Heads, 1900 (6)	175 - 200	200 - 225
Series 769 (6)	175 - 200	200 - 225
"1900 Grand Femme" (6)	120 - 140	140 - 160
BRUNELLESCHI	70 - 80	80 - 100
CAUVY, L. (Denmark)	25 - 30	30 - 35
DANIELL, EVA (British)		
R. Tuck		

Kiezkow

R. Kirschner
"Women in the Sun" Series

"Art" Series 2524 (6)	150 - 160	160 - 175
"Art" Series 2525 (6)	120 - 125	125 - 135
DOCKER, E.	35 - 40	40 - 50
FRUNDT, H.	25 - 30	30 - 35
HAGER, NINI (Austria)	50 - 55	55 - 65
JOZSA, KARL (Austria)	50 - 55	55 - 65
KEMPF, TH. (Austria)	25 - 30	30 - 35
KING, JESSIE M.	70 - 80	80 - 90
KIRCHNER, RAPHAEL		
M. Munk		
"Continental" Series 4003 (6)		
"Women in the Sun"	90 - 100	100 - 110
KOSA (Austria)	75 - 85	85 - 100
LAUDA, RICHARD (Denmark)	40 - 50	50 - 60
LIKARTZ, MARIA (Austria)	200 - 225	225 - 250
LESSIEUX, LOUIS	40 - 50	50 - 60
MACDONALD, A.K.	40 - 50	50 - 60
MEUNIER, HENRI (Belgium)	200 - 225	225 - 250
MOSER, KOLOMON		
Philipp & Kramer Series V	150 - 160	160 - 175
MUCHA, A. (Czech.)		

Waverley Cycles (sold in 1991 for $13,500–see back cover)		
Sarah Bernhardt Poster Cards	125 - 150	150 - 175
Months of the Year	175 - 185	185 - 200
Times of Day	175 - 185	185 - 200
"La Plume"	370 - 380	380 - 400
Primevere	370 - 380	380 - 400
Ages of Man	250 - 260	260 - 275
Cocirico	450 - 475	475 - 500
Aurore	440 - 450	450 - 475
Czech. Designs	35 - 40	40 - 50
NOURY, GASTON (France)	40 - 50	50 - 60
PATELLA, B.	40 - 50	50 - 60
SONREL, ELISABETH	200 - 225	225 - 250
STEINLEN, A.T. (France)		
Better	200 - 210	210 - 225
Others	30 - 35	35 - 45
PELLON, A.		
"Ideal" Series (6)	80 - 90	90 - 100
RAUH, LUDWIG (German)	30 - 40	40 - 45

A. Mucha
"Souv. Belle Jardiniere"

Elisabeth Sonrel

RYAN

A 633	"Folly"	10 - 12	12 - 15
A 634	"Joy"	10 - 12	12 - 15
A 638	"So Lonesome"	10 - 12	12 - 15

LADIES & DOGS

BARBER, COURT			
"Beauties"		8 - 10	10 - 12
BERTIGLIA			
Series 163 (6)		8 - 10	10 - 12
BIANCHI			
Series 483 (6)		8 - 10	10 - 12
Series 2020 (6)		10 - 12	12 - 14
BOMPARD, S.			
Series 11 (6)		10 - 12	12 - 15
Series 343 (6)		10 - 12	12 - 15
Series 457 (6)		12 - 14	14 - 17
Series 461 (6)		10 - 12	12 - 14
BUSI, ADOLFO			
Series 170 (6)		12 - 14	14 - 16
Series 533 (6)		12 - 15	15 - 18
CHIOSTRI 316		22 - 25	25 - 30
CHRISTY, EARL			
R & N 942, "Protected"		10 - 12	12 - 15
COLOMBO			
Series 330 (6)		12 - 14	14 - 16
Series 894 (6)		12 - 15	15 - 18
Series 1165 (6)		12 - 15	15 - 18
Series 1494 (6)		10 - 12	12 - 15
Series 1763 (6)		12 - 14	14 - 16
CORBELLA			
Series 117 (6)		10 - 12	12 - 14
Series 233 (6)		15 - 18	18 - 22
Series 237 (6)		12 - 14	14 - 16
Series 230 (6)		12 - 15	15 - 18
Series 464 (6)		12 - 15	15 - 18
Series 516 (6)		15 - 18	18 - 22
Series 530 (6)		12 - 15	15 - 18
Series 2224 (6)		22 - 25	25 - 30
Series 4646 (6)		15 - 18	18 - 20
DEGAMI			
Ultra Series 2195		20 - 25	25 - 28
DUNCAN, F.			

E. Colombo
CAD 1763-1

R&N 931 "A Reserved Seat"	10 - 12	12 - 15
R&N 934 "Call of the Country"	10 - 12	12 - 15
FRANZONI		
BKWI Ser. 369	10 - 12	12 - 15
BKWI Ser. 6309	12 - 15	15 - 18
GUZERONI	10 - 12	12 - 15
MAUZAN		
Series 453 (6)	8 - 10	10 - 12
Series 491 (6)	10 - 12	12 - 15
MONESTIER		
Series 36 (6)	12 - 15	15 - 18
NANNI		
Series 205 (6)	15 - 18	18 - 22
Series 300 (6)	15 - 18	18 - 22
PENNELL		
M. Munk "My Companion"	8 - 10	10 - 12
PLANTIKOW	8 - 10	10 - 12
RALPH, LESTER		
Knapp Co. "Weathering it Together"	8 - 10	10 - 12
"Diana of the Shore"	8 - 10	10 - 12
"Fellow Sports"	8 - 10	10 - 12
"A Stroll Together"	8 - 10	10 - 12
"Favored by Fortune"	8 - 10	10 - 12

RAPPINI	8 - 10	10 - 12
SCHUBERT		
M. Munk, Vienna	6 - 8	8 - 10
TERZI, A.		
Series 341 (6)	8 - 10	10 - 12
Series 349 (6)	8 - 10	10 - 12
Series 399 (6)	8 - 10	10 - 12
Series 457 (6)	10 - 12	12 - 15
Series 482 (6)	10 - 12	12 - 15
Series 973 (6)	10 - 12	12 - 15
Series 976 (6)	12 - 14	14 - 17
UNDERWOOD, C.		
M. Munk, Vienna "My Companion"	6 - 8	8 - 10
USABAL		
Series 1336 (6)	8 - 10	10 - 12
P.F.B.		
Series 3968 (6)	12 - 14	14 - 16

Usabal
PFB 3968-2

Nanni
Uff. Rev. Stampa 300-4

LADIES AND HORSES

BARBER, COURT

"Miss Knickerbocker"	8 - 10	10 - 12
"In Summer Days"	8 - 10	10 - 12
"Thoroughbreds"	8 - 10	10 - 12

BARRIBAL

Artisque Series 2234 (6)	10 - 12	12 - 15
Artisque Series 2236 (6)	10 - 12	12 - 15

BERTIGLIA

Series 227 (6)	8 - 10	10 - 12
Series 2132 (6)	10 - 12	12- 14
Series 2151 (6)	8 - 10	10 - 12

BIANCHI

Series 2020 (6)	8 - 10	10 - 12

BOERMEISTER | 8 - 10 | 10 - 12 |

BOMPARD

Series 343 (6)	12 - 14	14 - 16
Series 457 (6)	12 - 14	14 - 16

Simonetti
SWSB 6781-2

F. Kaskeline
SWSB 1119

Series 641 (6)	12 - 14	14 - 16
BUSI, ADOLFO		
Series 157 (6)	12 - 15	15 - 18
COLOMBO		
Series 202 (6)	12 - 15	15 - 18
Series 488 (6)	15 - 18	18 - 22
Series 813 (6)	15 - 18	18 - 22
Series 1676 (6)	15 - 18	18 - 22
Series 1869 (6)	15 - 18	18 - 22
CORBELLA, T.		
Series 117 (6)	12 - 15	15 - 18
Series 237 (6)	12 - 15	15 - 18
Series 316 (6)	12 - 15	15 - 18
Series 330 (6)	12 - 15	15 - 18
Series 464 (6)	10 - 12	12 - 15
Series 530 (6)	12 - 15	15 - 18
Series 532 (6)	15 - 18	18 - 22
CYRANICUS		
Series 150 (6)	10 - 12	12 - 15
Series 430 (6)	10 - 12	12 - 15
GUERZONI		
BKWI Ser. 710 (6)	8 - 10	10 - 12
HORSFALL, MARY	10 - 12	12 - 15
KASKELINE	8 - 10	10 - 12
MAUZAN		
Series 383 (6)	12 - 15	15 - 18
NANNI		
Series 116 (6)	12 - 15	15 - 20
Series 257 (6)	12 - 15	15 - 18
Series 307 (6)	15 - 18	18 - 22
Series 374 (6)	15 - 16	16 - 18
OPLATEK	8 - 10	10 - 12
PENNELL	8 - 10	10 - 12
PERINI, T.	8 - 10	10 - 12
PLANTIKOW	8 - 10	10 - 12
RAPPINI		
Series 1002 (6)	10 - 12	12 - 15
Series 1092 (6)	8 - 10	10 - 12
Series 2019 (6)	8 - 10	10 - 12
SANTINO		
Series 68 (6)	8 - 10	10 - 12
SIMONETTI	10 - 12	12 - 15
Series 41 (6)	12 - 15	15 - 18
Series 90 (6)	10 - 12	12 - 14

STOLTE, F.		
Series 25 (6)	8 - 10	10 - 12
TERZI, A.		
Series 320 (6)	10 - 12	12 - 15
USABAL		
Series 257 (6)	8 - 10	10 - 12
Series 320 (6)	7 - 8	8 - 9
Series 328 (6)	8 - 10	10 - 12
Series 345 (6)	8 - 10	10 - 12
Series 1182 (6)	7 - 8	8 - 10
WALLACE	8 - 10	10 - 12
WFA		
Series 204 (6)	6 - 8	8 - 10

COMICS

ANDERSON, M. (CYNICUS) (British)	6 - 8	8 - 10
BAIRNSFATHER, BRUCE (British)	6 - 8	8 - 10
BISHOP, P. (U.S.A.)		
"Ginks"	8 - 10	10 - 12
Others	4 - 5	5 - 6
BRADSHAW, P.V. (British)	6 - 8	8 - 9
BRILL, GEORGE (U.S.A.)	6 - 8	8 - 10
BROWNE, TOM (British)		
Davidson Bros.		
Ser. 2598 "Are We Downhearted ..." (6)	5 - 8	10 - 15
Ser. 2578 "Billiards made ..." (6)	8 - 10	10 - 12
Ser. 2618 "Baseball Ill." (6)	8 - 10	10 - 12
Ser. 2619 "Baseball Ill." (6)	10 - 12	12 - 15
Ser. 2585		
"Amateur Photographe"r (6)	10 - 12	12 - 14
Ser. 2627 "Diabolo" (6)	10 - 12	12 - 15
CARMICHAEL		
Series 668		
"Anybody Here Seen Kelly"	6 - 7	7 - 8
Ser. 565 "I Love My Wife ..."	7 - 8	8 - 10
Ser. 261 "Would You?" (6)	6 - 7	7 - 9
CARR, GENE (U.S.A.)		
Rotograph Co., NY		
4th of July Series	8 - 9	9 - 10
St. Patrick's Series	6 - 6	6 - 8
CAVALLY, F. (U.S.A.)	2 - 4	4 - 6
DISNEY, WALT		
Foreign Issues		

R.F. Outcault
Buster Brown and His Bubble, "Black or White"

French, 30's era	15 - 20	20 - 25
German, 30's era	20 - 25	25 - 30
Czech., 30's era	20 - 25	25 - 30
Hungarian, 30's era	20 - 25	25 - 30
Other 30's era issues	15 - 20	20 - 25
DONADINI, JR.		
Series 454 Black Comics (6)	12 - 15	15 - 18
Auto Driver Series (6)	10 - 12	12 - 15
Horse Racing Series (6)	10 - 12	12 - 15
DWIG C.V. DWIGGINS (U.S.A.)		
C. Marks		
Halloween Series 981 (12)	20 - 22	25 - 28
R. Tuck Series		
"Cheer Up" (24)	6 - 8	8 - 10
"Don't" (24)	6 - 8	8 - 10
"Everytime" (24)	6 - 8	8 - 10
"Follies" (12)	6 - 8	8 - 10
"If" (24)	6 - 8	8 - 10
"Help Wanted" (12)	6 - 7	7 - 8
"Never" (24)	6 - 7	7 - 8
"Jollies" (12)	6 - 8	8 - 10
"School Days" (24)	6 - 8	8 - 10
"Smiles" (24)	8 - 10	10 - 12
"Toast" (12)	8 - 10	10 - 12

"Zodiac" (12)	12 - 14	14 - 18
Charles Rose		
"Baby" (6)	8 - 10	10 - 12
"Moon" (6)	6 - 8	8 - 10
"Moving" (6)	8 - 10	10 - 12
"New York" (6)	8 - 10	10 - 12
"Oyster Girl" (6)	10 - 12	12 - 14
"Sandwich" (6)	8 - 10	10 - 12
"Superstition" (6)	8 - 10	10 - 12
"What are Wild Waves ..." (6)	10 - 12	12 - 14
"The Wurst Girl" (6)	10 - 12	12 - 14
R. Kaplan		
"Fortune Teller" (12)	8 - 9	9 - 10
"How Can You Do It?" (24)	6 - 7	7 - 8
"Mirror Girl" (24)	8 - 10	10 - 12
Sam Gabriel		
"If's & And's" (24)	6 - 7	7 - 8
"Leap Year" (12)	9 - 10	10 - 12

GIBSON, CHARLES DANA (U.S.A.)

Walt Disney
RKO Czech

Donald McGill
Bamforth Comics

Henderson Co. (36)	5 - 6	6 - 7
GRIGGS, H.B. **HBG**		
L & E Halloween Series	8 - 10	10 - 12
Others	7 - 8	8 - 9
HARDY, DUDLEY (British)	5 - 6	6 - 8
HORINA, H. (U.S.A.)		
Illustrated P.C. Co.	5 - 6	6 - 7
HUTAF, AUGUST		
P.C.K. "Advice to Vacationists"	5 - 6	6 - 7
KYD, J.C.C. (British)		
Dickens Characters	9 - 10	10 - 12
LEWIN, F.G. See Black Comics		
MARTIN, ABE		
Illustrated P.C. Co.	5 - 6	6 - 7
MAY, PHIL (British)	6 - 8	8 - 12
McGILL, DONALD (British)		
Blacks	6 - 8	8 - 10
Others	2 - 3	3 - 4
McMANUS, GEORGE		
Bringing Up Father Series	20 - 25	25 - 30
OPPER, F. (U.S.A.)		
"Happy Hooligan" Series	8 - 10	10 - 12
"Alphonse & Gaston" Series	6 - 8	8 - 10
"And Her Name Was Maud" Series	6 - 8	8 - 10
Others	5 - 6	6 - 8
Add $3 for Tuck issues		
OUTCAULT, R.F. (U.S.A.)		
Buster Brown Series	8 - 12	15 - 25
Yellow Kid Series	40 - 50	50 - 60
Souvenir Post Card Co.		
Buster Brown & His Bubble (10)		
1 "A Quiet Day in Town"	15 - 20	20 - 25
2 "Hands Up"	15 - 20	20 - 25
3 "Black or White"	20 - 25	25 - 30
4 "Looking for Trouble"	15 - 20	20 - 25
5 "A Good Bump"	15 - 20	20 - 25
6 "Over the Bounding Main"	20 - 25	25 - 30
7 "A Rise in Bear"	15 - 20	20 - 25
8 "A Smooth Bit of Road"	20 - 25	25 - 30
9 "The Constable"	20 - 25	25 - 30
10 "All Over"	15 - 20	20 - 25
Others	6 - 8	8 - 10
PIPPO		
Big Eyed Man Series	8 - 10	10 - 12

Barber	Gambler		
Blacksmith	Musician		
Cook	Rich Man		
Doctor	Sculptor		
POULBOT, F. (France)		10 - 12	12 - 15
RAEMAKERS (Netherlands)		6 - 8	8 - 10
REZNICEK (Denmark)		12 - 15	15 - 18
ROBIDA (France)		10 - 12	12 - 15
SCHULTZ, C.E. (Bunny)			
Foxy Grandpa Series		6 - 8	8 - 10
SHINN, COBB (U.S.A.)			
H.A. Waters Co.			
Foolish Questions Series		3 - 4	4 - 5
Ford Comics		6 - 8	8 - 10
See Art Nouveau			
SPURGIN, FRED (British)		5 - 6	6 - 8
THACKERAY, L.			
R. Tuck Oilette Ser. 8553			
"At the Seaside" (6)		8 - 9	9 - 12
"Game of Golf" (6)		12 - 14	14 - 18
THIELE, ARTH.			
L & P			
Fat Lady Series		10 - 12	12 - 14
Bathing Girl Series		12 - 14	14 - 16
UPTON, FLORENCE (British)			
Golliwogs		12 - 15	15 - 25
See Golliwogs			
WALL, BERNHARD			
Many Sets and Series		5 - 6	6 - 10
WEAVER, E. (U.S.A.)			
Ford Comics		8 - 10	10 - 12
Others		1 - 2	2 - 3
WELLMAN, WALTER (U.S.A.)		4 - 5	5 - 8
WELLS, C.			
Lounsbury Series 2025			
"Lovely Lilly"		6 - 7	7 - 8
WITT			
Ford Booster comics (10)		7 - 8	8 - 10
WOOD, LAWSON (British)			
Chimps, Parrots, etc.		6 - 8	8 - 10
See Suffragettes			
Bauman (Uns.)			
Ugly Girls - Days of the Week (6)		6 - 8	8 - 9
Irwin Kline (Uns.)			

Masonic (No number) (6)	6 - 7	7 - 8
P.F.B. (Uns.)		
Ser. 5897 Mother-in-Law (6)	8 - 10	10 - 12
Ser. 6307 Comic Lovers (6)	8 - 10	10 - 12
Ser. 6538 Domestic Riot (6)	8 - 10	10 - 12

SILHOUETTES

ALLMAHER, JOSEFINE	6 - 8	8 - 9
BECKMAN, JOHANNA	5 - 7	7 - 8
BURKE, PAUL	5 - 7	7 - 8
BORRMEISTER, R.	6 - 8	8 - 10
DIEFENBACH		
Fantasy Children	7 - 10	10 - 15
FORCK, ELISABETH	6 - 7	7 - 8
GRAF, MARTE		
Art Deco		
Series 1, 2, 3, 4 (743-754)	8 - 10	10 - 14
Others	8 - 10	10 - 12
GROSS, CH.	5 - 7	7 - 8
GROSZE, M.		
P.F.B. IN DIAMOND		
Deco Series 2041 "After Bath"	12 - 13	13 - 15
Nude Series 2042	12 - 15	15 - 16
Nude Series 3339	12 - 15	15 - 18
Series 3341 & 3342	10 - 12	12 - 15
Others	10 - 12	12 - 14
KASKELINE		
Art Deco, Ladies/Children	8 - 10	10 - 12
LAMP, H.		
Series 3, Deco Dancing	12 - 15	15 - 18
Series 4, Bathing	12 - 15	15 - 18
ROBA		
Deco Fantasy	12 - 15	15 - 18
SACHSE-SCHUBERT, M.	10 - 12	12 - 14
SCHONPFLUG, FRITZ	10 - 12	12 - 15
STUBNER, LOTTE	8 - 10	10 - 12
S.K.		
Meissner & Buch	8 - 10	10 - 12

BLACKS, SIGNED

ATWELL, MABEL L.

Valentine
Ser. 745, A331 (6)	8 - 10	10 - 12
Ser. 614, 615 (6)	10 - 12	12 - 14

BRUNDAGE, FRANCES
R. Tuck Oilettes
Ser. 2723 "Colored Folks" (6)	30 - 35	35 - 40
"Church Parade"		
"The Christening"		
"De Proof..."		
"Don't took de las' piece"		
"The Village Choir"		
"You is a Chicken"		
Ser. 4096 "Funny Folk" (4)	25 - 30	30 - 35
Other Signed Brundage	15 - 18	18 - 22
Unsigned	12 - 15	15 - 18

CLAPSADDLE, HELEN
Int. Art. Pub. Co.
Mechanical Ser. 1236	150 - 160	160 - 175

M. Greiner
Int. Art Series 704

PFB Series 7179

HERMAN, H.
    Ullman Series 106 (4)   10 - 12   12 - 15
K.V.
    L.P. Series 206 Black Kewpies   10 - 12   12 - 15
KEMBLE B&W Comics   6 - 8   8 - 10
LEVI, C.
    Ullman Series 165   8 - 10   10 - 12
LEWIN, F.G.
    Artisque Series   12 - 14   14 - 16
    Inter Art   8 - 10   10 - 12
    P. Salmon   10 - 12   12 - 15
    Bamforth   8 - 10   10 - 12
M.D.S.
    R. Tuck
    Ser. 9049 "Happy Little Coons" (6)   10 - 12   12 - 14
    Ser. 9050 "Happy Little Coons" (6)   10 - 12   12 - 14
    Ser. 9093 "Curley Coons" (6)   12 - 14   14 - 16
    Ser. 9227 "Happy Little Coons" (6)   10 - 12   12 - 14
    Ser. 9228 "Happy Little Coons" (6)   10 - 12   12 - 14
    Ser. 9229 "Happy Little Coons" (6)   12 - 14   14 - 18
McGILL, DONALD
    Bamforth   6 - 8   8 - 10
    D. Constance, Ltd.   6 - 8   8 - 10
MINNS, B.E.
    Carlton Pub. Co.
    "Glad Eye" Series (6)   10 - 12   12 - 14
O'NEILL, ROSE
    R. Tuck Series 2482 Oilettes
    "High Society in Coontown" (6)   100 - 110 110 - 120
    "Coontown Kids" Series (6)   80 - 90   90 - 100
OUTCAULT
    Ullman "Darktown" Ser. 76   12 - 14   14 - 16
SANFORD, H. DIX
    R. Tuck Oilette
    "Dark Girls & Black Boys"
    Ser. 9428, 9489 (6)   10 - 12   12 - 15
    "Seaside Coons" Ser. 9318 (6)   10 - 12   12 - 15
    "Seaside Coons" Ser. 9968, 9969 (6) 10 - 12   12 - 15
    Hildesheimer & Co.
    "Negroes" Ser. 5268   8 - 10   10 - 12
SHEPHEARD
    R. Tuck Oilette
    "Coon's Cooning" Ser. 9068 (6)   10 - 12   12 - 14
TEMPEST, D.

Bamforth & Co.	8 - 10	10 - 12
THIELE, ARTH.		
FED		
Head Studies, Series 306 (6)	20 - 22	22 - 25
Black Jockey Series 871 (6)	20 - 25	25 - 28
TWELVETREES, C.	6 - 8	8 - 10
WUYTS		
A. Noyer Series 76 (6)	10 - 12	12 - 14

BLACKS, UNSIGNED

Albertype Co.		
PMC "Greetings from the Sunny South" (12)	30 - 35	35 - 40
Detroit Pub. Co.		
Black Series	10 - 12	12 - 14
G. B. Co.		
Series G Husband & Wife (6)	8 - 10	10 - 12
Franz Huld		
Cake Walk, "Darkey Series" (PMC)	10 - 12	12 - 15
Ill. P.C. Co.		
"Darkies," Series 78	8 - 10	10 - 12
Langsdorf		
"Greetings from the Sunny South"	10 - 12	12 - 15
P.F.B. Series 7148 (6)	12 - 14	14 - 18
Series 7179 (6)		
Black Gents & Ladies (6)	20 - 25	25 - 30
Series 7942 (6)	12 - 14	14 - 18
Series 7946 (6)	12 - 14	14 - 18
Taggart		
Red Background Ser. 24 (6)	10 - 12	12 - 15
Thanksgiving Ser. 608 (6)	8 - 9	9 - 10
R. Tuck		
Oilette Ser. 9297 (6)		
"Among the Darkies"	8 - 10	10 - 12
"Negro" 1819 (6)	8 - 10	10 - 12
"Coon Studies" Ser. 2087, 2088 (6)	10 - 12	12 - 14
"Coon Studies" Ser. 9094, 9542 (6)	10 - 12	12 - 14
"Coontown Kids" Ser. 2843, 9092		
and 9412 (6)	10 - 12	12 - 14
"Happy Coons" Ser. 9457 (6)	10 - 12	12 - 15
"Happy Darkies" Ser. 2363 (6)	10 - 12	12 - 14
"Happy Little Coons"		
Ser. 8438, 9049 (6)	10 - 12	12 - 14
9050, 9227, 9228, 9229 (6)	10 - 12	12 - 14

"High Society in Coontown"		
Oilette Ser. 9411 (6)	15 - 18	18 - 22
Calendar Ser. 1043, Black Couples (6)	8 - 10	10 - 12
Negro Melodies Ser. 2398, 6909 (6)	12 - 14	14 - 16
Sunny South Coon Studies Ser. 2181 (6)	10 - 12	12 - 14
Negro Series 4400, 4401 (6)	10 - 12	12 - 14
"Seaside Coons" Ser. 9318 (6)	12 - 14	14 - 16
Ullman Mfg. Co.		
"Little Coons," Series 59 (6)	10 - 12	12 - 15
"Kute Koon Kids," Series 1065 (6)	10 - 12	12 - 14
Mechanical - "Pick the Pickaninnies" Puzzle	50 - 55	55 - 60
Valentine & Sons		
"Coonville" (6)	8 - 10	10 - 12
White Border, Real Life	5 - 7	7 - 10
Linen Cards		
1930-1949	2 - 3	5 - 8

COWBOYS & INDIANS

CRAIG, CHARLES (U.S.A.)		
Williamson-Hafner Indian Series	6 - 8	8 - 10
GREGG, PAUL Cowboy Series	4 - 6	6 - 8
INNES, JOHN		
Western Art Series (6)	6 - 8	8 - 9
"The Bad Man"		
"Pack Train"		
"The Portage"		
"Prairie Schooner"		
"Roping Bronco"		
"Warping the Fur Barge ..."		
MacFarlane Pub. Co.		
Trioilene Series	6 - 8	8 - 10
"Cattle Girl"		
"Warping the Air Barge Upstream"		
"Indians in a Snow Storm"		
"Indian Pony Race"		
"Roping a Steer"		
"The Town Marshall"		
"The War Canoe"		
PAXON, E.S.		
McKee Printing Co. Indian Series	5 - 6	6 - 8
PETERSON, L. (U.S.A.)		
H.H. Tammen Co. Indian Series		
3420 "Chief Sitting Bull"	10 - 12	12 - 13

John Innes
Troilene Series, "Town Marshall"

3421	"Chief Geronimo"	10 - 12	12 - 13
3422	"Chief Yellow Hawk"	8 - 10	10 - 12
3423	"Chief Eagle Feather"	8 - 10	10 - 12
3424	"Chief High Horse"	8 - 10	10 - 12
3425	"Starlight"	8 - 10	10 - 12
3426	"Chief Big Feather"	8 - 10	10 - 12
3427	"Sunshine"	8 - 10	10 - 12
3428	"Fighting Wolf"	8 - 10	10 - 12
3429	"Minnehaha"	8 - 10	10 - 12
3430	"Hiawatha"	10 - 12	12 - 15
3431	"Chief Red Cloud"	10 - 12	12 - 15
3432	"Eagle Feather & Squaw"	8 - 10	10 - 12
3433	"Chief Black Hawk"	10 - 12	12 - 15
Tammen	"Cow Girl Series"	6 - 8	8 - 10

REMINGTON, FREDERIC
Detroit Publishing Co.

14179	"Evening on a Canadian"	35 - 45	45 - 55
14180	"His First Lesson"	30 - 35	35 - 45
14181	"A Fight for the Water Hole"	35 - 45	45 - 55
14182	"An Argument W/Marshall"	35 - 45	45 - 55
14183	"Calling the Moose"	30 - 35	35 - 45

RHINEHART, F.A.
Indian Series   6 - 8   8 - 10
"Rain in the Face," Sioux

"Big Man"
"Chief Wolf Robe," Cheyenne
"Chief Red Cloud," Sioux
"Chief Sitting Bull," Sioux
"Eagle Feather & Papoose"
"Two Little Braves," Sioux & Fox
"Chase-in-the-Morning"
"Hattie Tom," Chiricahua Apache
RUSSELL, CHARLES M.
  Ridgley Calendar Co.   10 - 12   12 - 15
  "Are You the Real Thing?"
  "Antelope Hunt"
  "A Touch of Western High Life"
  "The Buffalo Hunt"
  "Roping a Grizzly"
  "Lone Wolf Piegan"
  "A Wounded Grizzly"
  "Roping a Wolf"
  "Blackfeet Burning ..."
  "The Wild Horse Hunters"

Hiawatha
R. Tuck 1330, "Tall of Stature"

F.A. Rhinehart
"Chief Wolf Robe"

Others	8 - 10	10 - 12
Raphael Tuck "Indian Chiefs"		
Series 2171 (12)	8 - 10	10 - 12
Series 9131	10 - 12	12 - 15
"Chief Charging Bear"		
"Chief Not Afraid of Pawnee"		
"Chief Black Chicken"		
"Chief Eagle Track"		
"Chief Black Thunder"		
"Chief White Swan"		
Series 9011 "Hiawatha" (6)	8 - 10	110 - 12
Series 1330		
"Hiawatha"	10 - 12	12 - 15
SCHULTZ, F.W. (U.S.A.)		
Cowboy Series 1728-1746	5 - 6	6 - 8

ANIMALS

CATS

ALDIN, CECIL (British)	6 - 7	7 - 8
BARNES, G.L.		
R. Tuck		
Series 9301 "Cat Studies" (6)	8 - 10	10 - 12
BOULANGER Series 586 (6)	6 - 8	8 - 9
International Art Pub. Co.		
Series 472 Large Image (6)	12 - 15	15 - 20
Series 473 Large Image (6)	12 - 14	14 - 18
R. Tuck		
"Merry Days" Ser. 122 (6) Uns.	6 - 8	8 - 10
COBBE, B. (British)	6 - 8	8 - 10
ELLAM		
R. Tucks "Mixed Bathing" Series	8 - 10	10 - 12
FEIERTAG (Austria)	4 - 6	6 - 8
FREES		
Rotograph Real Photo Cat Comics	6 - 8	8 - 9
HOFFMAN, A.	5 - 6	6 - 8
KASKELINE		
SWSB Series 4370	5 - 6	6 - 8
LANDOR		
R. Tuck Real Photo Studies		
Series 5088, 7006 (6)	4 - 5	5 - 6
SCHWAR Cat Studies	6 - 8	8 - 9
SPERLICH, T. (British)	6 - 7	7 - 8

Arth. Thiele
TSN 896

Louis Wain
R. Tuck, "Diabolo"

German Am. Novelty Co.
Series 648 (6)	6 - 8	8 - 10
STOCK, A.	5 - 6	6 - 7
STOCKS, M.	6 - 7	7 - 8

THIELE, ARTH.
TSN
Series 129 Dancing (6)	10 - 12	12 - 15
Series 134 Large Heads (6)	15 - 18	18 - 22
Series 915 Comic Cats (6)	12 - 15	15 - 18
Series 995		
Large Cupid Cats (6)	25 - 30	30 - 35
Series 1002 At Home (6)	10 - 12	12 - 15
Series 1077 Cat Families (6)	10 - 12	12 - 15
Series 1326 In Kitchen (6)	10 - 12	12 - 15
Series 1412 Large Image (6)	20 - 22	22 - 26
Series 1423 In School (6)	10 - 12	12 - 15
Series 1424 Large Image (6)	20 - 25	25 - 28

"Big Cleanup"
"Big Washday"
"Dressmaking"
"Going to Bed"

"Kitty Traveling"
"Writing"

Series 1602 Comical Kids (6)	10 - 12	12 - 15
Series 1825 Cat Kids (6)	10 - 12	12 - 15
Series 1826 Cat Kids (6)	12 - 14	14 - 18
Series 1827 Cat Kids (6)	12 - 14	14 - 18
Series 1852 Cat Kids (6)	10 - 12	12 - 15
Series 1882 In School (6)	10 - 12	12 - 15
Series 2030 In School (6)	10 - 12	12 - 15

WAIN, LOUIS
  Raphael Tuck

Oilette Ser. 3385, Series 5 Paper Doll Postcards (6)	200 - 250	250 - 275
Calendar Ser. 298, 304 (6)	35 - 40	40 - 45
Series 331 (6)	30 - 35	35 - 40
Series 644 (6) Japanese	35 - 40	40 - 45
Series 1003 (6) Write Away	30 - 35	35 - 40
Oilette Ser. 1412, 6444 (6)	30 - 35	35 - 40
8515, 9563 (6)	35 - 40	40 - 50
Tuck Ser. 6084, 6723, 6724 6727 (6)	30 - 35	35 - 40
"Diabolo" Series 9563 (6)	35 - 40	40 - 45
Series 8819, 9396 (6)	30 - 35	35 - 40
Davis Series	25 - 30	30 - 35
Ettinger		
Series 5376 (Uns.) Santa	75 - 85	85 - 100
Faulkner Series	30 - 35	35 - 40
National Series	25 - 30	30 - 35
Nister Series	30 - 35	35 - 40
J. Salmon Series	30 - 35	35 - 40
Wrench Series	25 - 30	30 - 35
Santa Claus Cats (6)	90 - 100	100 - 125

DOGS

BARTH, KATH	6 - 8	8 - 10
BUTONY		
BKWI Series 859 (6)	8 - 10	10 - 12
C.A.	6 - 8	8 - 10
CORBELLA		
Series 378 (6)	12 - 15	15 - 18
Others	10 - 12	12 - 15
DONADINI, JR. (Dog Studies) (6)	10 - 12	12 - 15
DRUMMOND, N.		
R. Tuck Series 9105 (6)		

"Sporting Dogs"	12 - 14	14 - 16
FEIERTAG (Austria)	4 - 5	5 - 6
FREES, H.W.		
Rotograph Comic Dog Photos	4 - 5	5 - 6
GREINER, A.		
Series 726 Dog Studies (6)	8 - 10	10 - 12
Series 727 (6)	8 - 10	10 - 12
GROSSMAN, A.	6 - 8	8 - 10
GROSSMAN, M.	8 - 10	10 - 12
HANKE, H.		
Series 4056 Dressed Dachshund	10 - 12	12 - 15
HANSTEIN		
R. Tuck		
Series 4092 "Favorite Dogs"	8 - 10	10 - 12
HARTLEIN, W.	6 - 7	7 - 8
HERZ, E. W. (Austria)	7 - 8	8 - 10
KIENE	10 - 12	12 - 15
KIRMBE		
R. Tuck		
"Racing Greyhounds" 3586	8 - 10	10 - 12
KUGLMEYER (Austria)	6 - 8	8 - 10
LITHONIAN		
T.S.N. Series 1961	8 - 10	10 - 12
MACGUIRE Head Studies (Pastels)	8 - 10	10 - 12
MAILICK, R. Dog Studies	8 - 10	10 - 12
MULLER, A.		
Series 3956 (6) Dackels	12 - 15	15 - 18
Other Dressed Series	10 - 12	12 - 15
Others	6 - 8	8 - 10
OHLER, J. Comics	6 - 8	8 - 10
P.O.E. (Austrian)	6 - 7	7 - 9
PANKRATZ Comical Dachshunds	10 - 12	12 - 15
REICHERT, C. (Austrian)		
T.S.N. Series 923 (6)	7 - 8	8 - 10
Series 1336 (6)	8 - 10	10 - 12
Series 1337 (6)	8 - 10	10 - 12
Series 1280 (6)	6 - 8	8 - 10
Series 1851 (6)	8 - 10	10 - 12
SCHNOPLER, A. (Austria) Classical Dachshunds	10 - 12	12 - 18
SPERLICH	5 - 6	6 - 8
STOLZ, A.		
Series 772 Dachshunds	8 - 10	10 - 12
STUDDY "Bonzo"		
W/Tennis or Golf	12 - 15	15 - 18

G. Studdy
Valentines 1131, "All Ours"

W/Black Dolls	12 - 15	15 - 18
Others	8 - 10	10 - 12
THIELE, ARTH.		
R. Tuck Ser. 9799 (6)	15 - 18	18 - 22
T.S.N.		
Series 843 (6)	18 - 22	22 - 25
Series 1128 (6)	10 - 12	12 - 15
Series 1893 In School	10 - 12	12 - 15
German American Novelty Co.		
Series 806 Large Image	18 - 22	22 - 25
THOMAS		
R. Tuck		
Ser. 6990 "French Poodles" (6)	10 - 12	12 - 14
WAIN, LOUIS		
R. Tuck		
Series 6401 Comical Dogs (6)	35 - 40	40 - 45
Series 6402 (6)	35 - 40	40 - 45
Series 9376 (6)	35 - 40	40 - 45
WATSON, MAUDE WEST		
R. Tuck "Dog Sketches"		
3346, 8682, E8837, 9977 (6)	8 - 10	10 - 15
WEBER, E. Dachshund Comics	8 - 10	10 - 12
WOMELE		
M. Munk Series 883	8 - 10	10 - 12

HORSES

ADAMS		
Meissner & Buch	8 - 10	10 - 12
BARTH, W.	8 - 10	10 - 12
CASTALANZA Series 342	8 - 10	10 - 12
DONADINI, JR.		
Series 237 Racing Comics	10 - 12	12 - 15
DRUMMOND, NORAH		
R. Tuck		
Series 9065, 9138 (6)	7 - 8	8 - 10
Series 9561 (6)	12 - 15	15 - 18
Series 3109, 3603 (6)	8 - 10	10 - 12
FENNI (Racing Series)	10 - 12	12 - 15
FRIEDRICH, H. Series 464 (6)	6 - 8	8 - 10
HANSTEIN		
R. Tuck Steeple Chase Series (6)	8 - 10	10 - 12
HERMAN		
R. Tuck Oilettes "The Horse" (6)	10 - 12	12 - 14
KOCH, A.		
BKWI		
Trotter Series 473 (6)	10 - 12	12 - 15
Ser. 377, 566 (6)	8 - 10	10 - 12
Ser. 660, 739, 865 (6), (6), (8)	10 - 12	12 - 14
Ser. 966 Circus Studies (6)	12 - 14	14 - 18
KOCH, LUDWIG		
BKWI		
Series 493 (6)	10 - 12	12 - 15
Series 948 (6)	10 - 12	12 - 15
O.G.Z.-L Series 280-285	10 - 12	12 - 15
KOCH, PROF. G.		
R. Tuck Oilette 588B (6)	10 - 12	12 - 15
LITHONIAN		
Series 1935, w/dogs (6)	8 - 10	10 - 12
Series 5826, E1935 (6)	10 - 12	12 - 14
MERTE, O.		
A.M.S.		
Series 589, 599, 660 (6)	8 - 10	10 - 12
Series 623 Circus Horses (6)	10 - 12	12 - 15
Series 729 (6)	8 - 10	10 - 12
R. Tuck		
Ser. 9946 "Circus Horses" (6)	9 - 10	10 - 15
MULLER		
T.S.N.		

Nora Drummond
R. Tuck 9561, "A Hackney Stallion"

Series 128, 133 (6)	8 - 10	10 - 12
Series 333, 411, 509 (6)	10 - 12	12 - 14
SWSB Series 6919 (6)	6 - 8	8 - 10
PAYNE, HARRY		
R. Tuck	10 - 12	12 - 14
R.K.		
BKWI Ser. 350, 380, 386 (6)	6 - 8	8 - 10
REICHERT, C.		
T.S.N.		
Series 934, w/dogs (6)	8 - 10	10 - 12
Series 1359 (6)	8 - 10	10 - 12
Series 1605 (6)	8 - 10	10 - 12
Series 1606, w/dogs (6)	7 - 8	8 - 10
Series 1732, w/dogs (6)	8 - 10	10 - 12
Series 1782, 1870 (6)	10 - 12	12 - 14
Series 1422 Unsigned (6)	6 - 8	8 - 10
M. Munk		
Series 268, 771 (6)	8 - 10	10 - 12
Series 1165 (6)	10 - 12	12 - 14
SCHULZ Series 972 (6)	6 - 8	8 - 9
Alfred Stiebel Co.		
Series 430 (6)	10 - 12	12 - 15
Series 438 (6)	10 - 12	12 - 15

SHILLING, F.
    A.R & C.i.B. Series 1136 (6)   8 - 10   10 - 12
Stokes, Vernon
    Photochrom Co.
    Celesque Series (6)   7 - 8   8 - 9
TENNI
    Harness Racing Series   8 - 10   10 - 12
THAMSE
    R. Tuck   6 - 8   8 - 10
THOMAS, J.
    R. TUCK
    Trotter Series 575-B   10 - 12   12 - 15
    Steeplechase Ser. 579 (6)   8 - 10   10 - 12
    Racing Series (6)   10 - 12   12 - 15
    Series 9254 (6)   8 - 10   10 - 12
TRACH, E.
    Series 466, 788 (4)   8 - 10   10 - 12

O. Merté
AMS Series 589

P. Thomas
W&L Berlin, 1182,

Series E463, 1175 (4)	8 - 10	10 - 12
WALKER		
R.Tuck		
Series 9544 "Chargers"	8 - 10	10 - 12
WRIGHT, ALAN		
Series 12219 (6)	10 - 12	12 - 14
WRIGHT, GEORGE		
E.W. Savory, Ltd.		
Series 2118 (6)	8 - 10	10 - 12

MISCELLANEOUS

BANKS, E.C. (U.S.A.) See Halloween		
BAKST, LEON (Russia)		
Ladies, Ballet Costumes (12)	40 - 45	45 - 50
Others	20 - 25	25 - 30
BENOIS (Russia)		
Ballet Costume Series	30 - 35	35 - 40
Others	15 - 20	20 - 25
BERTHON, PAUL (France)		
"Music" Series	60 - 70	70 - 80
BILLIBINE (Russia)		
Heroes, Costumes, Opera	15 - 20	20 - 25
BUNNELL, C.B. (See Fourth of July)		
CASSIERS, H. (Belgium)		
Red Star Lines Posters	15 - 20	20 - 25
Other Ship Paintings	8 - 10	10 - 12
Costumes	5 - 6	6 - 7
CLARK, ROSE (U.S.A.) See Teddy Bears.		
CHAPMAN, C. (U.S.A.) Patriotic	6 - 8	8 - 10
CRAMER, RIE		
Mode, Fashions	8 - 10	10 - 12
DUPUIS, EMILE (France)		
Lady & Men Military Series	8 - 10	10 - 15
FIELD, EUGENE "Lovers Lane" Series (12)	3 - 4	4 - 5
GOLAY, MARY Fruits, Flower Studies	3 - 4	4 - 6
HALLER, A. Flowers	2 - 3	3 - 4
HAMPEL, WALTER (Austria)		
Philip & Kramer	30 - 35	35 - 40
HOHENSTEIN, A. (Italy)		
Operas, Commemoratives	20 - 25	30 - 40
INNES, JOHN (Canada) See Cowboys/Indians.		
KIRK, M.L.		
National Art Days of the Week	6 - 7	7 - 8
KLEIN, CATHERINE		

Flowers	2 - 3	3 - 5
Birds	3 - 5	5 - 7
Parrots	5 - 7	7 - 9
Flowered Alphabet	12 - 15	15 - 18

MAILICK (Denmark)
See Santas, Children, Animals

ORENS, D. (France)	15 - 20	20 - 25

PARRISH, MAXWELL (U.S.A.)

Scenic Landscapes	20 - 30	30 - 40
Fairy Tales	60 - 70	70 - 80

PAYNE, HARRY (British)
R. Tuck   English Military Series

Ser. 8625 "The Scots Guards" (6)	10 - 12	12 - 14
Ser. 8738 "Types of the British Army" (6)	10 - 12	12 - 14
Ser. 9937 "The Argyll & Sou. H'landers" (6)	10 - 12	12 - 14
Ser. 9993 "The Coldstream Guards" (6)	10 - 12	12 - 14
Ser. 9994 "The Blackwatch" (6)	10 - 12	12 - 14
Others	10 - 12	12 - 14
London Life - Policemen, etc.	10 - 12	12 - 14
English Views and Landscapes	5 - 6	6 - 7

See Western and Indians for Wild West Series.

REMINGTON, FREDERIC (U.S.A.)
See Cowboys and Indians.

ROBINSON, FLORENCE (U.S.A.)

R. Tuck Views of U.S. Cities	10 - 12	12 - 15

ROBINSON, WALLACE (U.S.A.)
Heininger Co.

"Patriotic Kids"	10 - 12	12 - 15

ROCKWELL, NORMAN
Whitney

"Help Him Through the Game ..."	30 - 35	35 - 40
"The Fatherless Children of France"		
1 "Help the Fatherless Children ..."	30 - 35	35 - 40
2 "Polly Voos Fransay"	30 - 35	35 - 40
3 Mobilize for Defense Poster	35 - 40	40 - 45
Fisk Tires Advertising	15 - 18	18 - 22

RUSSELL, CHARLES M. (U.S.A.)
See Western and Indians.

VEENFLIET, R. (U.S.A.)

S. Garre Patriotics	6 - 8	8 - 10

Signed L.D.
Meissner & Büch

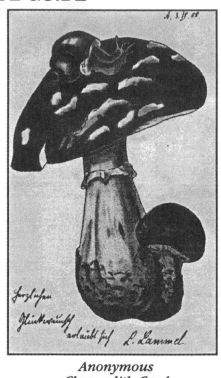

Anonymous
Chromolith Card

"Little Mushroom Girl"

German Elf and Mushroom

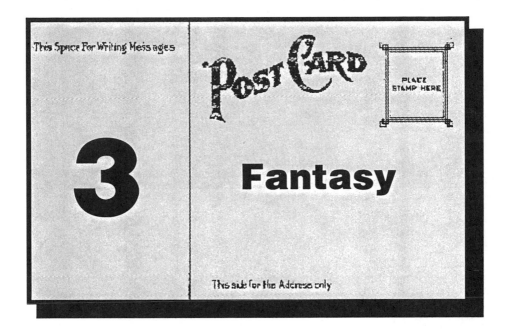

Fantasy, according to **Webster,** means imagination or fancy; wild visionary fancy; an unnatural or bizarre mental image; illusion, phantasm; an odd notion, whim, caprice; a highly imaginative poem, play; mental images as in a daydream... all of these definitions come to life on beautiful and wonderful fantasy postcards.

Most of the fantasies bring to life the days of our youth... of fairies and fairy tales, of frog kings and sleeping princesses, of dolls and teddy bears and dressed animals doing people things... of mermaids and sea creatures, of vixens and voluptuous nudes... which came later. These make a wonderful fantasy world for us all!

Before the influx of foreign cards to the U.S. in the late 70's and 80's, collectors of fantasy had to be content with the works of Dwig and a handful of other artists, a few nursery rhymes and fairy tales, some exaggerations of big fish, mosquitoes and farm produce, etc.–not too great for a fantasy collector.

Slowly the beautiful and desirable imports began appearing in auctions and finally in dealer stocks, and now everyone has discovered them. Prices have spiraled and most all types are in great demand. The most desirable are listed in these pages. Have a Fantasy time!

FAIRIES

The Fairy family includes Brownies, Elves,
Gnomes, Goblins, Fairies, Leprechauns,
Pixies, and Sprites.

BAUMGARTEN, FRITZ
  Oppel & Hess, Jena

Series 1509	10 - 12	12 - 15
Other Series	10 - 12	12 - 15
Other Publishers	10 - 12	12 - 15

CLOKE, RENE

Valentine & Sons "Fairies" (6)	12 - 15	15 - 20
Series 1002	12 - 15	15 - 18
Series 1183	12 - 15	15 - 18
Series 1848	12 - 15	15 - 18
J. Salmon		
Series 4626 (6)	10 - 12	12 - 15
Series 4627 (6)	10 - 12	12 - 15

Uns. Schulz
Andersen's Fairy Tale, BKWI 435-3

Anonymous
German, "The Fairy"

COWHAN, H.		
C.W. Faulkner "The Fairy Glen" Ser. (6)	10 - 12	12 - 15
DAUSTY (Nymphs)		
C. & P. & Co. Series 704 (6)	8 - 12	10 - 12
GIRIS, CESAR		
R. Tuck		
Ser. 2365 "Madame Butterfly" (6)	18 - 20	20 - 25
MARSHALL, ALICE		
R. Tuck 3490 "Fairyland Fancies" (6)	15 - 18	18 - 25
Series 3489 (6)	18 - 20	20 - 26
MARSH, HGC		
C.W. Faulkner Ser. 1510 (6)	12 - 15	15 - 18
MAUSER, PHYLLIS		
P. Salmon Ser. 5159		
"Brownies & Fairies" (6)	10 - 12	12 - 15
MAYBANK, THOMAS		
R. Tuck		
Ser. 6683 "Midsummer Dreams" (6)	20 - 22	22- 25
MILLER, HILDA		
C.W. Faulkner		
Series 1690 - Fairies	12 - 15	15 - 18
Series 1693 - Fairies	12 - 15	15 - 18
Series 1822 - Peter Pan	12 - 15	15 - 18
MULLER, PAUL LOTHAR		
Oscar Heierman, Berlin (Novitas)		
Gnomes Ser. 550	8 - 10	10 - 12
OUTHWAITE, IDA		
A & C Black, London		
Series 76 "Elves & Fairies"	15 - 18	18 - 22
Mermaid - "Playing With Bubbles"	20 - 25	25 - 30
SCHULZ, E.		
B.K.W.I.		
Series 391 (6)	18 - 20	20 - 25
M. Munk, Vienna		
Series 1363 (6)	15 - 18	18 - 22
Series 1364 (6)	15 - 18	18 - 22
Series 1365 (6)	15 - 18	18 - 22
SOWERBY, M.		
Humphrey Milford, London		
Woodland Games - Fairies (6)	15 - 18	18 - 22
Flowers & Wings - Elves (6)	12 - 15	15 - 18
Merry Elves (6)	12 - 15	15 - 20
Sky Fairies (6)	15 - 18	18 - 22
STEELE, L.R.		

Andreas Untersburger
Emil Kahn 1155, "The Snail"

Flora White
"Little Mermaid"

Salmon & Co.		
"Famous Fairies" 5050-5055	8 - 10	10 - 12
TARRANT, MARGARET		
Medici Society		
PK 120 "The Fairy Troupe"	8 - 10	10 - 12
PK 184 "The Enchantress"	8 - 10	10 - 12
UNTERSBERGER, ANDREAS		
Emil Kohn, Munchen		
Fairy and Gnome Series (12)	10 - 12	12 - 15
WATKINS, DOROTHY		
Valentine & Sons		
"The Dance of the Elves" Ser. 6	8 - 10	10 - 12
WHEELER, DOROTHY		
Bamforth & Co.		
Series 1 "Fairy Secret" (6)	8 - 10	10 - 14
WEIGAND, MARTIN		
Gnomes, Mushroom Series (12)	15 - 18	18 - 20
R. Tuck Oilette Ser. 6683		
"Mid Summer Dreams" (6)	15 - 20	20 - 25
"Valentine Series" 108 (6)	10 - 12	12 - 14

ANONYMOUS

Elves	5 - 8	8 - 15
Fairies	8 - 10	10 - 15
Gnomes	6 - 8	8 - 12
Goblins (Usually Halloween)	6 - 8	8 - 12
Leprechauns	5 - 7	7 - 12
Pixies	8 - 10	10 - 15
Sprites	7 - 8	8 - 10

FAIRY TALES

ANDERSEN, HANS

"The Little Mermaid"	15 - 20	20 - 25

BORRIS, MARGARET

"Hansel and Gretel" (6)	8 - 10	10 - 12
"Pied Piper" (6)	8 - 10	10 - 12
"Puss-in-Boots" (6)	8 - 10	10 - 12

HERRFURTH, OSCAR (German)
   Brothers Grimm Fairy Tales (6 cards per Series)

Pinggera
Schulverin 239, "Sans Däumling"

Flora White
"Who are you?"

Published by **UVA Chrom, Stuttgart**

Ser. 125 "Hansel & Gretel"	6 - 7	7 - 8
Ser. 128 "Rotkappchen"		
(Little Red Riding Hood)	7 - 8	8 - 9
Ser. 139 "Frau Holle" (Lady Hell)	4 - 5	5 - 6
Ser. 140 "Dornroschen" (Sleeping Beauty)	7 - 8	8 - 9
Ser. 147 "Schneewittchen" (Snow White)	7 - 8	8 - 9
Ser. 154 "Aschenbrodl" (Cinderella)	6 - 7	7 - 8
Ser. 223 "Der Gestiefelte Kater" (Puss-in-Boots)	5 - 6	6 - 7
Ser. 241 "Die Gansemagd" (The Goose Maid)	5 - 6	6 - 7
Ser. 242 "Der Rattenfanger von Hameln"		
(Pied Piper)	7 - 8	8 - 9
Ser. 252 "Der Schweinhirt" (The Pig Herdsman)	5 - 6	6 - 7
Ser. 254 "Siebenschon" (Seven Lovelies)	5 - 6	6 - 7
Ser. 264 "Der Tannenbaum" (The Fir Tree)	4 - 5	5 - 6
Ser. 265 "Der Wolf und die Sieben Geisslein"		
(Goats)	4 - 5	5 - 6
Ser. 266 "Marienkind"	4 - 5	5 - 6
Ser. 267 "Tischlein deck dich"	4 - 5	5 - 6
Ser. 268 "Die Sieben Schwaben"	5 - 6	6 - 7
Ser. 269 "Bruderchein und Schwesterchen"	6 - 7	7 - 8
Ser. 285 "Die Bremer Stadtmusikanten"	5 - 6	6 - 7
Ser. 298 "Hans im Gluck" (Jack & Jill)	5 - 6	6 - 7
Ser. 299 "Das Tapfere Schneiderlein"	5 - 6	6 - 7
Ser. 311 "Der Kleine Daumling" (Tom Thumb)	6 - 7	7 - 8
Ser. 319 "Hase und Igel - Das Lumpengesindel"	5 - 6	6 - 7
Ser. 320 "Die Sieben Raben" (The 7 Ravens)	6 - 7	7 - 8
Ser. 324 "Munchausen I"	4 - 5	5 - 6
Ser. 325 "Munchhausen II"	4 - 5	5 - 6
Ser. 354 "Das Schlaraffenland"		
(Milk & Honey Land)	4 - 5	5 - 6
Ser. 355 "Der Frosch Konig" (The Frog King)	6 - 7	7 - 8
Ser. 363 "Die Heinselmannchen"	5 - 6	6 - 7
Ser. 369 "Till Eulenspiegel" (12 cards)	4 - 5	5 - 6

Tales (Sagen) (6-Card Series)
Sage - A fantastic or incredible tale.
HERRFURTH, OSCAR

Ser. 127 "Die Nibelungen - Sage"	6 - 7	7 - 8
Ser. 141 "Parzival" (Parsifal)	7 - 8	8 - 9
Ser. 157 "Rübezahl I"	4 - 5	5 - 6
Ser. 161 "Rübezahl II"	4 - 5	5 - 6
Ser. 158 "Wilhelm Tell" (12)	5 - 6	6 - 7
Ser. 239 "Die Tristan - Sage"	6 - 7	7 - 8
Ser. 247 "Die Parzival - Sage I"	6 - 7	7 - 8

E. Kutzer
Der. Sudmark, "Rübezahl"

KUTZER, E.

Der. Sudmark	12 - 15	15 - 18
Ser. 253 "Die Parzival - Sage II"	6 - 7	7 - 8
Ser. 248 "Walther von der Vogelweide"	5 - 6	6 - 7
Ser. 258 "Die Lohengrin - Sage"	7 - 8	8 - 9
Ser. 259 "Die Tannehauser - Sage"	7 - 8	8 - 9
Ser. 263 "Aus der Zeit der Minnesanger"	6 - 7	7 - 8
Ser. 361 "Der Lichtenstein" (12)	4 - 5	5 - 6

LEETE, F. (Poster Cards)

H.K. & M. Co. "Seigfried" (6)	8 - 10	10 - 12

PINGGERA (Poster Card)

Series 239 "Sans Daumling" (Tom Thumb)	12 - 15	15 - 18

SCHULZ, E.

B.K.W.I. (Poster Cards)

Series 435 (6) Andersen's Fairy Tales	15 - 18	18 - 22

Deutscher Schulverein (Poster Cards)

Card 319 "Rumpelstilzchen"	15 - 18	18 - 25
Card 320 "Schneewittchen" (Snow White)	18 - 20	20 - 25
Card 321 "Rotkappchen" (Red Riding Hood)	18 - 20	20 - 22
Card 322 "Die Sieben Raben" (The 7 Ravens)	15 - 18	18 - 22
Card 564 "Aschenbrodel" (Cinderella)	20 - 22	22 - 25
Card 653 "Der Frotchkonig" (The Frog King)	20 - 22	22 - 25
Card 862 "Dornroschen" (Sleeping Beauty)	18 - 20	20 - 22

WAIN, LOUIS

R. Tuck "Oilette" Ser. 3385		
"Paper Doll Cats"	225 - 250	250 - 300
"Aladdin"		
"Beauty and the Beast"		
"Cinderella"		
"Dick Whittington"		
"Little Red Riding Hood"		
"Robinhood"		
WHITE, FLORA		
Ilfracombe Mermaid, "Who are You?"	20 - 25	25 - 30
Poster Series	12 - 15	15 - 18
"Cinderella"		
"Dick Whittington"		
"Goose Girl"		
"Hop-O-My-Thumb"		
"Peter Pan"		
"Puss-in-Boots"		
P.F.B. Fairy Tale Series		
"Cinderella"	15 - 18	18 - 22
"The Hose of Sweets"	15 - 18	18 - 22
"Little Red Riding Hood"	15 - 18	18 - 22
"Sleeping Beauty"	15 - 18	18 - 22
"Snow White"	15 - 18	18 - 22
"Tom Thumb"	15 - 18	18 - 22
Ullman Mfg. Co.		
1752-1757 "Little Red Riding Hood"	8 - 10	10 - 12
1759-1762 "Mary & Her Lamb"	8 - 10	10 - 12
Anonymous		
Paper Doll Cut-outs		
"Little Bo-Peep" Ser. 3382	40 - 45	45 - 55
"Little Boy Blue" Ser. 3383	40 - 45	45 - 55

DRESSED ANIMALS, INSECTS, BIRDS

Bears See Teddy Bears		
Birds	5 - 6	6 - 8
Bugs	10 - 12	12 - 15
Cats See Artist-Signed Cats		
Cows, Bulls, etc.	10 - 12	12 - 15
Dogs See Artist-Signed Dogs		
P.F.B. Ser. 8168 (6)	15 - 18	18 - 22
Ullman Mfg. Co.		
"Br'er Rabbit" Series 112	6 - 8	8 - 10
"Bunny Girl" Series 84	6 - 8	8 - 10

Art Nouveau
Dressed Pig, No Caption

German Dressed Bunny
No Caption

Embossed German Miakafirs

Embossed German Frog

"Jungle Sports" Series 72	8 - 10	10 - 12
"Monkey Doodle" Series 196	8 - 9	9 - 10
Elephants	15 - 20	20 - 22
Frogs	12 - 15	15 - 25
Goats	12 - 15	15 - 18
Grasshoppers	10 - 12	12 - 15
Hippopotamus	15 - 20	20 - 25
Horses	12 - 15	15 - 18
May Bugs (Miakafirs)	12 - 15	15 - 22
Pigs	10 - 12	12 - 18
Pig Chimney Sweeps	12 - 15	15 - 20
Rabbits	6 - 8	8 - 15
Rats, Mice	10 - 12	12 - 15

MISCELLANEOUS FANTASY

AUTOS FLYING ABOVE CITY	8 - 10	10 - 12
BUSI, ADOLFO		
Ser. 3059, Women/Snowmen (6)	18 - 20	20 - 25
P/Kaplan		
Ser. 57 Women's Heads in Clouds (12)	12 - 15	15 - 20
DEATH HEADS	8 - 12	12 - 18

Fritz Baumgarten
Oppel & Hess, Jena 1503-1

Embossed German Snowman
Wezel & Nauman S. 274

German Snowman
P.P.

ELVES, GNOMES	5 - 6	6 - 10
FACES IN MOUNTAINS	10 - 12	12 - 18
FLOWER FACES	6 - 8	8 - 12
GIANT PEOPLE	5 - 6	6 - 7
GOLLIWOGS		
Humphrey Milford, London		
"Dreams & Fairies" Signed A. Govey	12 - 14	14 - 18
H.K. & Co.		
"Jack in the Box" Signed M. Stocks	12 - 14	14 - 18
R. Tuck Signed F.K. Upton		
Series 1793, 1794 (6)	20 - 25	25 - 30
Series 1791, 1792 (6)	20 - 25	25 - 30
Series C2006 Signed A. Richardson (6)	15 - 18	18 - 20
R. Tuck "Art" Ser. 1281 (6)	15 - 18	18 - 20
R. Tuck Rescued Ser. 1282 (6)	18 - 20	20 - 22
R. Tuck Oilette Ser. 1397 (6)	15 - 18	18 - 25
R. Tuck "Art" Ser. 1262 (6)	15 - 18	18 - 22
Valentine & Sons Signed Mabel L. Atwell		
Series A561 (6)	12 - 15	15 - 18
Series A579 (6)	12 - 15	15 - 20

Series 748 (6)	15 - 18	18 - 22
John Winsch		
1910 Issue	15 - 18	18 - 20
1912 Issue (Santa)	15 - 18	18 - 22
1913 Issue (Santa)	15 - 18	18 - 22
DEPICTING THE FUTURE	7 - 8	8 - 10
MAN IN THE MOON	5 - 8	8 - 10
MAPS-BODIES MAKING UP COUNTRIES	8 - 9	9 - 10
METAMORPHICS See Topicals		
MUSHROOMS, GIANT	6 - 8	8 - 12
MUSHROOM PEOPLE	8 - 10	10 - 15
NUDES/ANIMALS		
R.S.M. Ser. 784		
S/Zandrino (6)	15 - 18	18 - 22
SKELETONS, DEPICTING DEATH	8 - 10	10 - 12
SNOWMEN	6 - 10	10 - 20
S/A. Thiele Snowman Ser. 1297 (6)	15 - 18	18 - 22
SOLOMKO		
UN 1015 "Dream of Icarius"	12 - 15	15 - 18
1019 "Blue Bird"	15 - 18	18 - 20
STICK OR WOOD PEOPLE	6 - 8	8 - 10

WAGNER OPERA SERIES

B.K.W.I.		
Series 438 (6)	12 - 15	15 - 18
E.S.D. Art Nouveau Borders		
8157 "Die Walkure" (6)	10 - 12	12 - 15
8158 "Siegfried" (6)	10 - 12	12 - 15
8159 "Das Rheingold" (6)	15 - 18	18 - 22
8160 "Gotterdammerung" (6)	8 - 10	10 - 12
8161 "Die Meistersinger" (6)	8 - 10	10 - 12
8162 "Tristan und Isolde" (6)	10 - 12	12 - 15
8163 "Der Fliegende Hollander" (6)	8 - 10	10 - 12
8164 "Lohengrin" (6)	10 - 12	12 - 15
GOETZ		
M. Munk, Vienna		
Series 861		
"Die Feen"	8 - 10	10 - 12
"Die Meistersinger"	8 - 10	10 - 12
"Die Walkure"	8 - 10	10 - 12
"Gotterdammerung"	10 - 12	12 - 14
"Lohengrin"	8 - 10	10 - 12
"Parsifal"	10 - 12	12 - 14

E. Schulz
BKWI 205-1, "Parsival"

E. Schulz
BKWI 438-1, "Tannhaüser"

"Rienzi"	8 - 10	10 - 12
"Rheingold"	10 - 12	12 - 14
"Siegfried"	8 - 10	10 - 12
"Tanhaüser"	8 - 10	10 - 12
Series 982 (12)	6 - 8	8 - 10
Series E984 (12)	6 - 8	8 - 10
KUTZER, E. (Poster Cards)		
Vercides Sudmark 245-256	15 - 18	18 - 22
LEETE, F. (Poster Cards)		
L. Pernitzch		
"Wagner's Heldengestalten" (24)	12 - 15	15 - 18
PINGGERA (Poster Cards)		
Deutches un Niederosterrich 242-252	12 - 15	15 - 18
M. Munk, Vienna		
Wagner's Series 28		
Ladies in Wagner's Operas	10 - 12	12 - 14
T.S.N.		
"Lohengrin" Series 141 (6)	8 - 10	10 - 12
R. Tuck "Wagner" Postcard Series		
690 "Siegfried" (6)	12 - 15	15 - 20
691 "Lohengren" (6)	12 - 15	15 - 20

692 "Gotterdammerung" (6)	10 - 14	14 - 18
693 "Tristan and Isolde" (6)	12 - 15	15 - 20
694 "The Rheingold" (6)	15 - 20	20 - 25
695 "The Flying Dutchman" (6)	10 - 14	14 - 18
"Moderner Meister" Ser. XX, 1219 (6)	12 - 15	15 - 18

Ottmar Ziehr

Wagner's Operas (6)	25 - 28	28 - 32

FANTASY NUDES

BENDER

"La Femme" (Snakes)	12 - 15	15 - 18

BOCKLIN, A.

Bruckmann A.G. 21 "Triton & Nereide" (Merman)	10 - 12	12 - 15
Bruckmann A.G. 6 "The Nereid" (Snake Serpent)	12 - 15	15 - 18

BRAUNE, E.

Amag Kunst 63 "Walkure" (Horse)	10 - 12	12 - 15

Eduard Stella
BRW 354, "Diana"

Susan Meunier
Marque L.E. Series 64-7

C.A. Geiger
Marke J.S.C. 6109, "Liebeskampf"

E.A. Dussek
J.K. 69, "Der Forschkonigs Braut"

CABANEL, A.
Salon J.P.P. 2206 "Nymph & Faun"
(Man/Goat)   12 - 15   15 - 18
COURSELLES-DUMONT
Lapina 564 "In der Arena" (Lion)   12 - 15   15 - 18
DUSSEK, E.A.
J.K. 69 "Froschkonigs Braut" (Frog)   15 - 18   18 - 22
FISCHER-COERLINE
M.K. 2475 "Salome" (Severed Head)   12 - 15   15 - 18
GIOVANNI, A.
ARS Minima 119 "Salome" (Severed Head)   12 - 15   15 - 18
GLOTZ, A.D.
BKWI 1009 "Lebensluge" (Ghost of Dead)   10 - 12   12 - 15
GEGLAR, C.A.
Marke J.S.C. 6109 "Liebeskampf"
(Man/Sea Beast)   15 - 18   18 - 22
Marke J.S.C. 6112 "Salome
(Severed Head)   12 - 15   15 - 18
HOESSLIN, GEORGE
NPG 491 "Die Schaumgebstene"
(Nude in Oyster Shell)   10 - 12   12 - 15

E. Schulz
BKWI, 165-5, "Blumenkönigin"

KELLER
 Russian 076 "Finale" (Death Head)   12 - 15   15 - 18
LEETE, F.
 Munchener Kt. 3113 "Nire und Wasserman"
 (Water Creature)   10 - 12   12 - 15
 Munchener Kt. 3114 "Gefangene Nymphe"
 (Dwarfs)   10 - 12   12 - 15
 Munchener Kunst 3117 "Triton Belaufde
 Nereide" (Merman)   10 - 12   12 - 15
LENOIR, CH.
 Lapina 5122 "Victory" (Octopus)   15 - 18   18 - 22
LEOPAROVA
 KV 1183 "Salome" (Severed Head)   10 - 12   12 - 15
MANDL, J.
 Minerva 177 "Printemps" (Wings)   10 - 12   12 - 15
MASTAGLIO
 Galerie Munchener Meister 380 "Duell"
 (Nudes Fencing)   10 - 12   12 - 15
MASTROIANNI, C.
 198 "Fievre d'Amore" (Waterfall)   10 - 12   12 - 15
MEUNIER, S.
 MARQUE L.E. Series 64 (6)   28 - 32   32 - 40
MUHLBERG
 Nude Riding a Seahorse   12 - 15   15 - 18
MULLER-BAUMGARTEN
 FEM 161 "Faun & Nymphe" (Man/Goat)   8 - 10   10 - 12
MUTTICH, C.V.
 V.K.K.V 2077 "Sulejka" (Peacock)   10 - 12   12 - 15
PENOT, A.
 Lapina 1340 "Red Butterfly"
 (Red-Winged Nude)   12 - 15   15 - 18
PIOTROWSKI, A.
 Minerva 1028 "Salome" (Severed Head)   10 - 12   12 - 15
 Manke JSC 6082 "Charmeuse de Serpents"
 (Snake)   15 - 18   18 - 22
REINACKER, G.
 PFB 6032 "Schlangen-Bandigerin"
 "Snake"   12 - 15   15 - 18
ROWLAND, FR.
 SVD 379 "Sirenen" (Snakes)   12 - 15   15 - 18
ROTHAUG
 LP 2815 "Pan and Psyche" (Man/Beast)   15 - 18   18 - 22
ROYER, L.
 Salon de Paris 374 "La Sirene"
 (Death Head)   12 - 15   15 - 18

SAMSON, E.
A.N., Paris 243 "Diane" (Wolf Dogs)	10 - 12	12 - 15

SCALBERT, J.
S.P.A. 48 "Leda & the Swan"	10 - 12	12 - 15

SCHMUTZLER
Russian, Richard 245 "Salome" (Severed Head)	12 - 15	15 - 18

SCHIFF, R.
W.R.B. & Co. Ser. 22-74 "Leda & Swan"	15 - 18	18 - 22
W.R.B. & Co. Ser. 22-74 "Head in Clouds"	12 - 15	15 - 18

SCHULZ   Poster Cards
BKWI 41 "The Frog King" (Big Frog)	15 - 18	18 - 22
BKWI 885-2 Gothe's "Der Fischer" Mermaid	25 - 28	28 - 32
BKWI 885-2 "God & the Baiadere"	18 - 20	20 - 25
BKWI 979-5 "Die Forelle" Mermaid	25 - 28	28 - 32
BKWI 205-6 Wagner's "Parsival"	15 - 18	18 - 22
BKWI 557-6 "Lotusblume" Nude in flower	18 - 20	20 - 25
BKWI Series 165 (6) Nudes on Giant Flowers	22 - 25	25 - 30

STELLA, EDUARD
BRW 354 "Diane" (Dogs)	18 - 20	20 - 22

STYKA, JAN
Lapina 810 "Good Friends" (Horse)	10 - 12	12 - 15

SZYNDIER, P.
Mal. Polskie 22, "Eve" (Snakes)	20 - 22	22 - 25

SOLOMKO
TSN Nude in Peacock Feathers	18 - 20	20 - 22

WARZENIECKI, M.
WILSA 90 "Une Nouvelle Esclave" (Death)	10 - 12	12 - 15

WOLLNER, H.
BKWI 1101 "Sadismus" (Death Head)	10 - 12	12 - 15

VEITH, E.
BKWI 1101 "Teasing" (Man/Goat)	10 - 12	12 - 15

ZANDER
SSWB 4790 "Sieg der Schonheit" (Tiger)	10 - 12	12 - 15

ZATZKA, H.
Panphot, Vienne 1284 "La Lerle" (Nude in Large Oyster Shell)	12 - 15	15 - 18

TEDDY BEARS

REAL PHOTO TEDDY BEARS
W/Children (Large T. Bears)	20 - 25	25 - 35

R. Tuck Little Bears
Series 118, "Your Good Health"

M. Greiner
"Molly and Her Bears"

W/Children (Small T. Bears)	12 - 18	18 - 25
W/Ladies (Large T. Bears)	18 - 22	22 - 28
W/Ladies (Small T. Bears)	12 - 15	15 - 20
ARTIST-SIGNED TEDDY BEARS		
W/Children (Large T. Bears)	10 - 15	15 - 20
W/Children (Small T. Bears)	8 - 12	12 - 15
W/Ladies (Large T. Bears)	10 - 12	12 - 18
W/Ladies (Small T. Bears)	8 - 12	12 - 15
BUSY BEARS		
J.I. Austen Co.	6 - 8	8 - 10

427 Monday, Hanging the Wash
428 Tuesday, Ironing Clothes
429 Wednesday, Sweeping
430 Thursday, Mopping the Floor
431 Friday, Baking Bread
432 Saturday, Darning
433 "Learning to Spell"
434 "Playing Leap Frog"
435 "Off to School"
436 "Getting it in the Usual Place"
437 "Something Doing"

438 "Vacation"

BUSY BEARS, DAYS OF THE WEEK

S/Bernhard Wall	6 - 8	8 - 10
1905 Sunday		
1906 Monday		
1907 Tuesday		
1908 Wednesday		
1909 Thursday		
1910 Friday		
1911 Saturday		

CRACKER JACK BEARS

Rueckheim & Eckstein

1 At Lincoln Zoo	20 - 25	25 - 30
2 In Balloon	20 - 25	25 - 30
3 Over Niagara Falls	20 - 25	25 - 30
4 At Statue of Liberty	20 - 25	25 - 30
5 At Coney Island	20 - 25	25 - 30
6 In New York	20 - 25	25 - 30
7 Shaking Teddy's Hand	30 - 35	35 - 40
8 At Jamestown Fair	20 - 25	25 - 30
9 To the South	20 - 25	25 - 30
10 At Husking Bee	20 - 25	25 - 30
11 At the Circus	20 - 25	25 - 30
12 Playing Baseball	30 - 35	35 - 40
13 Cracker Jack Time	20 - 25	25 - 30
14 Making Cracker Jacks	20 - 25	25 - 30
15 At Yellowstone	20 - 25	25 - 30
16 Away to Mars	20 - 25	25 - 30
17 - 32	30 - 35	35 - 40

ROSE CLARK BEARS

Rotograph Co., N.Y.	8 - 10	10 - 12
307 "Bear own Cadet"		
308 "Is That You Henry?"		
309 "Henry"		
310 "The Bride"		
311 "The Groom"		
312 "A Bear Town Spot"		
313 "A Bear Town Dude"		
314 "I'm Going a Milking"		
315 "I Won't be Home ..."		
316 "C-c-come on in"		
317 "Fifth Avenue"		
318 "Hymn No. 23"		

DOGGEREL DODGER BEARS

Paul Elder Co.		
Signed - A. Wheelan	6 - 8	8 - 10
D.P. Crane, DAYS OF THE WEEK		
H.G.Z. Co.	8 - 10	10 - 12
WM. S. Heal, DAYS OF THE WEEK	6 - 8	8 - 10
D. Hillson, DAYS OF THE WEEK	6 - 8	8 - 10
LITTLE BEARS		
Raphael Tuck Series 118 (12)	12 - 15	15 - 18
"A Morning Dip"		
"A Very Funny Song"		
"Breaking the Record"		
"Kept in at School"		
"Missed Again"		
"Oh! What a Shock"		
"Once in the Eye"		
"The Cake Walk"		
"The Ice Bears Beautifully"		
"The Jolly Anglers"		
"Tobogganing in the Snow"		
"Your Good Health"		
McLaughlin Bros. BEARS	6 - 8	8 - 10
MOLLY & TEDDY BEARS		
International Art Co.		
S/Greiner Series 791	8 - 10	10 - 12
MOTHER GOOSE'S TEDDY BEARS		
S/Fred Cavaly (16)	6 - 8	8 - 10
Ottoman Lithographing Co., N.Y.		
(Set of 10)	6 - 8	8 - 10
"Come Birdie Come"		
"Good Old Summertime"		
"Is Marriage a Failure?"		
"Many Happy Returns"		
"Never Touched Me"		
"Well, Well, You never can Tell"		
"Will She Get the Lobster"		
"Please Ask Pa"		
10th card is unknown at this time		
ROMANTIC BEARS		
Ullman Ser. 88 (4), S/M.D.S.		
1950 "Too Late"	6 - 8	8 - 10
1951 "Who Cares?"	6 - 8	8 - 10
1952 "The Lullaby"	6 - 8	8 - 10
1953 "A Letter to My Love"	6 - 8	8 - 10
SPORTY BEARS		

Ullman Series 83, S/M.D.S.

1923 "Love All"	10 - 12	12 - 14
1924 "Here's for a Home Run"	12 - 14	14 - 16
1925 "Out for a Big Game"	10 - 12	12 - 15
1926 "King of the Alley"	8 - 10	10 - 12
1927 "A Dip in the Surf"	8 - 10	10 - 12
1928 "An Unexpected Bite"	8 - 10	10 - 12
1929 "On the Links"	12 - 14	15 - 16

C. TWELVETREES BEARS

National Art Co.   8 - 10   10 - 12

206 "Little Bear Behind"
207 "Stung"
208 "The Bear on Dark Stairway"
209 "How can you Bear this Weather?"
210 "A Bear Impression"
211 "The Seashore Bear"

ROOSEVELT BEARS   20 - 25   25 - 30

1 "At Home"
2 "Go Aboard the Train"
3 "In Sleeping Car"
4 "On A Farm"
5 "At a Country School"
6 "At the County Fair"
7 "Leaving the Ballroom"
8 "At the Tailors"
9 "In the Department Store"
10 "At Niagara Falls"
11 "At Boston Public Library"
12 "Take an Auto Ride"
13 "At Harvard"
14 "On Iceberg"
15 "In New York City"
16 "At the Circus"
17 "Shooting Firecrackers"   30 - 35   35 - 40
20 "Dancing"
22 "In New York"
25 "Swimming"
29 "Go Fishing"
30 "Bears on a Pullman"
31 "Hunters"
   There may be others.

ST. JOHN BEARS

Western News Co.

161 "Spring"   4 - 6   6 - 8

162 "Summer"	4 - 6	6 - 8
163 "Autumn"	4 - 6	6 - 8
164 "Winter"	4 - 6	6 - 8
Tower M. & N. Co., TEDDY BEARS	8 - 10	10 - 12
"Beary Well, Thank You"		
"But We Are Civilized"		
"Did You Ever Wear..."		
"Don't Say a Word"		
"Hurrah for - Eagle"		
"Hurrah for the..."		
"I'm Waiting For You"		
"Our Birth, You Know"		
"We Wear Pajamas"		
"You Don't Say"		
T.P. & Co. TEDDY BEARS	8 - 10	10 - 12
"Out for Airing"		
"I Wonder if He Saw Me?"		
"Isn't He a Darling"		
"How Strong He Is"		
"Oh! My! - He's Coming!"		
"Off for the Honeymoon"		
"Little Girl w/Teddy"		
"Dolly Gets an Inspiration"		
"Lost, Strayed, or Stolen"		
B. WALL, DAYS OF THE WEEK		
Ullman Mfg. Co.		
Series 70	8 - 10	10 - 12

MERMAIDS

ATWELL, MABEL LUCIE		
Valentine's 951 (W/Black Doll)	12 - 15	15 - 18
SCHULZ		
BKWI Poster Cards		
391-3 Heine - "Der Mond ist ..."	18 - 20	20 - 25
434-1 Andersen's Marchen	18 - 20	20 - 25
766-2 Schubert - "Das Wasser ..."	20 - 25	25 - 30
885-5 Goethe - "Der Fischer"	25 - 28	28 - 32
979-5 Schubert - "Die Forelle"	25 - 28	28 - 32
R. TUCK, OILETTES		
Mermaid Series 6822 (6)	22 - 25	25 - 30
Wagner Series 694 (6)		
"The Rhine Gold" (6)	18 - 20	20 - 25
BOCKLIN, A.		

Signed Schulz
BKWI 979-5 Shubert, "Die Forelle"

Anonymous
German Wasser Nixen Series 643

F. Bruckmann A.G.		
"Play in the Waves"	12 - 15	15 - 18
CARTER, REG.		
Max Ettinger & Co.		
Diver Series 4453 (6)	15 - 18	18 - 22
CHIOSTRI, S.		
Deco Series 238 (6)	35 - 40	40 - 50
Deco Series 317 (6)	30 - 35	35 - 40
GILLAUME		
Art Moderne 764 "Seetrift"	15 - 18	18 - 22
GOHLER, H.		
Russian, "Richard"		
"Du Nixlein Wunderhold ..."	15 - 18	18 - 22
LEETE, H.		
Munchener Kunst 3116,		
"De Taufe des Fawn"	10 - 12	12 - 15
LIEBENWEIN, M		
BKWI 1028, "Der Verrufene Weiher"	15 - 18	18 - 22
OUTHWAITE		
Elves & Fairies Series 73		
"Playing with Bubbles"	20 - 25	25 - 30

SAGER, XAVIER		
"Un Baiser D'Ostende," Big Letter card	20 - 22	22 - 25
SCHMUTZLER, L.		
Hanfstaengl 203, "Flame of Love"	15 - 18	18 - 22
SOLOMKO, S.		
T.S.N. 93, "The Tale"	15 - 18	18 - 22
WHITE, FLORA		
W.E. Mack, Hampstead		
Poster - "The Little Mermaid"	15 - 18	18 - 22
P/S. HILDESHIMER & CO.		
Andersen's Fairy Tales, "The Little Mermaid"	20 - 25	25 - 30
P/MN Co., 1910		
Unsigned, Unnumbered (10)	15 - 18	18 - 25
P/M. & L.G.		
National Series, untitled		
Art Nouveau W/Seashell	25 - 30	30 - 35
ANONYMOUS		
Art Nouveau Series 643 (6)	50 - 55	55 - 65

Chiostri
Ballerini & Fratini 238

Hans Andersen's Fairy Tales
"The Little Mermaid"

R. Tuck Series 6822
"Mermaid"

SUPERIOR WOMEN/LITTLE MEN FANTASY

B.G.W. Series 123/1233 (6)	8 - 10	10 - 12
FASCHE		
M. MUNK (6) "Diabolo"	12 - 15	15 - 18
KYOPINSKI (6)	10 - 12	12 - 15
KURDNEY		
M.MUNK (6) Men Puppets	12 - 15	15 - 18
N.F. Series 160-165 (6)	8 - 10	10 - 12
PENOT, A.		
Lapina Little Men Series (6)	15 - 18	18 - 20
SAGER, XAVIER		
Series 43 Soldiers/Little Women (6)	18 - 20	20 - 25
SCHONPFLUG		
BKWI Series 4132 (6)	10 - 12	12 - 15
Marks, J.		
Series 155 "Summer Girl" (8)	8 - 10	10 - 12
BKWI		
Series 136 (6)	8 - 10	10 - 12
WBG 123 (6)	7 - 8	8 - 10

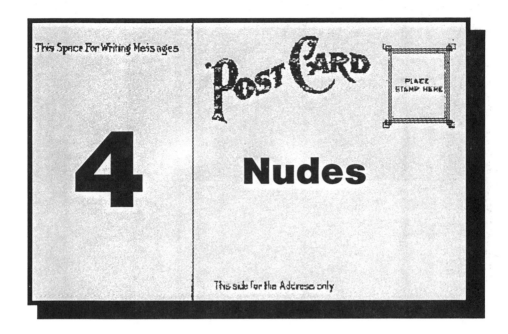

This Space For Writing Messages

POST CARD

PLACE
STAMP HERE

4 Nudes

This side for the Address only

COLOR NUDES

For many years, Color Nudes were completely neglected by the American postcard collector. The issues available were those of the Great Masters' reproductions of paintings housed in the big museums and art galleries throughout the world. Most of these were done by Stengel Art Co. of Dresden, Germany.

This gave color nudes a bad impression and repressed their growth until it was finally realized that there were hundreds of beautiful nudes and semi-nudes that were not museum reproductions. During postcards' Golden Years, European artists—especially the French and Germans—painted beautiful nudes relating to mythical, historical, Bibical, fairy tales, and fantasy motifs that were adapted to postcards. These cards have become highly collectible and are pursued by many American deltiologists.

As there was no demand in the United States from 1900 to 1920, color nudes by American artists are very rare. Therefore, most all of the nudes listed in this publication are those from Europe. Most cards of these artists were issued as single entities and there are very few sets or series available.

ALLEAUME, L.
    Lapina 59 "In the Rose"   12 - 15   15 - 18
      201 "Offering"   10 - 12   15 - 15
ASTI, A.
    JL & W 36/25, No Caption, Unsigned   12 - 15   15 - 18
    Salon 1897, "Songeuse"   15 - 18   18 - 22
AUER, R.
    Salon J.C.Z. 4 "Tender Flower"   12 - 15   15 - 18
    1 "Delight"   10 - 12   12 - 15
AXENTOWICZ, T.
    ANCZYC 110 "Noc"   20 - 25   25 - 30
    D.N. 29 "Studjum"   18 - 20   20 - 25
BARBER, COURT
    S.& G.S.i.B 1284 "Der Goldene Schal"   12 - 15   15 - 18
    1283 "Nach dem Bade"   12 - 15   15 - 18
BENDER, S.
    H.M., "La Femme Series (12)   15 - 18   18 - 25

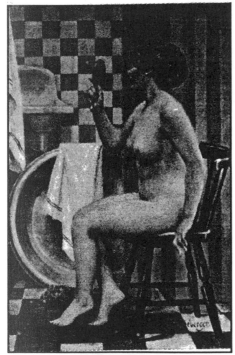

J. Seeberger
A.N., Paris 466, "After the Bath"

M. Bouland
A.N., Paris 446, "Femme a, l'echape"

BECAGLI, P.			
Salon de Paris "Paressguse"		12 - 15	15 - 18
BERNHARD			
"Bachante"		10 - 12	12 - 15
BORRMEISTER, R.			
Herman Wolff 1128 "Morgengruss"		10 - 12	12 - 15
Herman Wolff 1093 "Wald Marchen"		10 - 12	12 - 15
BOTTINGER, H.			
J.P.P. 1074 "Marchen"		12 - 15	15 - 18
BOULAND, M.			
A.N., Paris 446 "Femme a l'echape"		12 - 15	15 - 18
BRICHARD, X.			
A.N., Paris 404 "After the Bath"		12 - 15	15 - 18
BUBNA, G.			
Hermann Wolff 1135 "Ein Neugierger"		10 - 12	12 - 15
BUKOVAC, V.			
Minerva 21 No Caption		10 - 12	12 - 15
Minerva 28 "Koketa"		10 - 12	12 - 15
BUSMEY, S.			
Lapina 825 "The Dream of Love"		10 - 12	12 - 15
BUSSIERE			
Salon de Paris 744 "Salome"		10 - 12	12 - 15
CAYRON, J.			
Lapina 5433 "Repose"		12 - 15	15 - 18
CHANTRON, A.J.			
Salon de Paris 993 "The Bind Weed"		12 - 15	15 - 18
A.N., Paris 38 "Spring"		12 - 15	15 - 18
CHAPIN			
Stengel 29920 "Souvenirs"		8 - 10	10 - 12
CHERY			
"The Source"		10 - 12	12 - 15
COLLIN, R.			
Lapina 408 "Floreal"		8 - 10	10 - 12
COMERRE, LEON			
Palais des Beaux Arts "The Golden Rain"		10 - 12	12 - 15
A.N., Paris 164 "While the Artist ..."		8 - 10	10 - 12
COURTOIS, G.			
Lapina 526 "La Lecture"		8 - 10	10 - 12
CROZAT			
Galerie d'Art 117 "Apres le bal"		12 - 15	15 - 18
CUNICEL, EDW.			
O.F.Z.-L "Coquetry"		8 - 10	10 - 12
CZECH, E.			
"Apollon Sophia" 70 "Temptation"		8 - 10	10 - 12

DE BOUCHE

E.K.N. 1050 "The New Ornament"	8 - 10	10 - 12

DERVAUX, G.

Lapina 5412 "Naughty"	10 - 12	12 - 15

DEWALD, A.

Emgre-Sabn 229 "Eve"	10 - 12	12 - 15

DOLEZEL-EZEL, P.

F.H. & S. 5221 No Caption	10 - 12	12 - 15

DUPUIS, P.

Hanfstaengel 199 "The Wave"	12 - 15	15 - 18

DUSSEK, ED. ADRIAN

KPHOT Co.

JK51	"In Gedanken"	15 - 18	18 - 22
JK52	"Im Atelier"	20 - 22	22 - 25
JK53	"Studie"	20 - 22	22 - 25
JK54	"Das Model"	12 - 15	15 - 18
JK55	"The Hat"	15 - 18	18 - 22
JK56	"Studie"	18 - 20	20 - 25
JK57	"The Model"	12 - 15	15 - 18
JK58	"The Hat"	15 - 18	18 - 22
JK59	"In Gedanken"	15 - 18	18 - 22
JK60	"Schwuller Tag"	12 - 15	15 - 18
JK61	"Koketterie"	15 - 18	18 - 22
JK62	"Die Gold Gube"	15 - 18	18 - 22
JK63	"Vertraumt"	15 - 18	18 - 22
JK64	"Jugendstil Akstudie"	18 - 20	20 - 22
JK65	"Im Abendlicht"	15 - 18	18 - 22
JK66	"Halbakt"	25 - 28	28 - 32
JK67	"Erwachen"	18 - 22	22 - 25
JK68	"Blonder Akt"	20 - 22	22 - 25
JK69	"Frosch Koenigs Bride"	22 - 25	25 - 28
JK70	"Gross Toilette am Land"	12 - 15	15 - 18
JK25	"Modelpause"	12 - 15	15 - 18
JK18	"Das Neue Modell"	10 - 12	12 - 15

EICHER, MAX

O.G.Z-L 291 "Nach Dem Bade"	10 - 12	12 - 15

EINBECK "Nana" | 10 - 12 | 12 - 15 |

ENJOLRAS, E.

Lapina 718 "Repose"	12 - 15	15 - 18
Lapina "Ruth"	10 - 12	12 - 15
Lapina "Rest"	8 - 10	10 - 12

EVERART, M.

A.N., Paris 7 "The Woman With Ribbons"	10 - 12	12 - 15
SPA, Paris 4059 "The Woman With Lamp"	10 - 12	12 - 15

Ed. Adrian Dussek
J.K. 67, "Erwachen"

J.V.
Anonymous 67

SPA, Paris 76 "Young Woman at Mirror"	12 - 15	15 - 18
FAR-SI		
A.N., Paris "Oriental Perfume"	12 - 15	15 - 18
FEIKL, S.		
J.K.P. 236 "Akt"	10 - 12	12 - 15
FENNER-BEHMEL, H.		
Hanfstaengel's 194 "Ysabel"	15 - 18	18 - 22
FERRARIS, A.		
B.K.W.I. "Leda"	12 - 15	15 - 18
FOURNIER		
"Woman Bathing"	10 - 12	12 - 15
FREAND, E.		
Lapina 5415 "Familiar Birds"	8 - 10	10 - 12
FRIEDRICH, OTTO		
BKWI 1541 "Eitelkeit"	10 - 12	12 - 15
FRONTE, M.		
Lapina "Woman Lying Down"	12 - 15	15 - 18
FUCHS, RUDOLPH		
W.R.B.& Co. 738 "Blaue Augen"	10 - 12	12 - 15
GALAND, LEON		
Salon de Paris "A Sleeping Woman"	12 - 15	15 - 18

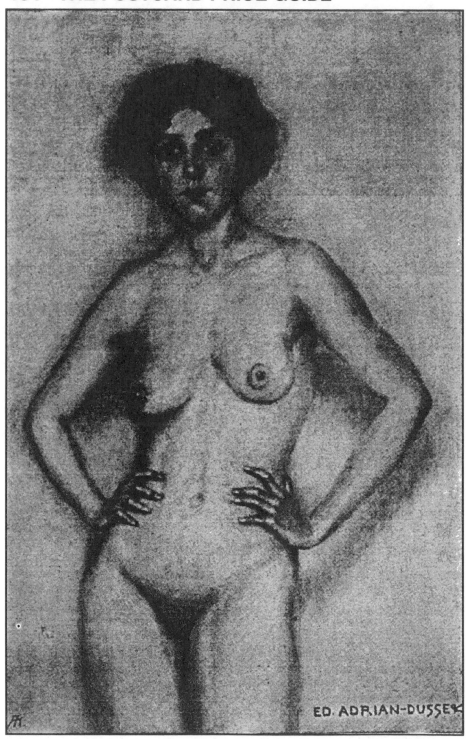

Ed. Adrian Dussek, J.K. 66, "Halbakt"

GALLELLI, M.			
P. Heckscher 143 "The First Pose"		10 - 12	12 - 15
GEIGER, C. AUG.			
NPG 453 "Eva"		10 - 12	12 - 15
GERMAIN			
"First Session"		12 - 15	15 - 18
GERVEX, H.			
Palais des Beaux-Arts 261 "Birth of Venus"		10 - 12	12 - 15
GITTER, H.			
Galerie Munchen Meister "Morgen"		8 - 10	10 - 12
Galerie Munchen Meister "Tag"		6 - 8	8 - 10
GLUCKLEIN, S.			
Hanfstaengel's 202 "Reposing"		10 - 12	12 - 15
GODWARD, J.W.			
Russia Richard 295 "A Fair Reflection"		10 - 12	12 - 15
GOEPFART, FRANZ			
301 "Ruhender Akt"		10 - 12	12 - 15
GOROKHOV			
N.P.G., Berlin "Wassernixe"		12 - 15	15 - 18
GRENOUILLOUX, J.			
Lapina "The Fair Summer Days"		12 - 15	15 - 18
Lapina "The Nymph with Flags"		12 - 15	15 - 18
Apollon 78 "Speil der Wellen"		8 - 10	10 - 12
Salon de Paris "The Nymph with Flags"		12 - 15	15 - 18
GUETIN, V.			
Lapina 799 "Das Bad"		8 - 10	10 - 12
GUILLAUME, R.M.			
Lapina 1400 "The Repose of the Model"		8 - 10	10 - 12
Lapina 1083 "Rapid Change"		10 - 12	12 - 15
Soc. des Artistes 58 "The Fly"		8 - 10	10 - 12
A.H.			
K.th W.II 636 "Lybelle"		10 - 12	12 - 15
HERVE, G.			
Lapina 44 "Resting"		12 - 15	15 - 18
Lapina 813 "Farniente"		12 - 15	15 - 18
Lapina "My Model and My Dog"		8 - 10	10 - 12
HEYMAN, RICHARD			
Heinrich Hoffman "Psyche"		10 - 12	12 - 15
HILSER			
Minerva 83 No Caption		10 - 12	12 - 15
Minerva 1130 "Siesta"		10 - 12	12 - 15
JANUSZEWSKI, J.			
ANCZYC 185 "Akt"		8 - 10	10 - 12
ANCZYC 455 No Caption		8 - 10	10 - 12

KASPARIDES, E.

BKWI 161-4 "A Warm Summer Morning"	8 - 10	10 - 12
BKWI 164-3 "The Airbath"	10 - 12	12 - 15
BKWI 164-10 "Forest Silence"	8 - 10	10 - 12
Others	8 - 10	10 - 12

KIESEL, C.

A.R. & C.i.B 463 "Salome"	8 - 10	10 - 12

KNOBLOCH, J.R.

O.G.Z.-l 1700 "Tired"	10 - 12	12 - 15

KNOEFEL

Novitas 668 (4) Illuminated Nudes	15 - 18	18 - 22

KLIMES

Minerva 1227 "Nymphe"	10 - 12	12 - 15

KORPAL, T.

ANCYZ 16 Bather "Au Ete"	10 - 12	12 - 15

KOSEL, H.C.

BKWI 181-3 "Kungstgeschlchte"	8 - 10	10 - 12
BKWI 181-8 "Nach im Bade"	8 - 10	10 - 12
BKWI 181-9 "Lekture"	8 - 10	10 - 12
BKWI 181-10 "Skaoin"	10 - 12	12 - 15

KRENES, H.

C1-12 "Danse"	8 - 10	10 - 12

KUTEW, CH.

Frist Ser. 90, 8 No Caption	8 - 10	10 - 12
Frist Ser. 90, 10 No Caption	12 - 15	15 - 18
AF.W. 111-2 "Ondine"	10 - 12	12 - 15

LANZDORF, R.

R. & J.D. 501 "Young Bedouin Girl"	8 - 10	10 - 12

LAUREN, P.A.

Lapina 2032 "Didon"	8 - 10	10 - 12

LEEKE, F.

Munchener Kunst 3114 "Bad de Bestalin"	12 - 15	15 - 18
Hans Koehler & Co. 76 "Bacchantalin"	12 - 15	15 - 18

LENDIR

P. Heckscher 366 "Die Zofe"	7 - 8	8 - 10

LENOIR, CH.

Lapina 853 "Stream Song"	12 - 15	15 - 18
A.N., Paris 19 "Tanzerin"	8 - 10	10 - 12
P. Heckscher 366 "Die Zofe"	8 - 10	10 - 12

L'EVEIL

Salon 1914 304 "The Awakening"	12 - 15	15 - 18

LIEBERMAN, E.

Emil Kohn 890 "At the Window"	8 - 10	10 - 12

LINGER, O.

G. Liersch & Co. 537 "Susses Nichtshen"		10 - 12	12 - 15
LUCAS, H.			
Lapina 890 "Happy Night"		10 - 12	12 - 15
MAKOVSKY, C.			
Russia 539 "Dans ie Boudoir"		8 - 10	10 - 12
MALIQUET, C.			
Lapina "Voluptuousness"		10 - 12	12 - 15
MANDL, JOS.			
Salon J.P.P. 2056 "L'Innocence"		8 - 10	10 - 12
MARECEK			
KV 1335 "Nach dem Bade"		8 - 10	10 - 12
VKKA 1201 "Toileta"		6 - 8	8 - 10
MARTIN, F.			
AR & CiB 395 "Vom dem Spiegel"		8 - 10	10 - 12
MARTIN-KAVEL			
Lapina "Nude on Tiger Rug"		8 - 10	10 - 12
Lapina 934 "Surprised"		8 - 10	10 - 12
MAX, G.			
Apollon Sophia 68 "Bacchante"		10 - 12	12 - 15

Susan Meunier
Marque L.E. Series 64-6

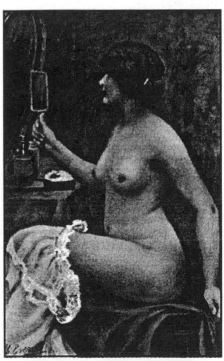

M. Everart, Salon de Paris,
"Young Woman at the Mirror"

MENZLER, W.
NPG 512 "Akt"	8 - 10	10 - 12

MERCIER
Art Moderne 748 "Nymphe Endormie"	10 - 12	12 - 15
Art Moderne "Nymph Reclining"	10 - 12	12 - 15

MERLE, K.
Moderner Kunst 2355 "After the Bath"	8 - 10	10 - 12

MIASSOJEDOW, J.
Russian 224 "Arab. Tanzerin"	10 - 12	12 - 15

MOHN, ROTER
Moderner Kunst 246 No Caption	8 - 10	10 - 12
Moderner Kunst 245 "Feuerlilien"	8 - 10	10 - 12

MORIN
Salon J.P.P. 1124 "Feu Follet"	8 - 10	10 - 12

MULLER, RICH.
Malke & Co. 25 "My Models"	15 - 18	18 - 22
SPGA 251 "Gold Fish"	15 - 18	18 - 22
SPGA 252 "Der Rote Ibis"	15 - 18	18 - 22
Others	15 - 18	18 - 22

NAKLADATEL, J.
J.P.P. 440-445 (6) Semi-Nudes	15 - 18	18 - 22

NEJEDLY
Salon J.P.P. "Erwachen"	10 - 12	12 - 15

NEMEJC, AUG.
Polish "Tragedie"	8 - 10	10 - 12

NISSL, RUDOLF
Novitas 388 "Akt im Mantel"	10 - 12	12 - 15

NONNENBRUCH, M.
Salon J.P.P. 2187 "La Sculpture"	10 - 12	12 - 15
O.G.Z.-L. 1174 "After Dancing"	10 - 12	12 - 15
Hanfstaengel's 49 "Flora"	10 - 12	12 - 15

OSTROWSKI, A.J.
Russian, **Phillips** 2172 "The Model"	10 - 12	12 - 15

OTTOMAN
Lapina "The Sleeping Courtesan"	8 - 10	10 - 12

PAPPERITZ, G.
Apollon 84 "Boa Neuf"	12 - 15	15 - 18
Apollon 237 "Bayadere"	12 - 15	15 - 18
Hanfstaengel's 197 "Chrysanthemums"	12 - 15	15 - 18

PAUSINGER
Russian 063 "Salome"	12 - 15	15 - 18

PENOT, A.
Lapina "Water Flower"	10 - 12	12 - 15
Lapina "Bayadera"	8 - 10	10 - 12

Lapina "A Young Girl"	10 - 12	12 - 15
Lapina "The Charm of Spring"	12 - 15	15 - 18
Lapina "Libelle"	10 - 12	12 - 15
Lapina 1340 "Red Butterfly"	12 - 15	15 - 18
Salon de Paris 229 "Repose"	10 - 12	12 - 15
PERRAULT		
Salon de Paris 727 "Der Erste Mai"	10 - 12	12 - 15
PETER, O.		
S.V.D. 292 "Das Kunstler Modell"	12 - 15	15 - 18
PRICE, J.M.		
Hanfstaengel's 117 "Odaliske"	12 - 15	15 - 18
R.R.		
M. Munk Ser. 684 (6)	12 - 15	15 - 18
M. Munk Ser. 873 (6)	15 - 18	18 - 22
REINACKER, G.		
Marke JSC 6054 "Am Morgen"	10 - 12	12 - 15
Marke JSC 6055 "Verkauft"	12 - 15	15 - 18
Marke JSC 6083 "Der Neue Schmuck"	12 - 15	15 - 18
PFB 6034 "Die Favoritin"	10 - 12	12 - 15
REIFENSTEIN, LEO		
Galzburger Kunst 45 "Schonhut"	10 - 12	12 - 15
RETTIG, H.		
Munchener Meister 568 "Im Spiegel"	10 - 12	12 - 15
RIESEN, O.		
A. Sch. & Co. 7152 "Unschuld"	10 - 12	12 - 15
S. & G. SiB 1471 "Am Morgen"	12 - 15	15 - 18
RITTER, C.		
Novitas 397 "Im Gotteskleid"	10 - 12	12 - 15
ROUSSELET, E.		
Lapina 1129 "Bathing"	12 - 15	15 - 18
Lapina "The Dream"	8 - 10	10 - 12
ROUSTEAUX-DARBOURD		
Salon 1912 571 "Am Feuer"	10 - 12	12 - 15
SAIZEDE		
Lapina "A Woman & Statuette"	8 - 10	10 - 12
SALIGER		
Haus der D. Kunst "Die Sinne"	10 - 12	12 - 15
SCALBERT, J.		
A.N., Paris 422 "The Shift"	8 - 10	10 - 12
Lapina 5158 "Hesitation"	10 - 12	12 - 15
SPA 30 "Satisfaction"	8 - 10	10 - 12
SCIHLABITZ, A.		
NPGA 30 "Akstudie"	10 - 12	12 - 15
SCHIVERT, V.		

TSN 801 "Der Liebestraube"	6 - 8	8 - 10
NPG 237 "Susanne"	8 - 10	10 - 12
NPG 238 "Akt"	12 - 15	15 - 18
Munchener Kunst 193 No Caption	12 - 15	15 - 18
Munchener Kunst 199 No Caption	12 - 15	15 - 18
PFB 42291 "Das Modell"	15 - 18	18 - 22
Arthur Rehn & Co. "Die Quelle"	15 - 18	18 - 22
SCHLEMO, E.		
TSN 889 "Beauty"	10 - 12	12 - 15
TSN 888 "Schonheit ist alles"	12 - 15	15 - 18
SCHLIMARSKI, H.		
BKWI 1805 "Vanity"	10 - 12	12 - 15
SCHMUTZLER, L.		
O.G.Z.L. 364 "Courtezan"	15 - 18	18 - 12
E.N. 810 "Passion"	15 - 18	18 - 22
Others	12 - 15	15 - 18
SCHNEIDER, E.		
"Die Windsbraut"	10 - 12	12 - 15
NPGA 54 "Halbakt"	10 - 12	12 - 15
AMAG Kunst 51 "Bacchantin"	10 - 12	12 - 15
SCHULZ, E.		
BKWI 885-1 Gothe's Der Got und Baidere"	15 - 18	18 - 22
SEEBERGER, J.		
A.N., Paris 466 "After the Bath"	10 - 12	12 - 15
A.N., Paris 470 "Smit with Love"	12 - 15	15 - 18
SEIGNAC, G.		
A.N., Paris "Gachucha"	8 - 10	10 - 12
A.N., Paris 597 "A Sprightly Girl"	10 - 12	12 - 15
A.N., Paris 760 "Indolence"	10 - 12	12 - 15
Lapina "The Birth of Venus"	12 - 15	15 - 18
SEZILLE, D.E.		
Lapina 913 "Annoying Accident"	12 - 15	15 - 18
SIEFERT, P.		
A.N., Paris "Diana"	15 - 18	18 - 22
SKALA		
Minerva 1117 "Eva"	10 - 12	12 - 15
SOLOMKO, S.		
TSN 153 "Circe"	15 - 18	18 - 22
SOUBBOTINE		
NPG 87 "Studie"	15- 18	18 - 22
Granbergs, Stock. 577 "Im Harem"	15 - 18	18 - 22
STACHIEWICZ, P.		
Wydann. Salon 152/23 "Kwiat Olean"	15 - 18	18 - 22
Wydann. Salon 152-24 "Zloty Zawoj"	12 - 15	15 - 18

Wydann. Salon "Ruth"	12 - 15	15 - 18
STELLA, EDUARD		
BRW 353 "Madame Sans Gene"	18 - 20	20 - 22
BRW 354 "Diana"	18 - 20	20 - 22
STEMBER, N.K.		
Russia, **Phillips** 1078 "Elegie"	18 - 20	20 - 25
Hanfstaengel's 56 "Jugend"	18 - 20	20 - 25
STENGEL NUDES		
Various Artists	8 - 10	10 - 12
STYKA, TADE		
Lapina 183 "Cinquecento"	6 - 8	8 - 10
SUCHANKE		
VKKA 1336 "Fruhlingslied"	6 - 8	8 - 10
SYKORA, G.		
G.Z. 032 "Der Necker"	8 - 10	10 - 12
URBAN, J.		
D.K. & Co. 678	12 - 15	15 - 18
VACHA, L.		
Minerva 1170 "Suzanne"	8 - 10	10 - 12
VALLET, L.		
Lapina 2498 "The Gourmet"	15 - 18	18 - 22
Lapina 2506 "Luxury"	15 - 18	18 - 22
Lapina 2507 "Pride"	15 - 18	18 - 22
Others	12 - 15	15 - 18
VASNIER, E.		
Lapina 779 "The Toilet"	12 - 15	15 - 18
VOLKER, ROB.		
Munchener Kunst 385 No Caption	10 - 12	12 - 15
Munchener Kunst 386 No Caption	10 - 12	12 - 15
VOWE, P.G.		
MBK 2546 No Caption	8 - 10	10 - 12
WALLIKOW, F.B.		
GK. v., Berlin 432 "Reifers Obst"	6 - 8	8 - 10
WEBER, E.		
BKWI 2363 "Akt"	10 - 12	12 - 15
WITTING, W.		
S.V.D. 358 "Auf Freier Hohe"	12 - 15	15 - 18
Dresdner KK "Jugend"	10 - 12	12 - 15
WOBRING, F.		
S.W.S.B. 4771 "Morgentau"	8 - 10	10 - 12
ZIER, ED.		
Russian, **Richard** "La Siesta"	12 - 15	15 - 18
ZMURKO, FR.		
ANCZYC 291, 297, 355, 448, 516	12 - 15	15 - 18

ANCZYC 280, 347, 449, 510, 648	10 - 12	12 - 15
ZOPF, C.		
O.G.Z.-L 865 "Curious"	8 - 10	10 - 12
ZWILLER, A.		
Salon de Paris "The Rest"	10 - 12	12 - 15

FRENCH GLAMOUR

Artists in America and many other countries were busy illustrating the faces, the big hats, and the mode of dress of their beautiful women; their French counterparts were equally busy showing her other bodily attributes, including her face. The mystique of the scantily and colorfully dressed beauties, showing lingerie, silk stockings, pajamas—and mostly nothing at all—made them the rage of the era. The French publishing firms of **Marque L-E** and **Delta** employed a varied group of talented artists to glorify the maiden form. Probably the most prolific and most popular of these was Susan Meunier with her renditions of numerous series of exotic nudes and semi-nudes. Jean Tam and his saucy, and sometimes comical, ladies also have become favorites of many collectors. Louis Icart and Umberto Brunelleschi, better known for their works in the Art Deco classification, each contributed a series in this glamorous field. For some unknown reason, most all of the different series by the two publishers contained seven cards, where normally there are 6, 8, 10 or 12. The highest priced and most desirable series, 31 by Brunelleschi, contains only 6 cards.

Delta Series are noted. The other publisher is **Marque L.E.**

BRUNELLESCHI, UMBERTO		
Series 31 (6)	80 - 90	90 - 110
CHARLET		
Delta Ser. 4	15 - 18	18 - 20
CREMIEUX, ED.		
Delta Ser. 44	15 - 18	18 - 20
Series 27	15 - 20	20 - 25
FABIANO		
Delta Ser. 5	12 - 15	15 - 18
Series 7, 11, 15	18 - 22	22 - 28
Series 32, 59, 63	15 - 18	18 - 22
FONTAN, LEO		
Series 17, 80	20 - 25	25 - 30
Series 23, 95, 5016	15 - 18	18 - 22
GALLAIS, P.		
Semi-Nude Series	20 - 22	22 - 26

Leo Fontan
Marque L.E. 5016

Herouard
Marque L.E. Series 55

GAYAC		
Series 290	18 - 20	20 - 25
GERBAULT		
Series 36	15 - 18	18 - 22
HEROUARD		
Series 55, 300	20 - 25	25 - 30
ICART, LOUIS		
Series 48 (6)	60 - 70	70 - 80
JARACH, A.		
Delta Ser. 156, 158	18 - 20	20 - 22
Series 18	18 - 20	20 - 25
KIRCHNER, RAPHAEL		
Series 1, 5	35 - 40	40 - 50
KOISTER		
Delta Series 71	15 - 18	18 - 22
LAFUGIE		
Series 45	15 - 18	18 - 22
LEONNEC		
Series 8	20 - 22	22 - 25
MANUEL, HENRI		
Series 51, 55	18 - 20	20 - 25

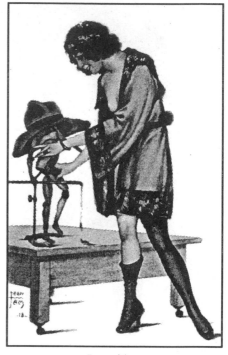

M. Pepin
Delta Series 23-113

Jean Tam
Marque L.E. Series 67-3

MEUNIER, SUSAN

Series 11, 20, 22	18 - 22	22 - 26
Series 26, 42, 77	22 - 25	25 - 35
Series 29, 32, 35	20 - 25	25 - 30
Series 32, 56, 74	18 - 22	22 - 26
Series 24, 52, 60	18 - 22	22 - 26
Series 64, 96, 98	25 - 30	30 - 35
Series 42, 99	18 - 22	22 - 26
Delta Ser. 90	20 - 22	22 - 26

MILLIERE, M.

Series 6, 21, 30, 37	18 - 22	22 - 26
Series 34, 54	20 - 25	25 - 30

NEY

Delta Ser. 24	20 - 25	25 - 30

PELTIER

Delta Ser. 28	20 - 25	25 - 28

PENOT, A.

Series 10, 28	18 - 22	22 - 26
Series 16, 25	18 - 20	20 - 25
Series 97, 98, 109	15 - 18	18 - 22

PEPIN

Delta Ser. 16, 21, 30	20 - 25	25 - 30

M. Milliere
Marque L.E. Series 6-5

Series 23	22 - 26	26 - 32
PERAS		
Series 68	15 - 18	18 - 22
SAGER, XAVIER		
P/Noyer		
Series 131 - Pajamas	15 - 18	18 - 22
Series 138 - Lingcric	18 - 22	22 - 25
Series 156 - Lesbian Dancers	22 - 27	27 - 35
Other Glamour Series	18 - 22	22 - 25
Erotic/Nudes	20 - 25	25 - 30
TAM, JEAN		
Series 39, 47,50	18 - 22	22 - 25
Series 57, 67	20 - 25	25 - 30
Series 70, 78, 81	18 - 22	22 - 25
VALLET, L.		
P/Lapina Nude Series	18 - 22	22 - 25

REAL PHOTO NUDES

Real photo nude postcards were first made famous by French publishers who selected bountiful beauties of the day to pose sans clothes. The more important publishing Salons were **AN, Corona, Noyer, PC, SAPI,** and **Super.** Others such as **AG, BMV, CA, ER, GP, JA, JB, JOPA, J.R., Leo, Lydia, MAH, SDK, S.I.C., SOL, Star, VC,** and **WA** added to the many cards produced.

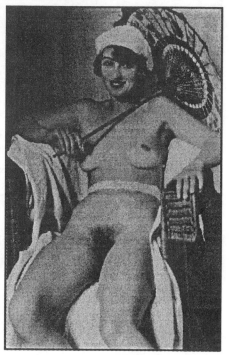

German Nude
No Airbrushing

Full Frontal German Nude
No Airbrushing

Although not always the norm, many publishers used airbrushing to obliterate any pubic or underarm hair from the photos and painted on lingerie for the prudish buyers in some markets. Tinting, especially those by **SOL, Paris,** enhanced the eye appeal and quality of selected series but, for today's collector, these are not quite as popular as the untouched material.

The cards were usually published and sold in sets of 6, 10 or 12, and from these many classical nudes exist. Various studio props were used for background affect. Chairs, tables, chests with mirrors, hanging tapestries, vases, and statues were among the favorites.

The most popular nudes, however, are those that were not profession- ally posed...were not airbrushed...and therefore left nothing to the imagination. Although the French did their share, cards of this particu- lar type were produced mainly in Germany and Austria, and normally do not have publisher bylines. A small number of cards in this group may also have been done in the U.S.

French Full Frontal
No Airbrushing

French Full Fontal
No Airbrushing

Non-Professionally Posed

Full Frontal, w/pubic hair	20 - 28	28 - 35
Full Frontal, w/underarm hair	22 - 30	30 - 40
Semi-Nude	12 - 15	15 - 20
Semi-Nude, w/underarm hair	20 - 25	25 - 30
Rear View	15 - 18	18 - 22
With Stockings	15 - 18	18 - 22
Lesbian Types	18 - 22	22 - 30
Tinted	15 - 18	18 - 22

Professionally Posed

Full Frontal, w/pubic hair	15 - 20	20 - 25
Full Frontal, no pubic hair	12 - 16	16 - 22
Semi-Nude, w/underarm hair	18 - 22	22 - 25
Semi-Nude, no underarm hair	15 - 20	20 - 25
Rear View	12 - 15	15 - 18
Lesbian Types	15 - 18	18 - 25
Tinted	12 - 15	15 - 18

Deduct $2 for non-postcard backs.

Lesbian Tendencies
Professionally-Posed
French J.R. Series 42

No Airbrushing
Professionally Posed
French J.R. Series 54

AFRICAN AND ASIAN SEMI-NUDES

Ethnic African and Asian nude postcards have become very popular in recent years. A quality group entitled "Afrique Occidental" seems to be the most popular. Cards are lightly colored and numbering has been seen from 0 up into the 1400's. The name of the particular tribe and whether the pictured semi-nude is a maiden (fille) or a woman (femme) is usually captioned on each card.

The publishers **L & L** produced a numbered colorful series of Arabians, Algerians, Tunisians, etc., that are also very collectible. Others, titled "Scenes et Types," "Egyptian Types," and a group of "Deutsch Sud West Africa" natives by **Albert Aust**, are also commanding good prices from collectors interested in this type material.

Black and white or sepia copies of many series were also produced. These are not as popular and prices are around 50% less than those produced in color. Real photo types, if original, tend to be priced higher.

African Native
Afrique Occ., 1378

African Native
Afrique Occ., 1351

Afrique Occidental

Filles	12 - 14	14 - 18
Femmes	10 - 12	12 - 14
Others	8 - 10	10 - 12
L & L	8 - 10	10 - 12
Scenes et Types	8 - 10	10 - 12
Egyptian Types	8 - 10	10 - 12
P/Albert Aust	12 - 14	14 - 18
Others	6 - 8	8 - 15

Greeting cards are those sent to recognize a Holiday, Birthday, or just to say "Hello." These were, by far, the largest single type of early postcards printed; there are millions still available today.

Many were beautifully printed and very desirable, while others were poorly designed and bland, unwanted by collectors, and destined today to postcard dealers' "25 cent" boxes. The majority of cards in huge accumulations or the remnants of a dealer's stock are represented in this group. Easter, Birthday, Thanksgiving, and common flowered greetings make up the greater proportion.

On the other hand, there are high quality Greeting cards by Signed Artists such as Helen Clapsaddle, Rose O'Neill, Frances Brundage, S.L. Schmucker, H.B. Griggs, Dwig, Grace Drayton/Wiederseim and others. Outstanding cards were also produced by publishers such as Winsch, Paul Finkenrath (PFB), Raphael Tuck, Nash, Santway, and Gabriel.

GREETINGS

NEW YEAR

Common	$ .50 - 1	$ 1 - 1.50
W/Children, uns.	2 - 3	3 - 5

HBG
L&E 2225

©Winch 1911
Uns. Schmucker

W/Pigs	4 - 6	6 - 8
W/Dressed Pigs	7 - 8	8 - 12
W/Chimney Sweeps	7 - 8	8 - 12
W/Pigs/Chimney Sweeps	8 - 10	10 - 15
W/Elves/Mushrooms/Gold, etc.	3 - 6	6 - 10
W/Big Snowmen	5 - 8	8 - 15
W/Year Date - See Year Dates		
W/Dressed Mushrooms, Gnomes	5 - 8	8 - 12
Sam Gabriel S/Brundage		
Ser. 300, 302, 316 (10)	10 - 12	12 - 14
International Art Pub. Co. S/Clapsaddle		
Common	4 - 5	5 - 6
W/Children	7 - 8	8 - 12
L & E S/H.B.G.		
Series 2225, 2227, 2266 (6)	8 - 9	9 - 10
Series 2276 (6)	8 - 9	9 - 10
P.F.B.		
Series 9501 Children/Auto (6)	6 - 8	8 - 10
R. Tuck Various Series		
Simple	0.50 - 1	1 - 2
W/Children	2 - 3	3 - 4

Series 601 (Uns. Brundage)   8 - 10   10 - 12
Wolf S/Clapsaddle, Uns./Clapsaddle
Add $3-5 per card to **Int. Art Pub. Co.** prices.

EASTER

Common	0.50 - 1	1 - 1.50
W/Children, unsigned	2 - 3	3 - 6
W/Chicks, Lambs, Bunnies	2 - 3	3 - 5
W/Dressed Chicks	3 - 5	5 - 7
W/Dressed Bunnies	4 - 6	6 - 12
W/Transportation	3 - 6	6 - 10
Easter Witches (Scandinavian) Normal	8 - 10	10 - 15
Easter Witches (Scandinavian) Small	10 - 12	12 - 18

See Artist-Signed
International Art. Pub. Co. S/Clapsaddle
Children   7 - 8   8 - 12
P.F.B.

Series 5837 (6)	5 - 6	6 - 8
Series 8270 (6)	6 - 7	7 - 9
Series 8684 (6)	6 - 7	7 - 9

Wolf S/Clapsaddle, Uns./Clapsaddle
Add $2-3 per card to **Int. Art Pub. Co.** prices.

PFINGSTEN (WHITSUN)

Embossed German Miakafirs, No Caption

Common	3 - 5	5 - 7
W/Children	4 - 6	6 - 8
W/Miakafirs (May Bugs)	8 - 10	10 - 16
W/Dressed Miakafirs	10 - 12	12 - 20
W/Bugs, Insects	7 - 10	10 - 12
W/Frogs	10 - 12	12 - 16
W/Dressed Frogs	12 - 18	18 - 25

Pfingsten cards have become very popular in recent times.

ST. PATRICK'S DAY

Common	1 - 1.50	1.50 - 2
W/Children, Ladies	3 - 5	5 - 7
W/Comics	2 - 3	3 - 5
W/Uncle Sam	4 - 6	6 - 8
W/Flags, Pipes	2 - 3	3 - 5
W/Ethnic Slurs	4 - 6	6 - 10
ASB Ser. 340 (6)	3 - 4	4 - 5

Helen Clapsaddle
Int. Art. Pub., No Number

Unsigned HBG
L&E 2253

Anglo American (AA)

Ser. 776, 815 (6)	3 - 4	4 - 5
Jules Bien Ser. 740 (6)	3 - 4	4 - 5

Sam Gabriel Ser. 140

Uns./Brundage (10)	8 - 10	10 - 12
Series 141 (10)	3 - 4	4 - 5

Gottschalk, Dreyfus & Davis

Ser. 2040, 2092, 2190, 2410	3 - 4	4 - 6

International Art Pub. Co. S/Clapsaddle

Children	6 - 9	9 - 12
Others	4 - 5	5 - 7
L & E S/H.B.G.	8 - 10	10 - 12

See Artist-Signed

Wolf S/Clapsaddle, Uns./Clapsaddle
Add $2-3 per card to **Int. Art Pub. Co.** prices.

VALENTINES DAY

Common	1 - 1.50	1.50 - 2
W/Children, Ladies	3 - 4	4 - 6
W/Comics	2 - 3	3 - 4
W/Animals	2 - 3	3 - 4

A.S.B.

Ser. 227, 229, 267 (6)	1 - 2	2 - 3
B.B. London Series 1501 (6)	1 - 2	2 - 3
B.W. Many Series (6)	1 - 2	2 - 3
S. Bergman Many Series (6)	1 - 2	2 - 3
Jules Bien Series 335 (6)	1 - 2	2 - 3
L.R. Conwell Ser. 329, 409 (6)	1 - 2	2 - 3

Sam Gabriel

S/J. Johnson Ser. 407 (6)	4 - 5	5 - 6
Uns./Brundage Ser. 413 (6)	8 - 10	10 - 12
Others	1 - 2	2 - 3

International Art. Pub. Co. S/Clapsaddle

Angels, Cherubs	4 - 6	6 - 8
Greetings	4 - 6	6 - 8
Children	8 - 9	9 - 18
E. Nash Many Series	1 - 2	2 - 3
P.F.B. Ser. 7185 Cupids	5 - 6	6 - 8
Samson Bros. Many Series	1 - 2	2 - 3

R. Tuck S/Brundage

Series 102 (6)	12 - 15	15 - 18
Blacks	22 - 25	25 - 30
Series 115 (4)	8 - 10	10 - 12
Blacks	22 - 25	25 - 30

Uns. Schmucker
©Winch 1910

Uns. HBG
L&E 2217

Series 11	8 - 10	10 - 12
Series 20 & 26 (uns.)	10 - 12	12 - 15
Series 100, 101 (6) (uns.)	10 - 12	12 - 14
Leatherette, 114, 116 (6)	3 - 5	5 - 7
Ser. 1033 Blacks	20 - 22	22 - 25
Other Uns./Brundage	8 - 10	10 - 12
Blacks	20 - 22	22 - 25
S/Outcault Series 106, 111, 112	8 - 10	10 - 12
Black Series 108 (6)	10 - 12	12 - 14
R. Tuck		
Series A, B, C, 5, 6, & 7	4 - 5	5 - 6
Winsch, Copyright		
Common	1 - 1.50	1.50 - 2
W/Children	4 - 5	5 - 6
W/Ladies, etc.	4 - 5	5 - 6
W/Uns. **Schmucker** Ladies	20 - 22	22 - 25
Booklet-types	5 - 6	6 - 8
Silk Inserts (Ladies)	10 - 12	12 - 15
W/Uns. **Schmucker** inserts	40 - 50	50 - 60
Rose Co. Comic Series	2 - 3	3 - 4
Illustrated P.C. Co. Comics		

S/**H. Horina** Series 5004	3 - 4	4 - 5
Aurochrome Co. Comics		
S/**Meyer**	3 - 4	4 - 5
Wolf S/Clapsaddle, Uns./Clapsaddle		
Add $3-5 per card to **Int. Art Pub. Co.** prices.		

BIRTHDAY

Common	0.50 - 1	1 - 1.50
W/Children	2 - 3	3 - 5
S/**Clapsaddle**	7 - 9	9 - 14
Winsch, Copyright	4 - 5	5 - 8
Wolf S/Clapsaddle, Uns./Clapsaddle		
Add $2-3 to **Int. Art Pub. Co.** prices.		

APRIL FOOL DAY

Henderson Litho Ser. 102	6 - 7	7 - 8
P.C.K. (Paul C. Kober)		
S/A. Hutaf	6 - 8	8 - 10
Ullman Mfg Co. S/B. Wall		
Ser. 156 (6)	6 - 7	7 - 8
Winsch Backs Ser. 1	6 - 8	8 - 10
FRENCH 1st of Avril Fish	6 - 8	8 - 12
P.F.B. Series 553	8 - 10	10 - 12
P.F.B. Series 6505	8 - 10	10 - 12

LEAP YEAR

S/**Brill,** B&W and Red (12)	3 - 4	4 - 5
D.P. Crane S/Zim	7 - 9	9 - 12
Sam Gabriel Ser. 401 S/Dwig	10 - 12	12 - 14
Grollman, 1908	6 - 8	8 - 10
H.T.M. 1060-1071 (12)	7 - 8	8 - 9
Illustrated P.C. Co. Ser. 217	6 - 7	7 - 9
P.C. Kober S/Hutaf	8 - 9	9 - 11
B.B. London Ser. E44, E81	8 - 9	9 - 10
E. Nash		
"Lemon" Series 1 (12)	7 - 8	8 - 9
"Diamond Ring" Ser., 1912	7 - 8	8 - 9
"Captured him in his lair"		
"Caught on the run"		
"Don't give up the ship"		
"Lay for him"		
"On the Trail"		
"Ring up the man you want"		
Rose Co. S/G. Brill (6)	5 - 6	6 - 7

P. Sanders, 1908	6 - 8	8 - 10
R. Tuck Ser. 7, S/ Curtis (12)	8 - 9	9 - 11
S/L. Thackeray	8 - 10	10 - 12

GROUND HOG DAY

Henderson Litho Co. (4)	120 - 125	125 - 150

MOTHER'S DAY

Metro Litho Co.

Series 446 (6)	10 - 12	12 - 14

Anonymous

Lady & Soldier, "Mother's Day"	8 - 10	10 - 15
Mother holds Baby, "Mother's Day"	8 - 10	10 - 15
Mother holds baby at arms length.	20 - 25	25 - 30

GEORGE WASHINGTON'S BIRTHDAY

Anglo American (AA)

Open Book Series	725 (6)	20 - 25	25 - 30

HBG
L&E 2242

Helen Clapsaddle
Int. Art Pub. 16209

	728 (6)	20 - 25	25 - 30
Jules Bien Series	605 (6)	6 - 8	8 - 10
	760 (4)	6 - 8	8 - 10
Gottschalk, Dreyfus and Davis	216 (12)	8 - 9	9 - 10
International Art Co.			
	51646 (8)	8 - 9	9 - 10
S/Clapsaddle	16208 (4)	7 - 8	8 - 10
	16209 (4)	7 - 8	8 - 9
Uns./Clapsaddle	16250 (6)	6 - 7	7 - 8
S/Clapsaddle	51896 (6)	7 - 8	8 - 9
S/Veenfliet	51766 (6)	8 - 9	9 - 10
L & E, S/H.B.G.	2242 (8)	10 - 12	12 - 15
Lounsbury	2020 (4)	10 - 12	12 - 15
E. Nash	1 (6)	6 - 7	7 - 8
	2 (6)	6 - 7	7 - 8
	4 (6)	6 - 7	7 - 8
W5, W6, W7 (4)		5 - 6	6 - 7
W9 (4)		5 - 6	6 - 7
W11 (4)		5 - 6	6 - 8
W14 (4)		5 - 6	6 - 7
W15 (4)		6 - 7	7 - 8
H.I. Robbins	329 (8)	6 - 8	8 - 10
P. Sander	414 (6)	6 - 8	8 - 10
M.W. Taggart, NY	605 (6)	6 - 8	8 - 10
Raphael Tuck Series	124 (6)	6 - 8	8 - 10
	156 (6)	6 - 8	8 - 10
	171 (6)	6 - 8	8 - 10
	178 (10)	6 - 8	8 - 10

DECORATION DAY/MEMORIAL DAY

Raphael Tuck Series	107 (12)	8 - 10	10 - 12
	158 (12)	8 - 10	10 - 12
	173 (12)	12 - 15	15 - 18
	179 (12)	12 - 15	15 - 18
Nash Series	1 (6)	6 - 8	8 - 10
	2 (6)	6 - 8	8 - 10
	3 (6)	6 - 8	8 - 10
	D4 (6)	6 - 8	8 - 10
	6 (6)	10 - 12	12 - 15
	21 (6)	8 - 10	10 - 12
Int. Art Co. Series			
S/Chapman	Ser. 6 (6)	6 - 8	8 - 10
S/Clapsaddle	6 (6)	8 - 10	10 - 12

S/Clapsaddle	973 (6)	6 - 8	8 - 10
S/Clapsaddle	2444 (6)	7 - 8	8 - 10
S/Clapsaddle	2935 (6)	8 - 10	10 - 12
S/Clapsaddle	4397 (6)	6 - 8	8 - 10
Lounsbury, S/Bunnell			
Series	2083 (4)	10 - 12	12 - 15
A.S.B. Series	283 (6)	5 - 6	6 - 8
Conwell Series	376-381 (6)	5 - 6	6 - 8
S. Gabriel Series	150 (6)	6 - 8	8 - 10
Santaway Series	157 (6)	8 - 10	10 - 12
Others		4 - 5	5 - 6

CONFEDERATE MEMORIAL DAY

R. Tuck's "Confederate" Series		
Divided Backs (12)		
"For though Conquered ..."	10 - 15	15 - 18
"Furl that Banner!"	10 - 15	15 - 18
General Joseph E. Johnson	15 - 18	18 - 22
General Robert E. Lee	20 - 25	25 - 28
General Stonewall Jackson	20 - 25	25 - 28
Headquarters, Army of N. Virginia	10 - 15	15 - 18
"In Memoriam ..." 2 flags	10 - 15	15 - 18
"In Memoriam ..." 3 flags	10 - 15	15 - 18
"The Hands that grasped ..." 4 flags	10 - 15	15 - 18
"The Warriors Banner takes its Flight"	10 - 15	15 - 18
"Twill live in Song and Story ..."	10 - 15	15 - 18
United Daughters Confederacy ..."	10 - 15	15 - 18
R. Tuck's "Heroes of the South"		
Series 2510	18 - 20	22 - 30
Souvenir P.C. Co.		
W/"Bee Brand" (6)	10 - 12	12 - 15
Jamestown A & V Co.		
Jamestown Expo Cards (11)	30 - 40	40 - 45
Veteran Art Co.		
"National Souvenir" Set	8 - 10	10 - 12
Winsch-back, No Publisher	10 - 12	12 - 15
Two Southern Generals Card	12 - 15	15 - 18

ABRAHAM LINCOLN'S BIRTHDAY

Anglo American (AA)		
Open Book Ser. 726 (6)	25 - 30	30 - 35
Series 727 (6)	25 - 30	30 - 35
Century Co.		
Sepia Series (6)	8 - 10	10 - 12

Abraham Lincoln
Anglo-American Open Book Series 726-4

Int. Art Pub. Co. Ser. 51658 (6)	8 - 10	10 - 12
Lincoln/Contrabands (1)	10 - 12	12 - 15
Lounsbury Centennial (4)	8 - 10	10 - 12
Nash Series 1 (6)	7 - 8	8 - 10
Gold or Silver 2 (6)	7 - 8	8 - 10
P. Sander Series 415 (6)	7 - 8	8 - 10
Sheehan, M.A. Series (18)	7 - 8	8 - 10
Raphael Tuck Series 155 (6)	10 - 12	12 - 14

FOURTH OF JULY

Common	2 - 3	3 - 4
W/Children, Ladies	5 - 6	6 - 8
W/Uncle Sam See Uncle Sam below		
Jules Bien Series 700 (6)	7 - 8	8 - 9
Conwell Series 380 (6)	4 - 5	5 - 6
S. Garre Series 51668 (6)		
S/Chapman	7 - 8	8 - 9
Gottschalk, Dreyfus & Davis		
Ser. 2171, 2099 (6)	7 - 8	8 - 9
Int. Art Pub Co. S/Clapsaddle		
Series 974 (6)	8 - 10	10 - 12
Series 2443 (6)	8 - 10	10 - 12

Helen Clapsaddle
Int. Art Pub. 2936

Helen Clapsaddle
Int. Art Pub. 4398

Fred C. Lounsbury S/Bunnell		
Series 2076 (6)	8 - 10	10 - 12
Uncle Sam Series (4)	12 - 15	15 - 18
Nash Comic Series 1 (6)	6 - 8	8 - 10
1 "How to prevent your boy..."		
2 "Ye Spit-Devil is a wily..."		
3 "The Giant Cracker..."		
4 "Photograph your boy..."		
5 "Where ignorance is bliss"		
6 "The Dog ..."		
Series 4, 5 (6)	7 - 8	8 - 9
Series J6 (6)	6 - 7	7 - 8
Series J8 (6)	8 - 10	10 - 12
W/Uncle Sam	15 - 18	18 - 22
P.F.B. Series 8252 (6)	12 - 15	15 - 18
Series 9507 (6) S/Bunnell	15 - 18	18 - 22
Rotograph Co. S/Gene Carr		
Series 219 (6)	7 - 8	8 - 10
P. Sander Series 440 (6)	7 - 8	8 - 9
Steiner Series 129 (6)	6 - 7	7 - 8
Tower Series 106 (6)	4 - 5	5 - 6

R. Tuck Series 109 (12)	6 - 7	7 - 9
Series 159 (12)	6 - 7	7 - 9
Ullman Co. Series 124 (6)	5 - 6	6 - 7
Wolf S/Clapsaddle, Uns./Clapsaddle		

Add $2-3 per card to **Int. Art Pub. Co.** prices.

FLAG OF THE U.S.

Jules Bien Ser. 710, 716	5 - 6	6 - 8
Ill. P.C. Co. Series 207	5 - 6	6 - 7
Souvenir P.C. Co.	4 - 5	5 - 7

HALLOWEEN

AMP Company Series 303	8 - 9	9 - 12
AA (Anglo American)		
Witch Series (6)	9 - 10	10 - 14
S/E.C. Banks	9 - 10	10 - 14

©Winch 1911
Uns. Schmucker

Uns. Helen Clapsaddle
Wolfe & Co.

Uns. Frances Brundage
R. Tuck Series 74

B.B., London (Birn Bros.)	9 - 10	10 - 14
Jules Bien & Co.	8 - 10	10 - 14
Conwell	8 - 9	9 - 10
P.F.B. (Paul Finkenrath)		
Series 9442 (6)	12 - 15	15 - 20
Sam Gabriel		
Series 120 S/Brundage (10)	15 - 17	17 - 22
Series 121 S/Brundage (10)	15 - 17	17 - 22
Series 123 S/Brundage (10)	12 - 15	15 - 20
Series 125 S/Brundage (6)	15 - 18	18 - 22
Gottchalk & Dreyfus		
Ser. 2040, 2097, 2171 (12)	8 - 10	10 - 14
Ser. 2402 (6)	10 - 12	12 - 15
Ser. 2470 (6)	8 - 9	9 - 12
International Art Pub. Co.		
Signed by Clapsaddle		
Series 501 (4), 978 (6)	15 - 20	20 - 35
Series 1236 (4) Mechanicals		
White Children	100 - 115	115 - 135
Black Child	150 - 160	160 - 175
Ser. 1237, 1238 (4)	12 - 15	15 - 20
Ser. 1301 (12), 1393 (6)	12 - 15	15 - 20
Ser. 1667 (12)	12 - 15	15 - 20

Ser. 1815 (6)	12 - 15	15 - 20
Unsigned Cards	8 - 9	9 - 10
Signed B. Wall No Nos. (12)	8 - 9	9 - 10
Wolf & Co. (Uns./Clapsaddle)	20 - 25	25 - 30
L. & E. (S/H.B.G.)		
Series 2214, 2215 (6)	10 - 12	12 - 15
Series E2231, 2262 (12)	10 - 12	12 - 15
Unsigned Cards	10 - 12	12 - 15
C. Marks S/Dwig (12)	20 - 22	22 - 25
Nash Many Series of (6)	8 - 10	10 - 12
F.A. Owen Many Series	6 - 7	7 - 8
P. Sander	6 - 8	8 - 10
S.B. Many Series	8 - 9	9 - 10
Stecher Many Series (6)	8 - 9	9 - 10
Taggert Series 803, 806 (6)	9 - 10	10 - 12
Valentine & Sons	8 - 10	10 - 12
Whitney No numbers.	6 - 8	8 - 10
Raphael Tuck		
Series 150 (12)	8 - 10	10 - 12
Series 160 (12)	10 - 12	12 - 14
Series 174 (12) (Uns./Brundage)	12 - 14	14 - 18
Series 181 (10) w/cat	8 - 10	10 - 12
Series 183, 188, 190, 197	8 - 10	10 - 12
Series 803	8 - 9	9 - 10
Series 807 (6) (Uns./Wiederseim)	30 - 35	35 - 40
John Winsch, Copyright		
1911 Series (6) (Uns./Schmucker)	60 - 70	70 - 80
1912 Series (12)	30 - 35	35 - 40
1913 Series (12)	20 - 22	22 - 25
1914 Series (18-20) (Uns./Freixas)	25 - 30	30 - 35
1915 Series (6)	25 - 30	30 - 35
Others, not listed	6 - 8	8 - 10

THANKSGIVING

Common	0.50 - 1	1 - 1.50
W/Turkeys	1 - 1.50	1.50 - 2
W/Children, Ladies, etc.	2 - 3	3 - 5
A.S.B. Series 282, 290 (6)	0.50 - 1	1 - 3
AA (Anglo American) Ser. 875	0.50 - 1	1 - 3
B.B. London 2700, 2701 (6)	1 - 2	2 - 4
Conwell Series 637 (6)	0.50 - 1	1 - 2
Sam Gabriel S/Brundage		
Series 130, 132, 133 (10)	8 - 10	10 - 12
Series 135 (6)	6 - 8	8 - 10

Others	0.50 - 1	1 - 2
Ill. P.C. Co.	0.50 - 1	1 - 2
International Art. Pub. Co.		
S/Helen Clapsaddle		
W/Children	5 - 6	6 - 9
W/Pilgrims, Turkeys, Corn	3 - 4	4 - 5
Others	1 - 2	2 - 3
L. & E. S/H.B.G.		
Series 2212, 2213, 2233		
Series 2263, 2273 (6)	6 - 8	8 - 10
P.F.B.		
Series 8429 (6)	6 - 7	7 - 8
Series 8857 (6)	4 - 5	5 - 6
Taggart Blacks (6)	8 - 9	9 - 10
Others	2 - 3	3 - 5
R. Tuck	2 - 3	3 - 4
Winsch, Copyright		
Common	1 - 1.50	1.50 - 2
Indians	3 - 4	4 - 6
Ladies	5 - 7	7 - 10
Wolf S/Clapsaddle, Uns./Clapsaddle		
Add $2-3 per card to **Int. Art Pub. Co.** prices.		

LABOR DAY

Lounsbury Series 2046 (4)	125 - 150	150 - 175
Nash Labor Day Series 1		
1 "Service Shall With Steeled ..."	120 - 130	130 - 150
2 "Labor Conquers Everything"	120 - 130	130 - 150

CHRISTMAS

Common	0.50 - 1	1 - 2
W/Children, Animals	2 - 3	3 - 4
W/Children, w/Toys	4 - 5	5 - 7
Small Santas, Red Suit	4 - 5	5 - 6
Large Santas, Red Suit	6 - 9	9 - 12
Lady Santa	10 - 20	20 - 40
Sam Gabriel		
S/Frances Brundage		
Series 200, 208, 219 (10)	10 - 12	12 - 15
Santa	15 - 18	18 - 22
International Art Pub. Co. S/Clapsaddle		
Children	7 - 9	9 - 12
Wolf S/Clapsaddle	10 - 12	12 - 15
P.F.B.		

Series 7143 Boy/Girl (6)	7 - 8	8 - 10
Series 7422 Children/Tree (6)	10 - 12	12 - 14
Winsch, Copyright		
Common	1 - 1.50	1.50 - 2
W/Children	4 - 5	5 - 7
W/Ladies	8 - 10	10 - 12
W/Silk Inserts, Common	3 - 5	5 - 7
W/Silk Ladies	12 - 15	15 - 20
Booklets, Common	3 - 5	5 - 7
Booklets W/Ladies	5 - 7	7 - 10

SANTAS

Small Image, Red Suit	3 - 5	5 - 6
Large Image, Red Suit	6 - 8	8 - 12
Small Image, Other Colors	8 - 10	10 - 12
Large Image, Other Colors	12 - 15	15 - 20
Lady Santas **P. Sander** (4)	20 - 30	30 - 40
Child Santas	5 - 10	10 - 20
W/Silk applique		
Small image	15 - 20	20 - 25
Large image	25 - 30	30 - 35
W/Odd Transportation		
Add $2-5 to prices.		
AA (Anglo American)		
Series 705, 708, 709 (6)	8 - 12	12 - 15
B.W., Germany		
Series 291, 296, 305, 324 (6)	8 - 12	12 - 20
Ettinger Uns./Louis Wain		
Series 5376 Santa	75 - 85	85 - 100
Samson Bros.		
Series 31, Series 705 (6)	8 - 12	12 - 20
R. Tuck		
Series 4 (12) S/Frances Brundage	12 - 15	15 - 20
Series 512 (12), 535 (6)	8 - 10	10 - 15
Series 549 (6) S/M.B.H.	12 - 14	14 - 18
Series 8415 (6) S/Shepheard	12 - 14	14 - 18
John Winsch, Copyright		
Copyright, 1913 (4)	18 - 22	22 - 25
Copyright, 1914 (4)	18 - 22	22 - 25
German Santas, Father Christmas		
Small figure, Non-Red Suit	6 - 9	9 - 12
Large figure, Non-Red Suits	9 - 12	12 - 18
Small, Robes other than Red	8 - 12	12 - 15
Large, Robes other than red	15 - 18	18 - 30

German Santa
M&B Green Robe

Embossed German Santa
Series 87 Purple Robe

W/Christ Child - Add $5 per card.		
Lady Santas	15 - 18	18 - 25
W/Odd Transportation - Add $4-5 per card.		
W/Switches - Add $3-4 per card.		
Signed by Mailick	15 - 22	22 - 35
Mailick Hold-To-Light	140 - 150	150 - 175
Other H-T-L German Santas	100 - 125	125 - 150
Uncle Sam Santa (4)	175 - 225	225 - 275
Uncle Sam Santa H-T-L (4)	500 - 750	750 - 900
H-T-L Transparency	50 - 60	60 - 75

SAINT NICHOLAS

Real Photo Types	8 - 10	10 - 12
Wearing Red/white Robe		
Small figure	8 - 10	10 - 12
Large Figure	12 - 15	15 - 20
Wearing Robes other than red/white		
Small figure	12 - 15	15 - 18
Large figure	15 - 20	20 - 25
St. Nicholas & Krampus together		

Lady Santa
P. Sander 751

Saint Nicholas
Import 226

Small figure	15 - 20	20 - 22
Large figure	20 - 25	25 - 35

KRAMPUS

European
Red Background - pre-1915

Small figure	10 - 12	12 - 15
Large figure	12 - 15	15 - 20

Printed, Color - pre-1915

Small figure	12 - 15	15 - 18
Large figure	20 - 25	25 - 30

W/crying children - add $4-5
W/children in the bucket - add $4-5
Erotic, w/women - add $5-10
W/cloth applique - add $5-6

Red Background - 1915-1930	10 - 12	12 - 15
Printed, Color - 1915-1930	15 - 18	18 - 20

UNCLE SAM

Common	6 - 7	7 - 9

F. Rosten
Austrian, C.H.W. 2483

Austrian, Anonymous
Gruss vom Krampus

Better Publishers		10 - 12	12 - 18
Franz Huld Installment Set		20 - 22	22 - 25
See Fourth of July			
Uncle Sam Santa (See Santas)			

YEAR DATES

1894-1895		75 - 85	85 - 100
1896		50 - 60	60 - 75
1897		40 - 50	50 - 65
1898		35 - 40	40 - 50
1899		30 - 35	35 - 45
1900	Common	20 - 25	25 - 30
W/Animals, People		25 - 30	30 - 35
Hold-To-Light		50 - 55	55 - 65
1901	Common	15 - 20	20 - 25
W/Animals, People		20 - 25	25 - 28
Hold-To-Light		50 - 55	55 - 65
1902	Common	10 - 12	12 - 15
W/Animals, People		15 - 18	18 - 22
Hold-To-Light		30 - 35	35 - 40

German Hold-To-Light
Year Date

1903	Common	8 - 10	10 - 12
W/Animals, People		10 - 12	12 - 15
Hold-To-Light		25 - 30	30 - 35
1904	Common	7 - 9	9 - 12
W/Animals, People		9 - 12	12 - 14
Hold-To-Light		22 - 25	25 - 28
1905	Common	5 - 6	6 - 8
W/Animals, People		6 - 8	8 - 10
Hold-To-Light		20 - 22	22 - 25
1906-1911	Common	4 - 5	5 - 6
W/Animals, People		6 - 7	7 - 8
1912-1914	Common	8 - 10	10 - 12
W/Animals, People		12 - 14	14 - 16
1915-1918	Common	10 - 12	12 - 14
W/Animals, People		12 - 14	14 - 16
1919-1925		20 - 25	25 - 30
1926-1930		25 - 28	28 - 32

RELIGIOUS, VIRTUES, ETC.

CHILD'S PRAYER

Cunningham (6)	8 - 10	10 - 12
Geo. F. Holbrook (4)	10 - 12	12 - 15

GUARDIAN ANGEL

A.S.B. Series 250 (4)	8 - 10	10 - 12

German
1902 Year Date

Easter Angels
DRGM Hold-to-Light

Mark Emege Series 178 (4)	8 - 10	10 - 12
Birn Bros. Series 2109 (4)	7 - 8	8 - 10
PFB		
Series 8618 (4)	10 - 12	12 - 15
Series 8621 (4)	10 - 12	12 - 15
THE HOLY SCRIPTURE		
S/Leinweber		
Old Testament	4 - 5	5 - 6
LORD'S PRAYER		
A.S.B. Series 264 (8)	5 - 7	7 - 8
Series 350 (8)	5 - 6	6 - 8
DB Series 350 (8)	6 - 8	8 - 10
I.S. Co. Series (8)	6 - 7	7 - 8
PFB Series 7064-7070 (8)	10 - 12	12 - 15
Series 8415 (8)	10 - 12	12 - 15
Unknown Publisher		
Series N-700 G (8)	6 - 8	8 - 10
TEN COMMANDMENTS		
PFB Series 163 (10)	8 - 10	10 - 12
Series 8554 (10)	8 - 10	10 - 12
Taggart Series (10)	8 - 10	10 - 12

Rose Series (10)	10 - 12	12 - 15
R. Tuck Ser. 163 (10)	8 - 10	10 - 12
VIRTUES - FAITH, HOPE, CHARITY		
A.S.B. Series 178 (6)	6 - 8	8 - 10
E.A.S. Series	7 - 8	8 - 12
G.B. Series (6)	8 - 10	10 - 12
Langsdorf Series	7 - 9	9 - 12
PFB Series 8797, 8798	10 - 12	12 - 14
Rotograph P.96	5 - 6	6 - 7

One of the more exhilarating experiences in postcard collecting is:

The Thrill of the Hunt!

Paul Finkenrath, Berlin
(PFB) 7138

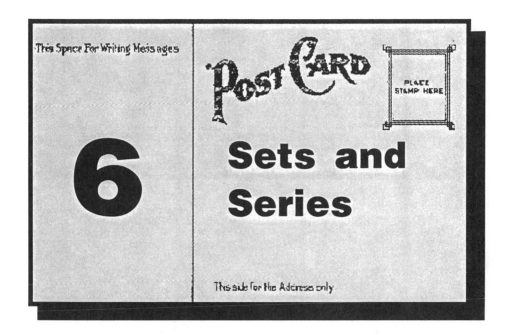

This Space For Writing Messages

POST CARD

PLACE
STAMP HERE

6

Sets and Series

This side for the Address only

Early publishers realized immediately the sales and manufacturing benefits of producing postcards in sets and series of like motifs. Artists and photographers were commissioned to submit their works in series or sets of 4, 6, 8, and 12, or more. They were then printed and packaged to sell this way. This method, as history has proven, turned out to be a very good merchandising scheme for the publishers and was very helpful, monetarily, to the aspiring artists of the day. It also greatly enhanced the interest and collectibility of postcards.

Collectors strive to complete sets or series and have been known to pay double or triple the value to obtain the last elusive card of a favorite subject. What a thrill it is to finally find that sixth card to complete the set!

Because of the comprehensive nature of this price guide, this section lists only a small number of the more important sets and series. Hundreds of others are listed in all other sections so they can be more easily found and identified.

The "Animals" motif is listed here and will be placed in another section in later editions.

American Colortype, 1909

"American Beauty" Series 12	$ 6 - 7	$ 7 - 8

Austin "Famous American" Series (12)

Theodore Roosevelt	6 - 8	8 - 10
Mark Twain	6 - 8	8 - 10
Robert Perry	6 - 8	8 - 10
George Dewey	6 - 8	8 - 10
John G. Whittier	6 - 8	8 - 10
U.S. Grant	8 - 10	10 - 12
Robert E. Lee	10 - 12	12 - 15
John Philip Sousa	6 - 8	8 - 10
Luther Burbank	6 - 8	8 - 10
Benjamin Franklin	6 - 8	8 - 10
Andrew Carnegie	6 - 8	8 - 10
George Washington	8 - 10	10 - 12

Austin "Tour of the World"	1 - 2	2 - 3
Bergman "College Girls"	6 - 7	7 - 8

Donaldson, H.M.

"American Heroes" (13)	10 - 12	12 - 15

David Farragut	Oliver H. Perry
Sam Houston	Israel Putnam

Langsdorf S541 Alligator Border
"On the Ocklawaha River, Florida"

R. Tuck State Belles 2669
"Massachusetts"

Platinachrome State Girls
"New York"

Andrew Jackson	Paul Revere	
John Paul Jones	Winfield Scott	
Gen. Robt. E. Lee	Philip Sheridan	
Abraham Lincoln	Capt. John Smith	
William Penn	George Washington	
"Paul Revere's Ride" (10) Anon.	4 - 5	5 - 6
American Historical Art Publishers		
"Colonial Heroes"		
Red, White, and Blue backs (40)	4 - 5	5 - 6
Illustrated P.C. Co.		
"State Capitols & Seals" (49)	6 - 7	7 - 8
Hudson-Fulton "Redfield Floats" (40)	5 - 6	6 - 7
L. Ferloni		
"Ferloni Popes," 1903	5 - 6	6 - 7
Johnson-Ayers, 1911 "President Series"		
Red, White, Blue	4 - 5	5 - 6
P.C. Kober (PCK)		
"Butterflies W/Views in Wings"	15 - 18	18 - 22
"Pansies W/Views in Petals"	12 - 15	15 - 18
J. Koehler "Hold-To-Lights"		
New York City (24)	32 - 35	35 - 40

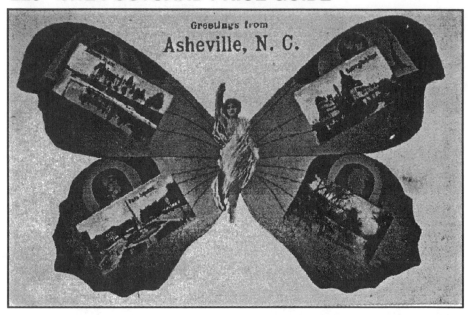

P.C.K. Butterfly View Series 9768

Cony Island (12)	32 - 35	35 - 40
Washington, D.C. (12)	25 - 28	28 - 32
Hudson River (12)	22 - 25	25 - 30
Philadelphia (12)	30 - 32	32 - 35
Boston (12)	30 - 32	32 - 35
Chicago (12)	30 - 32	32 - 35
Atlantic City (6)	32 - 35	35 - 38
Buffalo (6)	30 - 32	32 - 35
Niagara Falls (6)	22 - 25	25 - 30
Langsdorf		
"Alligator Borders" (165)		
Blacks	30 - 35	35 - 40
Views	25 - 30	30 - 32
"Shell Borders"	10 - 12	12 - 18
"State Girls" (31)	10 - 12	12 - 14
National Flag Series		
KVIB Woman in Flag Dress (18)	8 - 9	9 - 10
P.C.K.		
Butterfly Views	10 - 12	12 - 15
Platinachrome		
"State Girls"	8 - 10	10 - 12
Charles Rose, 1908		
Rose Song Cards (24)	5 - 6	6 - 8
Raphael Tuck		
"State Belles" Ser. 2669 (45)	10 - 12	12 - 14

"Portraits of the Presidents" Ser. 2328 (25) 8 - 10		10 - 12
"Homes of U.S. Presidents"		
Oilette Ser. 2900 (25)	6 - 7	7 - 8
"State Capitols & Seals"		
Oilette Ser. 2454 (45)	5 - 6	6 - 7
Wildwood Installment Sets	10 - 15	15 - 18

ANIMALS

CANTLE, J.M. (British)	6 - 7	7 - 8
COBBS, B. (British)		
R. Tuck Ser. 9539 "Bunnies"	5 - 6	6 - 7
DRUMMOND, N.		
R. Tuck		
Ser. 3297 "Faithful Friends"	7 - 8	8 - 12
See Dogs, Horses.		
ELLAM		
R. Tuck Ser. 9684		
"Dressed Elephants"	15 - 18	18 - 22
GEAR, MABEL (U.S.A.)	5 - 8	8 - 10
GREEN, ROLAND (British)	5 - 6	6 - 7
HORINA, H.		
Ullman Mfg. Co.		
Jimmy Pig Series 91		
1967 "This little pig went to market"	10 - 12	12 - 15
1968 "This little pig went in bathing"	10 - 12	12 - 15
1969 "This little pig stayed home"	10 - 12	12 - 15
1970 "This little pig went to school"	10 - 12	12 - 15
1971 "This little pig went to a party"	10 - 12	12 - 15
1972 "This little pig went to war"	12 - 14	14 - 16
1973 "This little pig went fishing"	10 - 12	12 - 15
1974 "This little pig worked in garden"	10 - 12	12 - 15
1975 "This little pig went sailing"	10 - 12	12 - 15
1976 "This little pig was a drummer boy"	10 - 12	12 - 15
JAMES, FRANK (British)	4 - 5	5 - 6
KEENE, MINNIE (British)	4 - 5	5 - 6
KENNEDY, A.E. (British) Comics	5 - 8	8 - 10
LANDSCER, SIR EDWIN (British)	5 - 8	10 - 15
LESTER, A. (British)	4 - 5	5 - 6
MAGUIRE, HELENA (British)	5 - 6	6 - 7
R. Tuck "Animal Studies"		
Series 6713, 6714 (6)	7 - 8	8 - 10
MULLER, A. (German) See Horse, Dogs.		
PERLBERG, F.		

Wildwood Installment Set, "The Fish Story"

R. Tuck Art Series 991 (6)	6 - 7	7 - 8
POPE, DOROTHY (British)	4 - 5	5 - 6
RANKIN, GEORGE (British)	4 - 5	5 - 6
SCRIVENER, MAUDE (British)	6 - 7	7 - 9
SHEPHERD, G. E. (British) See Comics		
STEWART, J.A. (British)	4 - 5	5 - 6
THIELE, ARTH.		
German American Novelty Art Co.		
Series 789 Pigs, Large Image	20 - 25	25 - 30
T.S.N.		
Series 919 Dressed Ducks	15 - 20	20 - 25
Series 1165 Dressed Chicks	15 - 20	20 - 25
Series 1352 Dressed Chicks	12 - 15	15 - 18
Series 1452 Dressed Chicks	15 - 20	20 - 25
Series 1020 Dressed Bunnies	15 - 20	20 - 25
Series 1021 Dressed Bunnies	15 - 20	20 - 25
Series 781 Dressed Monkeys	20 - 22	22 - 26
VALTER, EUGENIE (British)	5 - 6	6 - 7
WARDLE, ARTHUR (British)	4 - 5	5 - 6
WATSON, C.M. WEST (British)		
See Dogs, Horses.		
WEALTHY, R.J. (British)	4 - 5	5 - 6
WEST, A.L. (British)	5 - 6	6 - 7

ADDITIONAL SETS/SERIES ARE LISTED UNDER TOPICALS AND THROUGHOUT THIS BOOK.

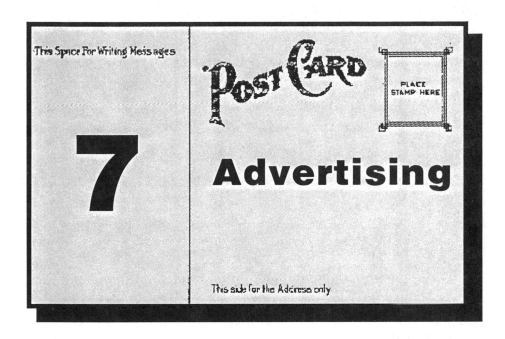

It all started in the early 1870's when salesmen began distributing tiny advertising trade cards that glorified their company's products in color. Each would leave several for the general store owner, merchants and other businessmen to give to their customers. This mode of advertising worked wonders and enhanced the sales of many products.

This means of advertising also stimulated the growth of advertising on letters that were sent through the mail. Businessmen of the time, however, felt that postage of three cents on the letters was a bit high for advertising.

The advent of the postcard as an advertising medium first came to fore in 1893 when cards were printed for vendors at the Columbian Exposition. Those visiting the Expo purchased these cards and sent them to their friends back home to prove their attendance. Many of these advertised products of the exhibitors.

This first trial was extremely successful and prompted owners of businesses throughout the U.S. to jump on the bandwagon. The reduced postage rates for postcards made the difference. Millions upon millions of advertising postcards, both color and black and white, were printed and mailed during the first year alone. Advertisers either mailed the cards themselves or gave them away to customers to use for their own personal use.

Competitiveness in all modes of product manufacturing and services prompted advertisers and merchants to publish beautiful sets and series by the artists of the day. Some of these companies are still in business; this, alone, makes them more collectible. The beauty and elusiveness of many of these cards have played a big role in making advertising postcards one of the favorites in the hobby.

ADVERTISING POSTCARDS

Absorbine Pain Killer	$ 6 - 8	$ 8 - 10
Albert Hosiery Co. (12)	6 - 8	8 - 10
Alexander, M.H. Co., Molasses	5 - 6	6 - 8
Allentown Adpostals (7)	35 - 40	40 - 45
American Enamel Co., 1906	5 - 6	6 - 7
American Journal Examiner		
Comics - by many Artists	5 - 6	6 - 12
American Fence Co.	4 - 5	5 - 6
American Lady Corsets	6 - 7	7 - 8
American Motor Co. (B&W)		
Motor Cycle Ad W/Miles per gal.	22 - 25	25 - 30
American Thermos Bottles (10)	4 - 5	5 - 6

American Motor Co.
Motorcycle

Angelus Player Pianos	8 - 10	10 - 12
Anheuser-Busch Brewing Co.(Western)	6 - 8	8 - 10
Anheuser-Busch Brewery Scenes	6 - 8	8 - 10
Anheuser-Busch Beer Wagon/Horses	8 - 10	10 - 12
Argand Stoves	5 - 6	6 - 8
Armour & Co. American Girl Series (12)		
German Publisher, (B & W)		
The Karl Anderson Girl	10 - 12	12 - 15
The Walter A. Clark Girl	10 - 12	12 - 15
The John C. Clay Girl	10 - 12	12 - 15
The Howard C. Christy Girl	15 - 20	20 - 25
The Harrison Fisher Girl	40 - 45	45 - 50
The C. Allen Gilbert Girl	15 - 20	20 - 25
The Henry Hutt Girl	15 - 20	20 - 25
The Hamilton King Girl	15 - 20	20 - 25
The F. S. Manning Girl	10 - 12	12 - 15
The Thomas M. Pierce Girl	10 - 12	12 - 15
The W. T. Smedley Girl	10 - 12	12 - 15
The G. G. Wiederseim Girl	30 - 35	35 - 40
Armour Star - "The Ham What Am"	6 - 7	7 - 8
Arbuckle Coffee	5 - 6	7 - 8
Do-Wa-Jack Paintings, S/Souler	12 - 15	15 - 18
5 A Horse Blankets	12 - 15	15 - 18

   "Athol"   "Bouncer"
   "Briar"   "Buster"
   "Essex"   "Fashion"
   "Myrtle"   "Paris Faun"
   "Stratton"   "Plush Robe" 1300
   "Plush Robe" 1652
   "Plush Robe" 1853
   Promotional Cards

"Great For Wear"	15 - 18	18 - 22
"They Make Philadelphia Famous"	15 - 18	18 - 22
Bakers Chocolate	6 - 7	7 - 8
Bear Brand Hosiery	6 - 8	8 - 9
Bell Telephone (12)		
R1 "Announces Unexpected Guests"	12 - 15	15 - 18
R2 "The Convenience of Marketing"	12 - 15	15 - 18
R3 "Keeps the Traveler in Touch"	12 - 15	15 - 18
R4 "Into the Heart of Shopping District"	12 - 15	15 - 18
R5 "When Servants Fail You"	12 - 15	15 - 18
R6 "The Social Call"	12 - 15	15 - 18
R7 "A Doctor Quick"	12 - 15	15 - 18
R8 "Guards the Home"	15 - 18	18 - 22

Campbell Soups, 10 ¢ a can
Grace Wiederseim

The DeLaval
Cream Separator

R9 "In Household Emergencies"	15 - 18	18 - 22
R10 "Relieves Anxieties"	12 - 15	15 - 18
R11 "Gives Instant Alarms"	15 - 18	18 - 22
R12 "When the Elements are Against You"	12 - 15	15 - 18
Ben-Hur Book	4 - 5	5 - 6
Ben-Hur Flour	6 - 7	7 - 8
Ben-Hur (Sears-Roebuck)	4 - 5	5 - 6
Bensdorp's Royal Dutch Cocoa (Dutch Life)	4 - 5	5 - 6
Costumed Children Series	10 - 12	12 - 15
Benjamin Suits	4 - 5	5 - 6
Berry Brothers Varnishes (18)	7 - 8	8 - 10
Bester Dairy Appliances	5 - 6	6 - 8
Bismark Beer	8 - 10	10 - 12
Blatchford Calf Meal Co.	4 - 5	5 - 6
Borden's (Elsie Says)	5 - 6	6 - 7
Boston Rubber Shoe Co. (10)	3 - 4	4 - 5
Boy's Newspaper	3 - 4	4 - 5
Brockton Shoe Industry	5 - 6	6 - 7
Brodrick Buggies	8 - 10	10 - 12
Brown's Bronchial Trochs	3 - 4	4 - 5
Brown Shoes		

Buster Brown, S\Outcault (12)	10 - 12	12 - 15
Buchan's Soap (6)		
White Bears and Children	10 - 12	12 - 15
Buckbee's Seeds (6)	2 - 3	3 - 4
Buchan's Soaps (6) W/White Bears	10 - 12	12 - 14
Budweiser Anheuser-Busch Beer Wagon (2)	10 - 12	12 - 15
Budweiser Barley Malt Syrup	12 - 15	15 - 18
Budweiser Beer (early)	12 - 15	15 - 18
Budweiser Yeast	8 - 10	10 - 12
Buffalo Bill's Wild West (6)	15 - 18	18 - 22
Bulte's Best Flour (6) Kids	6 - 8	8 - 10
1. "Bulte's Best"		
2 "Homeward Bound ..."		
3 "Into the Oven ..."		
4 "Of All the Flour ..."		
5 "Out Piping Hot ..."		
6 "Patty Cake"		
Bull Durham, S/Outcault (30 Countries)	22 - 25	25 - 30
Burke's Medicine	5 - 6	6 - 8
Burke's Whiskey	6 - 8	8 - 10
Busch Extra Dry Ginger Ale	20 - 25	25 - 30
Calumet Powder	4 - 5	5 - 6
Calumet Baking Powder, S/Outcault	10 - 12	12 - 15
Campbell Soup, (10 Cents a can)		
Uns. G. Wiederseim, large image (4)	80 - 90	90 - 100
Other Wiederseim, w/jingles (12)	50 - 55	55 - 60
Others w/jingles	40 - 45	45 - 50
Carnation Milk (A.Y.P. Expo)	8 - 10	10 - 12
Carswell Horse Shoe Nails	5 - 6	6 - 8
Canadian Club Whiskey	8 - 10	10 - 12
Candee Rubber Co. (Comics)	5 - 6	6 - 8
Case Steam Engines	8 - 10	10 - 12
Case Threshing Machines	8 - 10	10 - 12
Cauchois' Fulton Mills Coffee	5 - 6	6 - 8
Cherry Smash (On Lawn at Mt. Vernon)	70 - 75	75 - 85
Chesterfield Cigarettes		
Service Men, Uns./Leyendecker	25 - 30	30 - 35
Chocolate Lombart, Air Plane Series	8 - 10	10 - 12
Cleveland Six Automobile	15 - 18	18 - 22
Coca Cola (Girl Driving)	500 - 600	600 - 700
Coca Cola (Girl's Head) S/H. King	300 - 325	325 - 350
Cole Mercantile Co.	4 - 5	5 - 6
Continental Rubber Tires (Bike)	15 - 20	20 - 25
Continental Rubber Tires (Tennis)	20 - 25	25 - 30

DuPont Powders
DuPont Dog, "Joe Cummings"

Community Silver	3 - 4	4 - 5
Continental Pneumatic Tires	15 - 18	18 - 25
Corbin Coaster Brakes (Bicycles)	12 - 15	15 - 18
Cook Beer	5 - 6	6 - 7
Cracker Jack Bears (1 - 16)	18 - 20	20 - 25
Cracker Jack Bears (17 - 32)	25 - 30	30 - 35
Creamlac, Bicycle Cleaner (1898)	40 - 45	45 - 50
Crescent Flour	4 - 5	5 - 6
Crocker & Best Flour	4 - 5	5 - 6
Crown Millinery Co., 1910	4 - 5	5 - 6
Crown Flour	5 - 6	6 - 8
Curtis Publishing Co.	4 - 5	5 - 6
Daniel Webster Cigars	8 - 10	10 - 12
Daniel Webster Flour	4 - 5	5 - 6
Dannemiller's Royal Coffee	4 - 5	5 - 6
Derby's Croup Mix (w/Children)	5 - 6	6 - 7
Deward's Whiskey	12 - 15	15 - 18
De Laval Cream Separator	6 - 7	7 - 8
Diamont Rubber Co., Akron	4 - 5	5 - 7
Disinfectine Soap (Whole Dam Family)	6 - 8	8 - 10
Domino Sugar	6 - 8	8 - 10
Do-Wah-Jack, w/Indians - Months of Year Ser.	12 - 15	15 - 18
Dutch Boy Paints	7 - 8	9 - 12
Dupont Bird & Wild Game (12) "Blue Wing Teal"	25 - 30	30 - 35

"Canada Goose"		
"Canvas Back"		
"Gray Squirrel"		
"Jack Rabbit"		
"Jack Snipe"		
"Mallards"		
"Prairie Chicken"		
"Quail"		
"Ruffled Grouse"		
"Wild Turkey"		
"Woodcock"		
Wyeth Painting Card	30 - 35	35 - 40
Dupont Dogs (13)	50 - 60	60 - 70
"Joe Cummings"		
"Allmabagh"		
"Count Gladstone IV"		
"Count Whitestone"		
"Geneva"		
"Lady's Count Gladstone"		
"Manitoba Rap"		
"Mohawk II"		
"Monora"		
"Pioneer"		
"Prince - Whitestone"		
"Sioux"		
"Tony's Gale"		
Eastman Cameras	10 - 12	12 - 15
Eclipse Coaster Brakes (Bicycles)	12 - 15	15 - 18
Edison Phonograph (Famous Singers)	10 - 12	12 - 15
Egg Climax Incubator	4 - 5	5 - 6
Egg-O-See Cereals	6 - 7	7 - 8
Eldredge Rotary Sewing Machines	6 - 8	8 - 10
Elgin Watch Co.	12 - 15	15 - 18
Emerson Plows	6 - 7	7 - 8
EMF Auto (Glidden Tour)	12 - 15	15 - 18
Eskay's Foods	4 - 5	5 - 7
Excelsior Pneumatic Tires	15 - 20	20 - 25
Excelsior Stove & Mfg. Co.	5 - 6	6 - 7
F. A. Whitney Carriage Co.	5 - 6	6 - 7
Falstaff Beer	8 - 10	10 - 12
Faun Butters	4 - 5	5 - 6
Federal Cord Tires (3 1/2" x 6")	7 - 8	8 - 10
Firestone Tires	10 - 12	12 - 15
Fisk Tires	8 - 10	10 - 12

Fisk Red Top Tires	12 - 15	15 - 18
Fisk Removable Rims	8 - 10	10 - 12
Fitz Overalls	5 - 6	6 - 8
Fleischmann Co. Yeast	3 - 4	4 - 5
Flexible Flyer Sleds	5 - 7	7 - 8
Flood & Conklin & Co., Varnish		
P. Boileau Ladies Calendars	75 - 85	85 - 95
Formosa Oolong Tea	4 - 5	5 - 6
Force Food Co.	4 - 5	5 - 7
Foss Orange Extract	8 - 10	10 - 12
Foss Pure Extract	6 - 8	8 - 10
Fowler's Cherry Smash		
W/George Washington	200 - 250	250 - 275
Fox Head Lager Beer	5 - 8	8 - 10
Fralinger's Original Salt Water Taffy		
Beach Series	4 - 5	5 - 6
Nursery Rhymes (24), S/Burd	20 - 22	22 - 25
Others, S/Burd	10 - 12	12 - 15
Fralingers Salt Water Taffey - others	5 - 7	7 - 9
Franklin Davis Nursery Co.	2 - 3	3 - 4
Free Sewing Machine Co.	7 - 8	8 - 10
Frog in the Throat Lozenge Co.		
(PMC, 12, oversized)		
1 "A Social Success"	20 - 25	25 - 30
2 "A Universal Favorite"	20 - 25	25 - 30
3 "Don't Be Without It"	20 - 25	25 - 30
4 "Favorite at all Times"	20 - 25	25 - 30
5 "Fore Everybody"	25 - 30	30 - 35
6 "For Singers"	20 - 25	25 - 30
7 "Innocent and Instantaneous"	20 - 25	25 - 30
8 "My Old Friend Dr. Frog"	20 - 25	25 - 30
9 "Needs No Introduction"	20 - 25	25 - 30
10 "Nothing Better"	20 - 25	25 - 30
11 "Pleasant to Take"	20 - 25	25 - 30
12 "Popular Everywhere"	20 - 25	25 - 30
Cartoons (10) 3" x 5"	15 - 18	18 - 22
Fry's Chocolates, S/Tom Browne	10 - 12	12 - 15
Fry's Cocoa	5 - 6	6 - 7
Fuller Brush Co.	3 - 4	4 - 5
Fuller Floor Wax	4 - 5	5 - 6
Gales Chocolates (4" x 6")	4 - 6	6 - 8
German-American Coffee	10 - 12	12 - 15
Gilles Coffee	3 - 4	4 - 5
Gillette Safety Razor Co. (Child Shaving)	10 - 12	12 - 15

Elgin Watch Co.

Köhler German Sewing Machine

Gladwell's Lawn Mowers	10 - 12	12 - 15
Glidden Tour Autos	10 - 15	15 - 20
Globe-Wernicke Bookcases	4 - 6	6 - 7
Gold Dust Twins Wash Powders	20 - 25	25 - 30
Billboard Signs	8 - 10	10 - 15
Gold Label Beer	6 - 8	8 - 10
Golden Tree Syrup	3 - 4	4 - 5
Gold Medal Flour	3 - 4	4 - 5
Good Luck Baking Powder (Jamestown Expo)	10 - 12	12 - 15
Goodrich Silvertown Tires	8 - 10	10 - 12
Gorham Silver Polish (1903)	8 - 10	10 - 12
Great Northern Railway	5 - 7	7 - 8
Greenfield's Chocolate Sponge	5 - 7	7 - 8
Grollman Hats, 1918	3 - 4	4 - 5
Hackett Carbart & Co. Clothing	3 - 4	4 - 5
Happy Day Washers	5 - 7	7 - 8
Happy Thought Chewing Tobacco (12)	6 - 8	8 - 10
Hamm Brewing Co.	8 - 10	10 - 12
Hart Hats, S/Hoffman	4 - 5	5 - 6
Harley Davidson Motorcycles (6) - Govt. Postals	15 - 18	18 - 22
Hart Schaffner & Marx		

S\Ed. Penfield	12 - 15	15 - 18
Hathaway's Bread	3 - 4	4 - 5
Havana Club Rum	7 - 8	8 - 10
Heather Bloom Petticoats (E. Barrymore)	6 - 8	8 - 10
Heinz Foods, 57 Varieties (w/Product on Front)	12 - 15	15 - 18
Heinz Foods - others	3 - 4	4 - 5
Hendel Motorcycles	8 - 10	10 - 12
Herman Reel Co. (Indians)	6 - 7	7 - 10
Hershey's Cocoa & Chocolates	2 - 3	3 - 4
High Life Beer	8 - 10	10 - 12
Hinds Honey and Almond Cream	6 - 8	8 - 9
Hiram Walker & Sons Liquors	8 - 10	10 - 12
Holsum Bread (Cartoons)	8 - 10	10 - 12
Hires Root Bear	5 - 8	8 - 10
Hoods Sarsaparilla	6 - 8	8 - 10
Humpty-Dumpty Stockings (N. Rhymes)	5 - 6	6 - 8
Humphrey's Witch Hazel Oil	5 - 6	6 - 8
Hupmobile, 1911	20 - 25	25 - 28
Huyler's Candy (w/Children)	8 - 10	10 - 12
S/Von Hartman	10 - 12	12 - 14
I. X. L. Tamales	3 - 4	4 - 5
Imperial Diamond Needles	3 - 4	4 - 5
Independent Wall Paper Co.	3 - 4	4 - 5
India & Ceylon Tea	7 - 8	8 - 10
India Tea Growers	7 - 8	8 - 10
International Harvester, 1909 (12)	5 - 6	6 - 7
International Harvester, 1910 (12)	5 - 6	6 - 7
Iowa Seed Co.	2 - 3	3 - 4
Jack Sprat Oleomargarine	6 - 8	8 - 9
Japan Tea	4 - 5	5 - 6
Joplin Overalls (Girl)	5 - 6	6 - 8
Kalodont Toothpaste & Mouthwash (German)	15 - 18	18 - 25
Kelloggs Corn Flakes (Allentown Adpostal)	35 - 40	40 - 45
Kelloggs Corn Flakes, others	5 - 6	6 - 7
Kinsey Pure Rye Whiskey	5 - 6	6 - 8
Klumbacher Beer (German Beer)	15 - 18	18 - 25
Kodak Cameras	15 - 18	18 - 20
Kohler Sewing Machine (German)	20 - 22	22 - 26
Kohn Brothers Fine Clothing	3 - 4	4 - 5
Koch, W.J. Seed Co. (Dutch Kids)	3 - 4	4 - 5
Korn Kinks, H.O. Company	10 - 12	12 - 15

The Jocular Jinks of Kornelia Kinks
1   "Said Momma to Me ..."
2   "Man, Whar's Your Politeness"

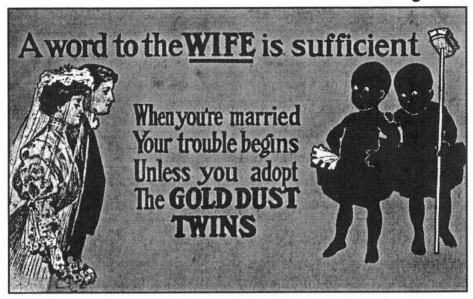

Gold Dust Twins Soap Powders

3 "Gran'pa done say dat ..."		
4 "I'se a going to be ..."		
5 "It ain't a bit o'use ..."		
6 "Susie done `through' ..."		
The Korn Kink Advertising cards (2)	15 - 18	18 - 22
Korvin Ice Cream, Jersey Shore Creamery	6 - 8	8 - 9
Kulmbacher Export Beer, Gruss Aus	20 - 25	25 - 30
Kuppenheimer Suits, Uns./Leyendecker	10 - 12	12 - 15
Laco Lamps (Children/Bulbs)	8 - 10	10 - 12
Lash Bitters (Laxative) Drunks	10 - 12	12 - 15
Lehr Pianos	3 - 4	4 - 5
Lemp Beer	12 - 15	15 - 20
Leonard's Bulk Seed	2 - 3	3 - 4
Lindholm Piano Co.	4 - 5	5 - 6
Lindsay Gas Light Mantles	4 - 5	5 - 6
Lipton Tea (6)	5 - 6	6 - 7
Listerated Pepsin Gum (10), Bears	8 - 10	10 - 12
Lowney's Chocolates (Indians)	8 - 10	10 - 12
Girl Golfers, S/Archie Gunn	8 - 10	10 - 12
Magic Curlers	3 - 4	4 - 5
Majestic Stove Ranges	5 - 6	6 - 7
Malt Breakfast Food	4 - 5	5 - 6
Malted Cereal Co.	4 - 5	5 - 6
Masons Automobile	15 - 18	18 - 22
Mauser's Best Flour	8 - 10	10 - 12
Maxwell Exclusive Line Wall Paper	3 - 4	4 - 5

Klumbacher German Beer

McCallum, D. & J. "Perfection" Scotch Whiskey	8 - 10	10 - 12
McPhail Pianos (Boston Views)	2 - 3	3 - 4
Mecca Cigarettes	12 - 15	15 - 18
Men-tho-la-tum Salve	6 - 7	7 - 9
Metz Motorcycles	15 - 18	18 - 22
Michelin Tires	15 - 18	18 - 22
Michelin Tires, s/Vincent	8 - 10	10 - 12
Middlebrook Razors	5 - 6	6 - 8
Miller High Life Beer - Kids in Auto	15 - 20	20 - 25
Mistletoe Margarine	12 - 15	15 - 18
Mogul Egyptian Cigarettes (La. Purch. Expo)	7 - 8	8 - 10
Monarch Typewriters	8 - 10	10 - 12
Moxie	30 - 35	35 - 40
20 Mule Team Borax	7 - 8	8 - 9
Mulford, H. K., Vaccine	5 - 6	6 - 7
Murad Cigarettes (Views)	4 - 5	5 - 6
National Girls	4 - 5	5 - 6
National Biscuit Co.	4 - 5	5 - 6
National Cash Register	4 - 5	5 - 6
National Light Oil	5 - 6	6 - 8
National Lead Paint (Dutch Boy)	10 - 12	12 - 14
Others	4 - 5	5 - 6
National Phonograph Co.	5 - 6	6 - 8
National Recording Safe Co.	4 - 5	5 - 6

Nestle's Baby Food	6 - 7	7 - 8
Nestle's Chocolate	6 - 7	7 - 8
New Departure Brakes (Jack & Jill)	12 - 15	15 - 18
New Idea Manure Spreader	12 - 15	15 - 18
New Home Sewing Machine	6 - 8	8 - 10
Northwestern Hide & Fur Co.	8 - 10	10 - 12
Nu-Life Cereal	5 - 6	6 - 7
Nuvida Springs, California (Indian Girl)	7 - 8	8 - 10
Nylo Chocolates	5 - 6	6 - 7
Ocherade Drink	5 - 6	6 - 7
Oil Pull Tractors	8 - 10	10 - 12
Old Style Lager	6 - 8	8 - 10
Oliver Farm Machinery	5 - 6	6 - 7
Old Prentice Whiskey	6 - 8	8 - 9
Overland 83B Touring Car	12 - 15	15 - 18
Pabst Breweries (Views)	6 - 7	7 - 8
Pacific Mail Steamship Co.	5 - 6	6 - 8
Palmolive Soap (Govt. Postal)	5 - 6	6 - 8
Parisian Belle Perfume	7 - 8	8 - 10

Triumphator Bürger-Bräu
German Beer

Mauser's Best Flour

Overland Model 83 B Touring Car

Parker Shot Guns	10 - 12	12 - 15
Pears Soap	6 - 7	7 - 8
Peter's Weatherbird Shoes (Months of Year)	8 - 10	10 - 12
Seasons	8 - 10	10 - 12
Halloween	12 - 15	15 - 18
Philadelphia Lawn Mowers	8 - 10	10 - 12
Pillsbury Flour	4 - 5	5 - 6
Pinkham, Lydia E., Medicine Co.	4 - 5	5 - 6
Piso's Cure for Colds	4 - 5	5 - 6
Polarine Oil	6 - 8	8 - 9
Post Toasties Cereal	7 - 8	8 - 9
Post Toasties Corn Flakes	8 - 10	10 - 12
Postum Cereal	3 - 4	4 - 5
Powell's N.Y. Chocolates	3 - 4	4 - 5
Premier Bicycles	20 - 25	25 - 30
Prisco Lantern	6 - 7	7 - 8
Private Estate Coffee	6 - 7	7 - 9
Purina Chick Chow	5 - 6	6 - 8
Puritan Blouses and Shirts	3 - 4	4 - 5
Quaker Oats, w/B&W foreign views	8 - 10	10 - 12
Quick Meal Gas Stoves	8 - 10	10 - 12
RCA, Dog & Mule Calendars	4 - 5	5 - 6
Rat Bis-Kit (Dog/Cat)	5 - 6	6 - 8
Red Bird Coffee	6 - 8	8 - 9
Red Horse Tobacco	5 - 6	6 - 7

Red Pig Knives (Posters)	15 - 18	18 - 22
Red Star Lines, s/Cassiers	8 - 10	10 - 15
Regal Shoe Co. (La. Purchase Expo)	8 - 10	10 - 12
Remington Arms	15 - 18	18 - 22
Remy Magnettos, 1910	4 - 5	5 - 6
Richardson Skates	6 - 8	8 - 10
Ringling Bros. Animals	4 - 5	5 - 6
Ringling Bros. Circus Ads	8 - 10	10 - 12
Robeson Cutlery		
"Red Pig" Knives	20 - 25	25 - 30
Rockford Watches Calendars, s/Outcault	10 - 12	12 - 15
Round Up Cigars	5 - 6	6 - 8
Rumford Baking Powder	5 - 6	6 - 8
Rumley Tractors	6 - 8	8 - 10
Samoset Chocolates (8) Indians		
S/Elwell	10 - 12	12 - 15
Sandeman Scotch Whiskey	9 - 10	10 - 12
Savannah Line, Coast Steamers	7 - 8	8 - 10
Sawyer Crystal Blue Laundry Soap	5 - 6	6 - 8
Schlitz Beer	8 - 10	10 - 12
Schraffts Chocolate	5 - 6	6 - 8
Schulze's Butter-Nut Bread	6 - 8	8 - 10
Scull, William S. Co., Coffee	6 - 8	8 - 10

Continental Tennis Balls, S/Fritz Schon, 1905

Teutonic Pneumatic Bicycles
with Golliwog

Selz Liberty Bell Shoes		5 - 6	6 - 8
Sen Sen Gum		10 - 12	12- 15
Sharples Cream Separator			
1	Boy and Girl	12 - 15	15 - 18
2	Cow and Ladies	12 - 15	15 - 18
3	Mother and Child	12 - 15	15 - 18
4	Farm Pleasures	12 - 15	15 - 18
5	Helping Gramma	12 - 15	15 - 18
6	Teddy	15 - 18	18 - 22
7	Modern Way	12 - 15	15 - 18
8	Dairyman's Choice	12 - 15	15 - 18
Shredded Wheat Cereal		6 - 8	8 - 10
Simple Simon Oleo		6 - 7	7 - 8
Simplex Cream Separators		5 - 6	6 - 8
Simplex Typewriters		6 - 8	8 - 10
Singer Sewing Machines		6 - 8	8 - 10
Sleepy Eye Milling Co. (9) Indians		50 - 60	60 - 70

"A Mark of Quality"
"Chief Sleepy Eye Welcomes Whites"
"Indian Artist"
"Indian Canoeing"
"Indian Mode of Conveyance"
"Pipe of Peace"
"Sleepy Eye Mills"
"Sleepy Eye Monument"

"Sleepy Eye, The Meritorious Flour"		
Snow Drift Cotton Oil Co.	5 - 6	6 - 8
Snow Drift Hogless Lard (Bunny & Pail or Lard)	15 - 18	18 - 22
Socony Gasoline	5 - 7	7 - 9
Sonora Phonographs	8 - 10	10 - 12
Solis Cigar Co. (Columbian Expo)	12 - 15	15 - 20
South Bend Lathes	5 - 6	6 - 8
Southern Cotton Oil Co. (Snowdrift)	5 - 6	6 - 8
Spillers Victorian Dog Food	8 - 10	10 - 12
Stanley Belting Corp. (B&W)	4 - 5	5 - 6
Sterling Ranges	5 - 6	6 - 8
Stiletto Lawn Mowers	6 - 8	8 - 10
Stukenbrok's Teutonia-Pneumatic Bicycles		
W/Golliwog, Gruss aus w/und/back	35 - 40	45 - 50
Suchard Cacao, Color Product, W/B&W views	10 - 12	12 - 15
Summit Shirts	5 - 6	6 - 8
Sunny Jim Whiskey	6 - 7	7 - 9
Swift & Co., 6-Horse Team	6 - 8	8 - 10
Swift's Premium Butterine	5 - 6	6 - 8
Swift's Premium Oleomargarine		
"Children of World"	6 - 8	8 - 10
Swift's Pride, s/Grace Wiederseim	25 - 30	35 - 40
Swift's Pride Soap (6) Shadows on Wall	6 - 8	8 - 10
Taylor's Headache Cologne	6 - 8	8 - 10
Templin's "Idea" Seeds	4 - 6	6 - 8
Teutonia-Pneumatic Bicycles W/Golliwog	25 - 30	30 - 40
Texaco Motor Oils	6 - 8	8 - 10
Thomas Brau Beer	10 - 12	12 - 15
Toledo Metal Wheel Co.	7 - 8	8 - 10
Toledo Scales	5 - 6	6 - 8
Troy Detachable Collars	4 - 5	5 - 6
True Fruit Flavors	5 - 6	6 - 8
Uhlen Baby Carriages	6 - 8	8 - 10
Uncle John's Syrup (Poster)	20 - 25	25 - 30
Underwood Typewriters	5 - 6	6 - 8
Universal Regulators	4 - 5	5 - 6
Utopia Yarns (Dutch Children)	5 - 6	6 - 7
Valentine's Varnishes (Auto)	10 - 12	12 - 15
Velvetlawn Seeders	6 - 8	8 - 10
Verbeck & Lucas Stoves	5 - 6	6 - 8
Vick's Quality Seeds, Rochester	4 - 5	5 - 6
Voss Brothers Washing Machine	8 - 10	10 - 12
Wales-Goodyear Bear Brand Rubbers	5 - 8	8 - 10
Walker House, Toronto	5 - 6	6 - 8
Walk-Over Shoes, (24) Famous Men	6 - 8	8 - 10

Walk-Over Shoes, Pilgrim Series	4 - 5	5 - 6
Walk-Over Shoes, Dutch Children	4 - 5	5 - 6
Watkins, J. R., Medical	5 - 6	6 - 8
Weatherbird Shoes	5 - 6	6 - 8
Westinghouse Cooper Hewitt Mercury Rectifier	8 - 10	10 - 12
Westinghouse Electric Iron	6 - 7	7 - 8
Weyerheuser Lumber Co.	5 - 6	6 - 8
White Brothers Bread	6 - 7	7 - 8
White House Coffee & Tea	6 - 8	8 - 10
Whitney, F.A. Carriage Co.	8 - 10	10 - 12
Wilbur Chocolates, S/Henkels (6)	10 - 12	12 - 14
Willys Overland, Model 59T	22 - 25	25 - 30
Wilson & Co., Meat Packers	6 - 8	8 - 10
Winchester Arms & Ammo, Folding card, 1906	10 - 12	12 - 15
Witch Hazel Ointment	5 - 6	6 - 8
Woods Electrics (Auto)	15 - 18	18 - 22
Woodstock Typewriters	6 - 7	7 - 9
Woonsocket Rubber Co. (10)		
Footwear of Nations	8 - 10	10 - 12
Rubber Shoe Boat	12 - 15	15 - 18
Wyandotte Cleaner & Cleanser	5 - 6	6 - 8
Youth's Companion Magazine	4 - 5	5 - 6
Zang's Beer	8 - 10	10 - 12
Zenith Watches	5 - 8	8 - 10
Zeno Gum Co.	5 - 6	6 - 8

Although there are around 500 listings in our Advertising Postcards section, this by no means includes all that were issued. For a more comprehensive listing we suggest that you obtain a copy of Fred and Mary Megson's fine book, **American Advertising Postcards, Sets and Series, 1890-1920, Catalog and Price Guide.** It may be obtained from the Postcard Lovers, Martinsville, NJ.

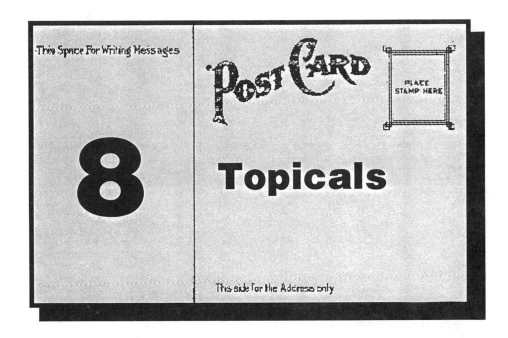

Topical postcards, as the name implies, are those of a particular place or subject and are any type not listed in a specific section of this publication. They are very special to the collecting fraternity, and make up a large part of every collection.

There were thousands of topics printed on postcards, and many are sure to appeal to any collector's fancy. As a general rule, collectors "specialize" in a particular subject or theme and try to obtain every card available, old or modern, until the collection is complete. Usually, because of their profound interest, they will also research the subject and become very knowledgeable about it and its history. This, in part, is one of the things that makes postcards so interesting, and that provides the momentum for the hobby to continue to grow and prosper.

Unless definite cards or sets are listed, values are for a generalized selection in each particular topic. There may be cards in each topic that will command higher, or even lower, prices.

TOPICALS

ACTORS, Pre-1930	$ 6 - 8	$ 8 - 10
1930-1945	4 - 5	5 - 8
Valentino	8 - 10	10 - 15

Catherine Klein
Alphabet Series 48, "F"

Real Photo, United Artists
Rudolph Valentino

ACTRESSES, Pre-1930	6 - 8	8 - 10
1930-1945	4 - 5	5 - 8
Greta Garbo	8 - 10	10 - 12
AESOP'S FABLES		
R. Tuck Propaganda		
"Aesop's Fables Up to Date" (6)	20 - 25	25 - 30
AIRPLANES, Military	5 - 6	6 - 8
AIRPLANES, Others	3 - 4	4 - 6
French Aviation Set - Plane & Pilot		
Glen Curtis	30 - 35	35 - 40
De La Grange	25 - 30	30 - 35
Henri Demanest	25 - 30	30 - 35
Hubert Latham	30 - 35	35 - 40
Orville Wright	30 - 35	35 - 40
Bleriot	25 - 30	30 - 35
Voisin	25 - 30	30 - 35
Roger Sommer	25 - 30	30 - 35
Santo Dumont	25 - 30	30 - 35
Robert E. Pelterie	25 - 30	30 - 35
Anonymous 39424 Sepia Series		
Glenn H. Curtis	20 - 25	25 - 28

Others	15 - 20	20 - 25
Early Pioneers, Named	15 - 20	20 - 25
R. Tuck		
Aviation Series 406 (6)	15 - 18	18 - 22
"Famous Aeroplanes" Ser. 9943 (6)	15 - 18	18 - 22
Series 3101 (6)	10 - 12	12 - 15
Series 3103 (6)	10 - 12	12 - 15
Series 3144 (6)	12 - 15	15 - 20
AIRPORTS	4 - 5	5 - 6
See Views.		
ALLIGATORS, CROCODILES	2 - 3	3 - 4
ALLIGATOR BORDER CARDS, 5500-5664		
Views	12 - 15	15 - 20
Blacks	20 - 25	25 - 30
ALPHABET		
Simple	2 - 3	3 - 4
W/Children, Ladies, Animals	4 - 5	5 - 6
Signed C. Klein, Flower Series 148	12 - 15	15 - 18
Letters U,V,W,X,Y,Z	20 - 22	22 - 25
Rotograph Co. Ser. B428	4 - 5	5 - 6
AMUSEMENT PARKS, Views	6 - 7	7 - 8
Rides, Shows	7 - 8	8 - 12
Real Photos, Views	10 - 12	12 - 15

Glenn H. Curtis, the American Aviator, and his Aeroplane in Flight.

Glenn H. Curtis, American Aviator

Real Photos, Rides, Shows	20 - 25	25 - 30
Real Photos, Merry-Go-Rounds	35 - 40	40 - 50
ANGELS	2 - 4	4 - 10
Signed by Mailick	10 - 12	12 - 15
ANIMALS, Domestic See Artist-Signed.	1 - 2	2 - 3
P.F.B. "Cake Walk" Ser. 3903 (6)	15 - 18	18 - 22
R. Tuck Ser. 6989 "Russian Greyhounds"	10 - 12	12 - 18
ANIMALS, Wild	2 - 3	3 - 6
Official New York Zoo	2 - 3	3 - 4
ANIMALS, Prehistoric	2 - 3	3 - 4
APPLIQUE (Add-Ons)		
Beads	1 - 2	2 - 3
Celluloid	2 - 3	3 - 4
Felt	2 - 3	3 - 4
Flowers	1 - 2	2 - 3
Glitter (Distracting on most cards)	1 - 2	2 - 3
Hair (On Beautiful Ladies)	15 - 18	18 - 25
Metal	3 - 4	4 - 5
Silk See Santas, Langsdorf Ladies, E. Christy.		
Others	4 - 5	5 - 8
ART MASTERPIECES		
Stengel	1 - 2	2 - 3
Nudes	6 - 8	8 - 10

Stengel & Co. 29358, "Abraham"

Battleship USS Tennessee, Real Photo by Hoffman

Sborgi	1 - 2	2 - 3
ASTROLOGY	3 - 4	4 - 6
ASYLUMS	3 - 5	5 - 7
AUTHORS	3 - 4	4 - 5
John Winsch	6 - 7	7 - 8
AUTO RACING, Early	10 - 15	15 - 25
AUTO SERVICE STATIONS See R. Photo, Views.		
BALLET DANCING	3 - 4	4 - 6
BALLOONS, Flying, Early	8 - 10	10 - 15
Real Photo	15 - 20	20 - 25
BANDS, Musical	5 - 6	6 - 10
Military	5 - 6	6 - 8
BANDSTANDS	3 - 4	4 - 6
BANKS See Views and Real Photos.		
BASEBALL PARKS, Major, 1900-1920	25 - 30	35 - 40
1920-1940	15 - 20	20 - 25
Linens - 1935-49	8 - 10	10 - 18
Minor - 1900-1920	10 - 12	12 - 15
1920-35	8 - 10	10 - 15
1935-49	5 - 6	6 - 8
BASEBALL PLAYERS, Major, 1900-1920	30 - 50	50 - 100
1920-1940	10 - 40	40 - 60
A.C. Dietsche, Detroit, 1907 (B&W)	35 - 40	40 - 45
Ty Cobb	150 - 160	160 - 175
Dormand	12 - 15	15 - 20

Embossed Coins of Denmark
M.H., Berlin

Hall of Fame Players	30 - 35	35 - 40
McCarthey	12 - 15	15 - 20
Hall of Fame Players	30 - 35	35 - 40
Rose Co.	40 - 50	50 - 100
H.M. Taylor (B&W)		
Detroit Tigers	70 - 80	80 - 90
Home Town Teams	8 - 10	10 - 12
Real Photo	15 - 18	18 - 25
Jules Bien Series 36 Comics	8 - 10	10 - 12
WILLIAMS, O.D. Baseball Comics		
"Boston Baseball Series" 103 (11)	8 - 10	10 - 12
Other Comics	6 - 8	10 - 20
BASKETBALL PLAYERS, Home Teams, Schools	8 - 10	10 - 12
Real Photo	12 - 15	15 - 18
BATHING BEAUTIES		
Illustrated P.C. Co. Ser. 80	7 - 8	8 - 10
Langsdorf & Co. (10)	6 - 7	7 - 9
Leighton & Co. (10)	6 - 7	7 - 8
J. Marks "Summer Girl" Ser. 155	6 - 7	7 - 8
P.F.B. Series 6271 (6)	7 - 8	8 - 10
Souvenir Postcard Co. Ser. 526 (6)	6 - 7	7 - 8
E.L. Theochrome Ser. 1035	5 - 6	6 - 7
W.M. Taggert Ser. 25	6 - 8	8 - 10
R. Tuck		

Ser. 116, 1363 (6)	8 - 9	9 - 10
Ser. 9414, E9466, 9494 (6)	8 - 9	9 - 10
Ullman Mfg. Co. "Seashore Girls" Ser. 90	7 - 8	8 - 9
Foreign Series 583 (6)	6 - 7	7 - 8
Foreign Series 1070 (6)	6 - 7	7 - 8
Others	4 - 6	6 - 8
BATTLESHIPS		
A.C. Bosselman	5 - 6	6 - 7
Albertype	7 - 8	8 - 10
Britton & Rey	6 - 7	7 - 8
Allen Fanjoy	5 - 6	6 - 7
Illustrated P.C. Co.	7 - 8	8 - 9
S. Langsdorf	7 - 8	8 - 9
Rotograph S/Muller	7 - 8	8 - 9
R. Tuck		
"U.S. Navy" Series 2323, 2324	6 - 7	7 - 8
BEACH SCENES	1 - 2	2 - 4
W/Bathers	3 - 4	4 - 6
Real Photo	6 - 8	8 - 12
BEARS	1 - 2	2 - 3
Teddy Bears, Artist-Signed	10 - 12	12 - 15
Teddy Bears W/Children, Artist-Signed	10 - 12	12 - 16
Real Photo, Large Image W/Children	20 - 25	25 - 35
Real Photo, Small Image W/Children	10 - 12	12 - 18
See Teddy Bear Section.		
BICYCLES	3 - 4	4 - 6
Real Photo	8 - 10	10 - 15
Advertising	10 - 15	15 - 20
BILLIARDS	4 - 6	6 - 8
Artist-Signed	8 - 10	10 - 12
BIRDS	2 - 3	3 - 4
Signed C. Klein	5 - 6	6 - 8
Audubon Society	1 - 2	2 - 3
BIRTH ANNOUNCEMENTS	4 - 5	5 - 6
BIRTHSTONES		
E. Nash Series 1	5 - 6	6 - 7
E.P.C. Co. Series 100, 200	2 - 3	3 - 4
BLACKS, U.S.A. (See Artist-Signed, Unsigned Blacks)	5 - 6	6 - 10
Foreign	4 - 5	5 - 6
BOATS, Large Image	2 - 3	3 - 4
Small	1 - 1.50	1 - 50 - 2
BOER WAR	8 - 10	10 - 15
BOOKS	1 - 1.50	1.50 - 2
BOWLING	3 - 4	4 - 6

BOXING, Early 1900-1920	15 - 20	20 - 40
Benham Co., 109		
Jim Jeffries	20 - 25	25 - 28
G. Henry Co.		
Jeffries-Johnston Match	18 - 22	22 - 26
Underwood RP 460		
Dempsey-Carpentier Fight	20 - 25	25 - 30
BOY SCOUTS		
Colortype Co., Chicago Sepia	12 - 15	15 - 18
Gartner & Bender, Chicago	12 - 15	15 - 18
Henninger Co., N.Y.		
Scouts Law (12)	12 - 15	15 - 20
Scouts Gum Co. S/H.S. Edwards (12)	15 - 18	18 - 22
R. Tuck Boy Scout Ser. 9950 (6)	70 - 75	75 - 85
Ser. 8745 S/Shepheard		
"Advice to Scouts" (6)	15 - 20	20 - 25
BREWERIES - Exteriors	6 - 8	8 - 12
Interiors	10 - 12	12 - 14
BROOKLYN EAGLE VIEWS	2 - 3	3 - 5
BULL FIGHTS	2 - 3	3 - 5
BUS DEPOTS	4 - 5	5 - 8
See Views and Real Photos.		
BUSES - 1900-1920	12 - 15	15 - 25
1920-1940	10 - 12	12 - 20
BUTTERFLIES	1 - 2	2 - 3
On Greetings	2 - 3	3 - 5
BUTTON FACES - BUTTON FAMILY		
George Jervis	18 - 20	20 - 25
CALCIUM LIGHTS		
J. Plant "Army-Navy Series"	3 - 4	4 - 5
CALENDARS, Pre-1904	8 - 10	10 - 12
1905-1910	4 - 6	6 - 8
1910-1915	3 - 5	5 - 7
1915-1940	2 - 3	3 - 4
CAMERAS		
Kodak Advertising	15 - 18	18 - 25
Artist-Signed	7 - 10	10 - 16
CANALS	1 - 2	2 - 3
Panama Canal Construction Views	5 - 7	7 - 10
CANOEING	1 - 2	2 - 3
CAPITOLS See Important Sets & Series		
State Capitals & Seals.		
CARNIVAL		
R. Tuck "Carnival" Series 117 (6)	12 - 15	15 - 18

Camera
Souvenir Postcard Co., "Peeping Tom"

Oilette Series 6435 (6)	12 - 15	15 - 18
Oilette "Mardi Gras" Ser. 2551 (6)	7 - 8	8 - 10
T. Gessner "Mardi Gras" Series	6 - 7	7 - 8
Real Carnivals		
Sideshows, Color	6 - 8	8 - 10
Sideshows, Real Photo	15 - 18	18 - 25
CAROUSELS Color	10 - 12	12 - 15
Real Photo	15 - 20	20 - 30
CARTS		
Goat, Pony	5 - 6	6 - 8
Horse, Oxen	4 - 5	5 - 7
See Real Photos		
CASTLES	1 - 2	2 - 3
CATHEDRALS	1 - 1.50	1.50 - 2
CATS See Artist-Signed Cats		
CATTLE	1 - 2	2 - 3
CAVES	1 - 2	2 - 3
CEMETERIES	1 - 2	2 - 3
CHESS/CHECKERS	5 - 7	7 - 12
CHICKENS	1 - 3	3 - 6
Dressed like people.	6 - 8	8 - 12
CHILDREN, Foreign	1 - 2	2 - 4
Playing	2 - 3	3 - 5
W/Dolls, Toys	7 - 8	8 - 15
W/Animals	6 - 7	7 - 10

See Real Photos		
CHINESE PEOPLE	2 - 3	3 - 5
CHRISTMAS TREES		
R. Tuck Series 529 (6)	7 - 8	8 - 10
CHURCHES See Views.		
CIGARETTES, CIGARS	4 - 5	5 - 8
CIRCUS		
Barnum & Bailey - 1900-1920	25 - 30	30 - 35
1920-1940	15 - 20	20 - 25
Other Circus	10 - 15	15 - 20
CIVIL WAR		
R. Tuck Series 2510		
"Heroes of the South"		
1. General Lee & Traveler	15 - 18	18 - 22
2. General Robert E. Lee	15 - 18	18 - 22
3. Lee in Confederate Uniform	18 - 20	20 - 25
4. Gen. Thomas J. "Stonewall" Jackson	18 - 20	20 - 25
5. Lee and Jackson	18 - 20	20 - 25
6. Prayer in "Stonewall" Jackson's Camp	15 - 18	18 - 22
Jamestown A&V Co, 1907		
Jamestown Expo Series 50-367		
Confederate Cards	15 - 20	20 - 25
CLOCKS	1 - 2	2 - 3
CLOWNS - Barnum & Bailey	15 - 20	20 - 25
Others	10 - 12	12 - 18
COAT-OF-ARMS	3 - 4	4 - 6
COIN CARDS, Emb.		
Walter Erhard	8 - 10	10 - 12
Flat Printed	7 - 9	9 - 12
H. Guggenheim	6 - 7	7 - 9
H.S.M.	8 - 9	9 - 10
COLISEUMS See Views.		
COLLEGES See Views.		
COMETS		
Halley's	10 - 12	12 - 16
COMPOSERS	2 - 3	3 - 5
CONFEDERATE STATES		
"Sheridan's Ride" (10)	8 - 10	10 - 12
CONVENTS	2 - 3	3 - 4
CORPSE, In Casket		
Real Photo	6 - 8	8 - 10
COSTUMES, Native	1 - 2	2 - 3
COURT HOUSES See Views.		
COVERED BRIDGES	5 - 6	6 - 8

COWBOYS	3 - 5	5 - 8
R. Tuck "Among the Cowboys" Ser. 2499	6 - 7	7 - 8
Real Photos	6 - 8	8 - 10
COWGIRLS	3 - 5	5 - 8
Real Photos	6 - 8	8 - 10
CRADLES	2 - 3	3 - 4
CROSSES	1 - 2	2 - 3
CUPIDS	2 - 3	3 - 5
DAIRIES See Views.		
DAMS	2 - 3	3 - 4
DANCING	3 - 5	5 - 6
Artist-Signed	6 - 8	8 - 12
DAYS OF WEEK	2 - 3	3 - 5
See Teddy Bears, Sunbonnet Girls		
DEATH	2 - 3	3 - 5
DEER	1 - 2	2 - 3
DENTAL	6 - 8	8 - 12
Artist-Signed	10 - 12	12 - 15
DEPARTMENT STORES	4 - 5	5 - 7
Interiors	5 - 6	6 - 8
Interiors See Real Photos.	8 - 10	10 - 12
DETROIT PUB. CO. VIEWS		
Early PMC Cards Better Views	15 - 20	20 - 25
Common	5 - 6	6 - 8
Others - Better Views	6 - 8	8 - 10
Common	1 - 2	2 - 3
DEVIL	4 - 5	5 - 8
DIABOLO		
Davidson Ser. 2627 S/Tom Browne	12 - 15	15 - 16
Langsdorf Ser. 711 S/Kinsella (6)	12 - 14	14 - 16
R. Tuck Ser. N49 S/G.E. Shepherd	12 - 14	14 - 15
LOUIS WAIN Ser. 9563, 9564 (6)	35 - 40	40 - 45
DICE	3 - 4	4 - 6
DIME STORES	2 - 3	3 - 5
DINERS See Views, R. Photos, Roadside America.		
DIONNE QUINTUPLETS	15 - 18	18 - 20
DIRIGIBLES, AIRSHIPS, ZEPPS	10 - 12	12 - 20
See Real Photos		
DISASTERS	6 - 8	8 - 12
See Real Photos		
DIVERS	2 - 3	3 - 5
DOG CARTS	6 - 8	8 - 12
Sleds	6 - 8	8 - 10
DOGS See Artist-Signed Dogs.	2 - 3	3 - 5

A.S.B. Ser. 245	6 - 7	7 - 8
A. & M. B. Ser. 54	6 - 7	7 - 8
B.B. London Ser. E32	6 - 7	7 - 8
H.S.M. Ser. 719	6 - 7	7 - 8
P.F.B. Ser. 8163 (6) Large Image	15 - 17	17 - 20
R. Tuck "Art" Ser. 855 (6)	10 - 12	12 - 15
"Connoisseur" Ser. 2546 (6)	10 - 12	12 - 15
DOLLS See Golliwogs, Real Photos, Children.		
Gartner & Bender		
Rag Doll Series	5 - 6	6 - 8
"A Wise Guy" (6)		
"Amybility" (6)		
"Antie Quate" (6)		
"Dolly Dimple" (6)		
"Epi Gram" (6)		
"Gee Whiz" (6)		
"Gee Willikens" (6)		
"Heeza Korker" (6)		
"Jiminy" (6)		
"Optomistic Miss" (6)		
"Phil Osopher" (6)		
DONKEYS, MULES, BURROS	1 - 2	2 - 3
DOVES	0.50 - 1	1 - 1.50
DREAMING	2 - 3	3 - 4
DRINKS Beer, Drunk Comics	2 - 3	3 - 4
DRUG STORES See Views and Real Photos.		
DRUNKS	2 - 3	3 - 4
DUCKS, GEESE	1 - 2	2 - 3
EARTHQUAKES	4 - 6	6 - 12
ELEPHANTS	4 - 5	5 - 6
Artist-Signed	8 - 9	9 - 12
Dressed like People	10 - 12	12 - 18
R. Tuck S/Ellam		
Series 9684	15 - 18	18 - 22
Series 9553 (6)	15 - 18	18 - 22
ELKS	2 - 3	3 - 4
Fraternal, Artist-Signed	6 - 7	7 - 10
EXAGGERATED		
Big Fish, Rabbits, Vegetables	3 - 5	5 - 8
Big Grasshoppers	5 - 6	6 - 9
Add $2-3 each to prices for Real Photos.		
FAB PATCHWORK SILKS		
W.N. Sharpe		
Kings & Queens	25 - 30	30 - 35

Scenes	20 - 25	25 - 28
FACTORIES, PLANTS See Views and Real Photos.		
FAIRY TALES See Fairy Tales.		
FAIRS, FESTIVALS	5 - 6	6 - 10
See Views.		
FAMOUS PEOPLE'S HOMES		
Movie Stars	2 - 3	3 - 5
FANS	2 - 3	3 - 4
FARMING	2 - 3	3 - 5
FARMING EQUIPMENT		
Horse Driven	5 - 6	6 - 8
Motor Driven	6 - 8	8 - 10
See Real Photos.		
FASHIONS	3 - 5	5 - 10
FAT PEOPLE, Real	5 - 6	6 - 8
Circus Side Shows See Real Photos.	7 - 8	8 - 10
COMICS	1 - 2	2 - 3
FENCING	3 - 4	4 - 6
FERRY BOATS See Real Photos.	6 - 7	7 - 10
FIRE ENGINES, Horse	8 - 9	9 - 12
Motor driven See Real Photos.	12 - 15	15 - 20
FIRE HOUSES See Real Photos.	8 - 10	10 - 12
W/Equipment	10 - 12	12 - 15
FIRES (Disasters)	5 - 6	6 - 8
Named See Real Photos.	6 - 8	8 - 15
FIREWORKS	4 - 5	5 - 6
FISH, FISHING	2 - 3	3 - 6
FLAGS, USA	4 - 5	5 - 6
Jules Bien Series 710	5 - 6	6 - 8
Ill. Post Card Co. Series 207	5 - 6	6 - 8
National Art Co. "Hands Across the Sea"	7 - 8	8 - 9
Real Photo	8 - 10	10 - 12
Foreign	2 - 3	3 - 4
FLOODS (Disasters)	5 - 6	6 - 8
Named See Real Photos.	8 - 10	10 - 12
FLOWER FACES	6 - 7	7 - 8
FOOTBALL Players	6 - 8	8 - 10
FORTS	2 - 3	3 - 4
FOREIGN VIEWS	0.50 - 1	1 - 1.50
FORTUNE TELLING	3 - 4	4 - 6
FRATERNAL		
Ullman Mfg. Co. Series 199	7 - 8	8 - 9
FREAKS, Animal	6 - 7	7 - 9
People	8 - 9	9 - 12

New York Fire Boat in Action
Illustrated Postcard Co. 96-56

FROGS See Dressed Animals.	1 - 2	2 - 3
FRUIT	1 - 1.50	1.50 - 2
FUNERAL HOMES See Views.		
GAMBLING	4 - 5	5 - 6
GEYSERS	1 - 2	2 - 3
GHOSTS See Fantasy.		
GIANTS	5 - 6	7 - 9
GIRL SCOUTS		
BALLINGER, E.		
Girl Scout Laws Ser. M572	10 - 12	12 - 15
GILLESPIE, JESSIE		
Silhouettes of Scout Activities (6)	12 - 14	14 - 18
EDITH B. PRICE		
The Four Seasons (4)	10 - 12	12 - 15
MARGARET EVANS PRICE		
Girl Scout Laws Series M-578	12 - 15	15 - 18
GOATS	1 - 2	2 - 3
Bergman Ser. 1052 Billy Goat Comics (6)	5 - 6	6 - 8
GOLF Players	3 - 4	4 - 5
Courses	3 - 4	4 - 5
Golf Comics	8 - 10	10 - 12
Artist-Signed Beautiful Ladies	15 - 18	18 - 25
EARL CHRISTY		
Knapp Co.		
"Always Winning"	15 - 18	18 - 22

"Goodbye Summer"	15 - 18	18 - 22
R&N		
367 "The Day's Work"	15 - 18	18 - 22
CORBELLA		
Series 316 (6)	15 - 18	18 - 22
GUTTANY		
E. Gross "A Tee Party"	12 - 15	15 - 18
NANNI Series 309 (6)	15 - 18	18 - 22
RELYA		
W.C. 9, 10	12 - 15	15 - 18
UNDERWOOD, C.		
M. Munk "Lost"	10 - 12	12 - 14
R. Tuck		
Ser. 697 "Golf Hints" (6)	12 - 15	15 - 18
Ser. 9499 "Humorous Golf" (6)	12 - 15	15 - 18
Ser. 3600 "Golf Humor" (6)	12 - 15	15 - 18
S/Thackeray Ser. 9304, 9305 (6)	15 - 18	18 - 22
Ser. 1627, 1628 (6)	15 - 18	18 - 22
Ladies/Men Artist-Signed	12 - 14	14 - 18

Mabel Lucie Atwell
Atwell Series

Court Barber 2023/5
"A Golf Champion"

Golliwogs, "Keep Off the Grass"
B.B. London 510

R. Tuck Ser. 9427 Blacks, "More Coons" (1)	20 - 22	22 - 26
Valentine & Co. S/C. Crombie		
"Etiquette," "Local Rule," etc. (6)	10 - 12	12 - 15
Advertising, product	12 - 15	15 - 25
GOOD LUCK SYMBOLS		
Horseshoes, Four-leaf Clover	1 - 2	2 - 3
Swastikas	4 - 5	5 - 6
GYMNASIUMS See Views.		
GYMNASTICS	3 - 4	4 - 5
GYPSIES	5 - 6	6 - 8
HANDBALL	3 - 4	4 - 6
HARBORS	2 - 3	3 - 4
W/Ships, Busy	4 - 5	5 - 7
HATS		
Ladies Big Hats	3 - 4	4 - 6
HERALDIC	4 - 5	5 - 10
R. Tuck		
"Boston"	8 - 10	10 - 12
"Philadelphia"	8 - 10	10 - 12
"Washington, D.C." PMC's	10 - 12	12 - 14
HITLER, Real Photo		
Postmarked	12 - 15	15 - 18
Unused	10 - 12	12 - 14
Color, Continental size, Common	15 - 18	18 - 25

Color, Continental size, Rarer issues	50 - 75	75 - 100
HOLD-TO-LIGHT, Die-Cut Issues		
Koehler See Special Sets and Series		
Other Publishers		
Santas	100 - 125	125 - 150
Uncle Sam Santa	800 - 900	900 - 1000
Year Dates - See Year Dates		
Children	20 - 25	25 - 30
Christmas Scenes	20 - 22	22 - 25
Easter, New Year	15 - 20	20 - 25
Statue of Liberty	25 - 30	30 - 35
Trains, Ships	30 - 35	35 - 40
Other Views, Bldgs., etc.	15 - 20	20 - 30
Comics	15 - 20	20 - 25
Foreign Gruss Aus City Views	20 - 25	25 - 30
Foreign War Issues (Belgian)	12 - 15	15 - 20
HOLD-TO-LIGHT, See-Through Issues		
Comics	10 - 12	12 - 18
1900 Year Date	20 - 25	25 - 30

Hold-to-Light Santa
German

Hold-to-Light Statue of Liberty

Fairy Tales	15 - 20	20 - 25
Others	12 - 15	15 - 20
HOROSCOPE		
Dietrich & Co.	5 - 6	6 - 8
Williamson-Haffner Ser. 985	6 - 7	7 - 8
Others	5 - 6	6 - 7
HORSE & BUGGIES, Large Image, Color	8 - 10	10 - 12
Small Image	5 - 6	6 - 7
See Real Photos.		
HORSES, Unsigned - Heads	5 - 6	6 - 8
Large Images	5 - 6	6 - 8
Small Images	2 - 3	3 - 4
See Artist-Signed Horses.		
Dan Patch		
Wright, Barnett, & Stilwell Co.	15 - 18	18 - 22
V.O. Hammond 155	15 - 18	18 - 22
T.P. & Co.	12 - 15	15 - 20
Real Photos	35 - 40	40 - 45
HOSPITALS See Views, Real Photos.		
HOTELS See Views, Real Photos.		
HOURS OF THE DAY		
Rose Co.	3 - 4	4 - 5
Warwick Co.	3 - 4	4 - 5
HOUSEBOATS	4 - 5	5 - 6
HUNTING	1 - 2	2 - 3
ILLUMINATED WINDOWS	5 - 6	6 - 8
ILLUSTRATED SONGS		
Bamforth Many different.	2 - 3	3 - 5
E. Nash "National Song" Series (6)	6 - 8	8 - 10
E.L. Theochromes	2 - 3	3 - 4
INCLINE RAILWAYS	3 - 5	5 - 7
INDIANS, Chiefs	6 - 7	7 - 10
Others	4 - 5	5 - 6
See Cowboys and Indians.		
INDUSTRY, Exterior	3 - 5	5 - 8
Interior	5 - 6	6 - 10
See Views and Real Photos.		
INSECTS	2 - 3	3 - 5
See Fantasy and Artist-Signed.		
INSTALLMENT CARDS		
W.M. Beach		
Cow (4)	7 - 8	8 - 9
Others	7 - 8	8 - 9
Huld		

1 Alligator (4)	7 - 8	8 - 10
2 Dachshund (4)	7 - 8	8 - 10
3 Uncle Sam (4)	25 - 28	28 - 30
4 Fish (4)	7 - 8	8 - 10
5 Sea Serpent (4)	7 - 8	8 - 10
6 Mosquito (4)	7 - 8	8 - 10
7 Rip Van Winkle (4)	7 - 8	8 - 10
8 New York City (4)	9 - 10	10 - 12
9 Santa (4)	20 - 25	25 - 30
10 Christmas Tree (4)	8 - 9	9 - 11
11 Fisherwoman (4)	7 - 8	8 - 9
12 Fisherman (4)	7 - 8	8 - 9
14 Rabbit (4)	7 - 8	8 - 10
15 Teddy Bear (4)	10 - 12	12 - 14
N.Y. Journal-American Comic Characters	6 - 8	8 - 9
H.M. Rose	6 - 7	7 - 8
Wildwood Co.	6 - 7	7 - 8
Wrench & Co.	6 - 7	7 - 8
Ottmar Zieher	8 - 9	9 - 10
Standup Napoleon (10) Sepia	10 - 12	12 - 14
Albert of Belgium (10) B&W	8 - 10	10 - 12
Joan of Arc (10) B&W	10 - 12	12 - 14
JAILS	4 - 5	5 - 8
JAPANESE GIRLS **P.C.K.** Series	3 - 4	4 - 5
JAPANESE NAVY **R. Tuck** Oilette Ser. 9237 (6)	5 - 6	6 - 8
JERUSALEM **R. Tuck** Oilette Ser 3355 (6)	5 - 6	6 - 7
JEWISH NEW YEAR		
Hebrew Pub. Co.	6 - 7	7 - 8
Others	4 - 5	5 - 6
JEWISH PEOPLE	3 - 5	5 - 8
Comics	8 - 10	10 - 15
JEWISH SYNAGOGUES	5 - 6	6 - 10
LAKES, Named	1 - 2	2 - 3
LANGUAGE OF FLOWERS	1 - 2	2 - 3
LARGE LETTERS, Cities, States Early	2 - 3	3 - 6
Linens	1 - 2	2 - 3
Names Early	5 - 6	6 - 8
Letters of Alphabet	4 - 5	5 - 6
LEATHER		
Greetings, Humor	3 - 5	5 - 8
Others, add $3-5 to card values of other topics.		
LESBIAN RELATED	10 - 12	12 - 15
Real Photo Nudes	18 - 22	22 - 30
LIBRARIES See Views.		

LIFE SAVING STATIONS	3 - 4	4 - 6
LIGHTHOUSES	2 - 4	4 - 5
LINENS		
Advertising, Product	3 - 5	5 - 9
Service	2 - 3	3 - 5
Blacks	2 - 3	3 - 8
Comics, Unsigned	.50 - 1	1 - 1.50
Comics, Signed	1 - 1.50	1.50 - 2
Comics, WW2	1 - 2	2 - 3
Hitler	2 - 3	3 - 5
Indians	1 - 2	2 - 3
Large Letters	1 - 1.50	1.50 - 2
Army Bases	2 - 3	3 - 4
Pin-up Girls	2 - 3	3 - 5
Political, Presidential	2 - 3	3 - 6
Court House, Post Office, etc.	1 - 1.50	1.50 - 2
Depots	2 - 3	3 - 4
Street Scenes, Small Town	1 - 2	2 - 3
See **Roadside America** for others.		
LIONS	1 - 2	2 - 3
LITERARY CHARACTERS	2 - 3	3 - 4
LOVERS	2 - 3	3 - 4
MACABRE	5 - 6	6 - 8
MAGICIANS	5 - 6	6 - 8
MAIN STREETS See Views and Real Photos.		
MAPS	1 - 2	2 - 4
MASONIC	3 - 4	4 - 6
National Art Co.		
Series 679	5 - 6	6 - 8
Series 1444	5 - 6	6 - 8
MECHANICALS, DIE-CUT		
Circle H 100 Series	12 - 15	15 - 20
P.F.B. Ser. 9526 Day-Month-Date	40 - 45	45 - 50
See Clapsaddle Halloween Mechanicals, others.		
MERRY WIDOW HATS		
Grollman	3 - 4	4 - 5
METAMORPHICS, Real Photos		
Skulls, "Diabolo"	25 - 30	30 - 35
Bismarck, Napoleon	15 - 20	20 - 25
Others	15 - 20	20 - 25
MEXICAN REVOLUTION	4 - 5	5 - 6
Real Photos	8 - 10	10 - 15
Pancho Villa	12 - 15	15 - 18
W.H. Horne - Add $2-3 per card.		

MIDGETS	5 - 6	6 - 8
MILITARY, Battles	2 - 3	3 - 4
Comics	3 - 4	4 - 5
Officers	3 - 5	5 - 8
Soldiers	2 - 3	3 - 4
Valentine Co.	4 - 5	5 - 6
R. Tuck "Military Life" Series (6)	5 - 6	6 - 7
"Military in London" (6)	6 - 7	7 - 8
Gale & Polden "Military Uniforms"	4 - 5	5 - 6
Langsdorf & Co. "Military Officers"	8 - 10	10 - 12
MILK CARTS	3 - 6	6 - 8
Real Photo	8 - 10	10 - 15
MILK WAGONS, TRUCKS See Real Photo		
MILLS, Industry	3 - 4	4 - 6
Real Photo Interior	10 - 15	15 - 20
Real Photo Exterior	8 - 10	10 - 15
MINING	5 - 6	6 - 8
Real Photo	8 - 10	10 - 12
MINING DISASTERS	8 - 10	10 - 15
MIRRORS	1 - 2	2 - 3
MONKEYS, APES	2 - 3	3 - 4
See Dressed Animals		
MONTHS OF YEAR	3 - 4	4- 6
MONUMENTS	1 - 2	2 - 3
MOTHER & CHILD	4 - 5	5 - 7
MOTORCYCLES	6 - 8	8 - 10
NAMED	10 - 12	12 - 15
Others	6 - 8	8 - 10
See Real Photos.		
MOTTOES	0.50 - 1	1 - 2
MOVIE STARS, Pre-1930	8 - 10	10 - 12
MOVIE STARS, 1930-45	4 - 6	6 - 10
MUSHROOMS	1 - 2	2 - 3
MUSICAL INSTRUCTORS	2 - 3	3 - 5
MYTHOLOGY	5 - 6	6 - 9
NAMES		
R. Tuck Series 131	5 - 6	6 - 7
Rotograph Co. Real Photos	5 - 6	6 - 7
NATIVES	3 - 4	4 - 6
SEMI-NUDES	8 - 10	10 - 14
NAVY		
R. Tuck		
U.S. Navy Series 2326	5 - 6	6 - 7
Illustrated P.C. Co.	4 - 5	5 - 6

NESBITT, EVELYN	10 - 12	12 - 15
NEWSPAPER	3 - 4	4 - 6
NORTH POLE EXPEDITION	8 - 10	10 - 12
NOVELTY		
APPLIQUED MATERIALS		
Feathered Birds	4 - 5	5 - 6
Feathered Hats	4 - 5	5 - 6
Flowers	1 - 2	2 - 3
Jewelry	3 - 4	4 - 5
Metal Models	7 - 8	8 - 10
Real Hair	10 - 15	15 - 20
Silk	3 - 4	4 - 10
Shells	2 - 3	3 - 4
Velvet	3 - 4	4 - 10
Miscellaneous	1 - 2	2 - 3
MECHANICALS		
Special Types	20 - 30	30 - 40
Kaleidoscopes	15 - 20	20 - 30
Lever-pull	5 - 10	10 - 15
Rotating Wheels	10 - 15	15 - 20
Miscellaneous	8 - 10	10 - 15
TRANSPARENCIES		
"Meteor"	10 - 15	15 - 30
Exhibitions	8 - 10	10 - 15
Comics, Views	8 - 10	10 - 15
Fairy Tales	10 - 15	15 - 18
Year Dates	10 - 15	15 - 20
MISCELLANEOUS		
Aluminum	4 - 6	6 - 10
Bas Relief	3 - 4	4 - 5
Royalty	10 - 12	12 - 18
Book Marks		
Common	1 - 2	2 - 3
Artist-Signed	3 - 5	5 - 10
Celluloid	5 - 6	6 - 8
Glass Eyes	2 - 3	3 - 4
Glitter	.50 - 1	1 - 1.50
Hold-to-Light		
See Koehler, Christmas, etc.		
Jig Saw Puzzles	7 - 8	8 - 15
Leather	2 - 3	3 - 5
Specials	6 - 10	10 - 20
Miniature Cards	4 - 5	5 - 8
Easter Witches	12 - 15	15 - 20

Peat	6 - 8	8 - 12
Perfumed	3 - 4	4 - 5
Photo Inserts	1 - 2	2 - 3
Pull-outs	2 - 3	3 - 4
Records	10 - 12	12 - 20
Satin Finish	4 - 5	5 - 6
Specials	8 - 10	10 - 20
Squeakers	2 - 3	3 - 4
Stamp Montage	6 - 7	7 - 10
Wood	2 - 3	3 - 5

NUDES - See Nudes

NURSERY RHYMES

BRETT, MOLLY
The Medici Society, Ltd., London

Series 145, 147, 155, 178 (6)	5 - 6	6 - 8
Series 178, 179, 185 (6)	5 - 6	6 - 8

JACKSON, HELEN

R. Tuck Series 6749 (6)	8 - 10	10 - 12

KENNEDY

C.W. Faulkner Series 1633 (6)	8 - 10	10 - 12

LeMAIR, WILLIBEEK
Augener, Ltd.

"Old Dutch Nursery Rhymes" (12)	10 - 12	12 - 15
"Old Rhymes W/New Pictures" (12)	10 - 12	12 - 15
"More Old Nursery Rhymes" (12)	10 - 12	12 - 15
"Our Old Nursery Rhymes" (12)	10 - 12	12 - 15
"Small Rhymes for Small People" (10)	8 - 10	10 - 12
"The Children's Corner" (12)	8 - 10	10 - 12

NIXON, K.
C.W. Faulkner & Co.

"Alice in Wonderland" (6)	10 - 12	12 - 15

NOSWORTHY, F.E.

F.A. Owen Ser. 160	10 - 12	12 - 14

SOWERBY, M.
Humphrey Milford, London

"Favorite Nursery Stories" (6)	10 - 12	12 - 15
"Flower Children" (6)	10 - 12	12 - 15
Jules Bien Series 40 (6)	6 - 8	8 - 10
C.S. Clark Series 2	6 - 8	8 - 10
F.H.S. Co. Series 9 (6)	6 - 7	7 - 9
National Art Co.	7 - 8	8 - 9
F. A. Owen Co. Series 161	7 - 8	8 - 9
P.F.B. Series 6943 (6)	12 - 14	14 - 16
Series 8666 (6)	12 - 15	15 - 18

R. Tuck

"Little Nursery Lovers" Ser. 9 (12)	8 - 10	10 - 15
"Nursery Don'ts" Ser. 12 (12)	8 - 10	10 - 15
"Nursery Rhymes" Ser. 3376 (6)	10 - 12	12 - 18
Series 3328, 3379, 3488 (6)	10 - 12	12 - 18

Ullman Mfg. Co.

"Nursery Rhymes" (uns.) 1664-1669	8 - 10	10 - 12
"Mary & Her Lamb" (uns.) 1759-1762	8 - 10	10 - 12
NURSES	5 - 6	6 - 8

OCEAN LINERS

R. Tuck "Celebrated Liners" (6-card sets)

Ser. 3378 "White Star Line"	6 - 8	8 - 10
Ser. 3379 "White Star Line"	6 - 8	8 - 10
Ser. 6228 "White Star Line"	6 - 8	8 - 10
Ser. 3592	6 - 7	7 - 8
Ser. 6229 "Orient Pacific"	7 - 8	8 - 10
Ser. 6230, 8960, 8961	7 - 8	8 - 9
Ser. 9106 "The Cunard Line"	8 - 9	9 - 10
Ser. 9112, 9124, 9125	7 - 8	8 - 9
Ser. 9126 "Atlantic Transport Line"	9 - 10	10 - 12
Ser. 9133 "Union Castle Line"	6 - 7	7 - 8
Ser. 914 "American Line"	9 - 10	10 - 12
Ser. 9151, 9155, 9213	7 - 8	8 - 9
Ser. 9215 "White Star Line"	8 - 10	10 - 12
Ser. 9268 "Cunard Line"		

The Cunard Liner Lusitania, *Davidson Brothers Real Photo*

'THE TITANIC' S. S.; 882 ft. long; the largest boat in the world; sunk April 15, 1912, at 2:20 A. M.; on her maiden trip; with a loss of about 1,500 passengers.

The Titanic, *B & W, Kraus Mfg. Co.*

1 "Mauretania"	8 - 10	10 - 12
2 "Lusitania"	15 - 20	20 - 25
3 "Carmania"	8 - 10	10 - 12
4 "Lusitania"	15 - 20	20 - 25
5 "Mauretania"	8 - 10	10 - 12
6 "Carpathia"	8 - 10	10 - 12
Ser. 9503 "White Star Line"	8 - 9	9 - 10
Ser. 9898 "White Star Line"		
"Titanic" (2 different)	25 - 30	30 - 40
Others	8 - 9	9 - 10
German-American Line	8 - 9	9 - 10
Holland-American Line	5 - 7	7 - 9
Red Star Line	6 - 7	7 - 8
S/Cassiers	7 - 8	8 - 10
Poster Series, S/Cassiers	12 - 15	15 - 20
American Line B&W	5 - 6	6 - 7
S/M.B.B., Paintings, B&W	6 - 7	7 - 8
Interiors	8 - 10	10 - 15
Real Photos	12 - 15	15 - 20
Lusitania	10 - 12	12 - 15
Real Photos	12 - 15	15 - 20
Titanic	30 - 40	40 - 50
Real Photos	40 - 50	50 - 75
White Fleet Series	6 - 8	8 - 9
OCCUPATIONS	6 - 8	8 - 12
OIL WELLS	3 - 4	4 - 6

OPERA SINGERS	4 - 6	6 - 8
OPIUM SMOKERS	4 - 6	6 - 8
ORANGES	1 - 2	2 - 3
ORCHESTRAS	5 - 6	6 - 8
ORGANS, MUSICAL	4 - 5	5 - 6
ORPHANAGES	4 - 5	5 - 8
OSTRICHES	2 - 3	3 - 4
OWLS	6 - 8	8 - 12
PALACES	2 - 3	3 - 4
PAPER DOLL CUT-OUTS		
R. Tuck "Window Garden" Ser. 3400 (6)	30 - 35	35 - 45
PARADES, Color	4 - 5	5 - 6
Real Photo	8 - 10	10 - 12
PASSION PLAY		
Conwell Red Borders	5 - 6	6 - 7
Others	4 - 5	5 - 6
PATRIOTIC	4 - 5	5 - 8
S/DeWees "Billy Possum" (6)	10 - 12	12 - 15
S/Crite "Billy Possum" (12)	7 - 8	8 - 10
Lounsbury		
Series 2514, 2517 "Billy Possum" (4)	8 - 10	10 - 12
National Song Series (6)	4 - 6	6 - 8
PENITENTIARIES	4 - 5	5 - 6
PENNANTS	1 - 2	2 - 3
PHONOGRAPHS	5 - 6	6 - 7
PHYSICIANS	5 - 6	6 - 8
PIANOS	3 - 4	4 - 5
PIGEONS	2 - 3	3 - 5
PIGS	3 - 4	4 - 5
See Dressed Animals		
PILGRIMS	2 - 3	3 - 4
PIN-UP GIRLS	3 - 4	4 - 7
PLAYING CARDS	4 - 6	6 - 7
POLICEMEN	4 - 5	5 - 7
POLITICAL, PRESIDENTIAL	10 -15	15 - 20
"Billikins" (Brown & Taft)	8 - 10	10 - 12
"Billy Possum" Ser. 2515, Emb., Sepia		
"Billy Possum & Jimmy Possum"	10 - 12	12 - 15
"Moving Day in Possum Town"	10 - 12	12 - 15
"The Only Possums that Escaped"	10 - 12	12 - 15
"Billy Possum" S/Crite		
"Give my Regards to Bill"	12 - 15	15 - 18
"Roast Teddy Bear"		
"Aw Don't Play Possum ..."		

Political/Billiken
Billiken Publishing Co.

Our Choice
Taft/Sherman, 1908

"Dear, Am Unavoidably Detained ..."
"I'm Having a High Old Time"
"Very Busy, Both Hands Full ..."
"Don't Play Possum Bur ..."
GROLLMAN POLITICAL SET
Fuller & Fuller Co.
Bryan & Taft, 1908 (16) W/Uncle Sam
Presidential Race, Baseball Game,

Winners & Losers	20 - 22	22 - 25
Third Party Jugates	30 - 35	35 - 40
Lounsbury Series 2515		
Taft/Roosevelt Sepia	20 - 22	22 - 28
"Our Choice" Taft-Sherman, 1908	15 - 18	18 - 22
"Our Choice" Bryan-Kern, 1908	15 - 18	18 22
Pres. Roosevelt	12 - 15	15 - 20
Pres. Taft	12 - 15	15 - 20
POSTCARD SHOPS	15 - 20	20 - 25
Advertising Postcards	8 - 10	10 - 12
POSTMEN	6 - 7	7 - 9
POULTRY		
H.K. & Co.		

Series 356	4 - 5	5 - 7
T.S.N. Series 540	4 - 5	5 - 7
PRESIDENTS, SETS/SERIES		
Cromwell "Roosevelt in Africa" (16)	6 - 7	7 - 8
Hugh C. Leighton		
Unnamed Series		
Similar to **Tuck's** below. (25)	6 - 7	7 - 9
W.R. Gordon, Phila Unnumbered (25) B&W	4 - 5	5 - 6
M.A. Sheehan (1940's) (32)		
Serigraphs by Paul Dubosclard (32)	3 - 4	4 - 5
R. Tuck Ser. 2328		
S/L. Spinner		
"Presidents of the United States" (24)	6 - 8	8 - 10
President Taft - Added Later	12 - 15	15 - 18
"President Theodore Roosevelt" Ser. 2333	15 - 18	18 - 22
Underwood & Underwood		
"Roosevelt's African Hunt" (40)	4 - 5	5 - 6
PRISONS	5 - 6	6 - 7
PROPAGANDA	7 - 9	9 - 12
PUZZLES	3 - 4	4 - 5
QUEEN'S DOLL HOUSE		
R. Tuck		
Series 4500 Set 1 (8)	6 - 8	8 - 9
Series 4501 Set 2 (8)	6 - 7	7 - 8
Series 4502 Set 3 (8)	6 - 7	7 - 8
Series 4503 Set 3 (8)	6 - 7	7 - 8
Series 4504 Set 4 (8)	6 - 7	7 - 8
Series 4505 Set 5 (8)	6 - 7	7 - 8
QUOTATIONS	1 - 2	2 - 3
RABBITS	1 - 2	2 - 3
Dressed	5 - 8	8 - 12
RACING, Auto	8 - 10	10 - 12
Dog	5 - 6	6 - 7
Horse	7 - 8	8 - 10
RADIO STARS, Early years	6 - 7	7 - 8
RAILROAD STATIONS - See Depots, & Real Photos.		
RAILROAD TRAINS, Large Image	5 - 6	6 - 8
Real Photo	8 - 10	10 - 15
Small Image	2 - 3	3 - 5
Real Photo	5 - 6	8 - 12
Wrecks	8 - 10	10 - 15
Also see Trains		
RAINBOWS	3 - 4	4 - 6
REBUS CARDS	5 - 6	6 - 8
REGIMENTAL BADGES	4 - 6	6 - 8

Dus ist ja unerhört!

W. Fialkowski, AVM 1197, "The New Radio"

Anonymous German Snowman   *Embossed German Snowman*
Santway 1223

RELIGIOUS See Religious	1 - 3	3 - 5
REPTILES	2 - 3	3 - 4
RESTAURANTS See Views and Real Photos.		
RETIREMENT HOMES	2 - 3	3 - 4
RIVERS	0.50 - 1	1 - 1.50
RODEOS	3 - 4	4 - 5
Real Photos	6 - 8	8 - 10
ROWING	3 - 4	4 - 5
ROYALTY, British	4 - 6	6 - 12
French	4 - 5	5 - 8
German	6 - 8	8 - 12
Others	3 - 5	5 - 7
R. Tuck		
Kings & Queens of England		
Series 614, 615, 616 (12)	8 - 10	10 - 12
Series 617 (3)	10 - 12	12 - 14
SAILORS	2 - 3	3 - 5
SAILBOATS	1 - 2	2 - 3
SALVATION ARMY	3 - 4	4 - 5
SAN FRANCISCO EARTHQUAKE	3 - 4	4 - 10
SANTA CLAUS See Christmas Greetings.		

Embossed Stamp Card 51, "New South Wales"

SNAKES	3 - 4	4 - 6
SNOWMEN See Fantasy		
SPOONS	3 - 4	4 - 5
STADIUMS, Football, Early	6 - 7	8 - 15
Others	3 - 4	4 - 8
See Baseball		
STAGE		
Maude Adams	8 - 10	10 - 12
Lillian Russell	12 - 14	14 - 18
Others	4 - 5	5 - 8
SPANISH AMERICAN WAR	5 - 8	8 - 10
STAMP CARDS		
Kunzli Bros., Paris Series	8 - 9	9 - 10
Ottmar Ziehr Series	8 - 10	10 - 12
Menke-Huber Series	8 - 10	10 - 14
Others	7 - 8	8 - 10
STAMP MONTAGE	5 - 6	6 - 8
STATE GIRLS		
Platinachrome Co. (45)	7 - 8	8 - 9
STATE CAPITALS & Seals		
Illustrated P.C. Co. Ser. 97	4 - 5	5 - 6
Gold Embossed Ser. 97	5 - 6	6 - 7
E.C. Kropp	5 - 6	6 - 7
Langsdorf	6 - 7	7 - 8
STATUE OF LIBERTY	2 - 4	4 - 8
Hold-To-Light	25 - 30	30 - 40
STATUES	1 - 2	2 - 4
STORKS	2 - 3	3 - 5
STREET SCENES See Views and Real Photos.		
STRIKES, Labor	8 - 10	10 - 12
STUDENTS	2 - 3	3 - 5
STUNTMEN	4 - 5	5 - 8
SUBMARINES	4 - 6	6 - 10
SUBWAYS	3 - 5	5 - 10
SUFFRAGETTES		
AA Pub. Co.		
698/12 "Stumping For Votes"	10 - 12	12 - 15
Attwell, Mabel Lucie		
Little Girl, "Where's My Vote"	18 - 20	20 - 25
LEVI, C.		
"Komical Koons" Ser. 210, 3308	20 - 22	22 - 25
Bergman Co.		
Series 6342 S/B. Wall	12 - 14	14 - 16
Cargill Co, Michigan		

Series 103-129	12 - 15	15 - 18
Campbell Art Co. S/Chamberlin (6)	15 - 18	18 - 22
Dunston-Weiler Litho Co.		
1 "Suffragette Madonna"	18 - 20	20 - 25
2 "Electioneering"	18 - 20	20 - 25
3 "Pantalette Suffragette"	18 - 20	20 - 25
4 "Suffragette Vote-Getter"	18 - 20	20 - 25
5 "Suffragette-Coppette"	18 - 20	20 - 25
6 "Uncle Sam-Suffragette the Easiest Way"	20 - 25	25 - 30
7 "Election Day"	18 - 20	20 - 25
8 "I Don't Care"	18 - 20	20 - 25
9 "Queen of the Poll"	18 - 20	20 - 25
10 "Where, Oh Where is My ..."	18 - 20	20 - 25
11 "I Want to Vote ..."	18 - 20	20 - 25
12 "I Love My Husband, But Oh You Vote"	18 - 20	20 - 25
L. & E., New York S/H.B.G.	40 - 50	50 - 60
Nash Suffragette Madonna		
"Crop of 1910"	12 - 16	16 - 20
GRACE O'NEILL		
Campbell Art Card	110 - 125	125 - 140
National Woman Suffrage Card	225 - 250	250 - 275
Roth & Langley, 1909 Issues	12 - 15	15 - 18
WALTER WELLMAN Issues	20 - 25	25 - 30
SUPERLATIVES - Largest-Smallest	2 - 3	3 - 5
SWANS	1 - 2	2 - 3
SYNAGOGUES	4 - 6	6 - 10
TARTANS	3 - 4	4 - 5
TELEGRAMS	1 - 2	2 - 3
TELEPHONES	5 - 7	7 - 12
TEMPERANCE	4 - 6	6 - 10
SHIRLEY TEMPLE		
Real Photos	6 - 8	8 - 10
Black & White, Color	10 - 12	12 - 14
TENNIS, Courts	5 - 6	6 - 8
Matches in progress	6 - 7	7 - 8
Artist-Signed,		
W/Beautiful Women, Lovers, Animals	10 - 12	12 - 20
BUTCHER, A.		
A.R.i.B. 1963	12 - 15	15 - 18
CHRISTY, EARL		
R&N 173 "Love All"	15 - 18	18 - 22
FIDLER, ALICE L.		
American Girl 73	12 - 14	14 - 16
FISCHER, PAUL	12 - 14	14 - 16

FISHER, H.		
R&N 834 "Her Game"	20 - 25	25 - 30
R&N 839 "A Love Score"	20 - 25	25 - 30
GRAF, M. Deco Silhouettes	15 - 18	18 - 22
NANNI Series 324 (6)	18 - 20	20 - 25
Series 434, 480 (6)	18 - 22	22 - 26
NAST, T. "Love Game"	10 - 12	12 - 15
REYNOLDS, A. "The Lady Plays Tennis"	10 - 12	12 - 15
UNDERWOOD, C.		
R.C. Co. 1443 "Victoria"	15 - 18	18 - 25
USABAL Series 336 (6)	15 - 17	17 - 20
Advertising Tennis Product	12 - 15	15 - 25
THEATRES See Views and Real Photos.		
TIGERS	2 - 3	3 - 5
TOLL GATES	3 - 4	4 - 6
TORNADOES	6 - 8	8 - 12
TRAINS		
Identified		
Large Image	8 - 10	10 - 12

E.P. Kinsella
Langsdorf & Co., "Game"

Anonymous
Sport, Tennis

Lake Shore & Michigan Southern Railway, "20th Century Limited"

Small Image	2 - 3	3 - 5
R. Tuck		
"Famous American Expresses" (6)	10 - 12	12 - 15
Series 8619 (6)	8 - 9	9 - 12
Series 9274 (6)	8 - 9	9 - 12
Series 9316 (6)	8 - 9	9 - 12
Series 9662 (6)	8 - 9	9 - 12
Series 9687 (6)	8 - 9	9 - 12
See Real Photos.		
TRAMPS	2 - 3	3 - 4
TROLLEYS, Large Image	8 - 10	10 - 12
Horse Drawn, Large Image	10 - 12	12 - 18
Horse Drawn, Small Image	6 - 7	7 - 10
See Real Photos.		
TUNNELS	2 - 3	3 - 4
TURKEYS	1 - 2	2 - 3
TYPEWRITERS	3 - 4	4 - 6
UMBRELLAS	2 - 3	3 - 4
UNCLE SAM See Greetings.		
U.S. NAVY		
R. Tuck Series 2326	5 - 6	6 - 8
Illustrated P.C. Co.	4 - 5	5 - 6
VIEWS See Views and Real Photos.		
VOLCANOS	2 - 3	3 - 4
WANTED POSTERS	8 - 12	12 - 15

WAR BOND CAMPAIGNS POSTERS	12 - 15	15 - 20
WEDDINGS	3 - 5	5 - 6
Real Photos	5 - 6	6 - 8
Jewish	6 - 7	7 - 9
WHALES	3 - 5	5 - 8
WHOLE DAM FAMILY (Many)	4 - 5	5 - 7
WINDMILLS	2 - 4	4 - 6
WINERIES	3 - 5	5 - 8
WITCHES	4 - 6	6 - 8
Artist-Signed	8 - 10	10 - 15
Easter Witches, Scandinavian	10 - 12	12 - 14
Miniature cards	15 - 18	18 - 22
WORLD WAR 1	3 - 5	5 - 10
WRESTLING	3 - 5	5 - 6
YACHTING	2 - 3	3 - 5
YMCA	3 - 5	5 - 6
YWCA	4 - 5	6 - 7
ZODIAC		
Jules Bien		
"Your Fortune" Ser. 37 (12)	5 - 6	6 - 8
Anonymous		
Published 1907 Zodiac Series (12)	5 - 6	6 - 7
ZOOS	2 - 3	3 - 4

Underwood & Underwood, "On a Hike, Camp Jackson, Columbia, S.C."

The majority of all postcard collectors begin their participation in the hobby by collecting views of their home town. They have this interest because of their familiarity with the town or community as it is today...and the desire to know its history and what it looked like in earlier years.

This desire prompts the enthusiast to search every possible avenue for these collectible gems. They find a court house, a post office, a hotel, and then they wonder if there might be a depot, a barber shop, or.... As the search goes on, the interest expands to other views, maybe of a nearby town, a popular city and finally the entire state. By this time the enthusiast is a full-blown postcard collector.

Most collectors, knowing how hard they are to obtain, will not part with their collection of views, other than duplicates, and they really become rarities when other enthusiasts begin their search.

Although small town views are the most popular and, therefore, command the highest prices, they, plus large town and city views of trolleys, banks, depots, main streets, etc., are continually pursued by topical collectors who care not whether the town is large or small, whether in Idaho or South Carolina...it just doesn't really matter. This elevates the prices of the topicals and also makes the small town views much dearer.

On the other side of the coin, however, views of large cities such as New York, Washington, D.C., Philadelphia, etc.; tourist attractions such as Niagara Falls, Mount Vernon, Watkins Glen, Grand Canyon, Yellowstone Park and others, have very little value because of the millions produced. Only special views in these areas are of any value.

THE PUBLISHER

There were many **great and illustrious** publishers of view cards from 1900 to 1940...names like **A.C. Bosselman, Valentine & Sons,** and **Rotograph** of New York, **Curt Teich of Chicago, Detroit Publishing Co., Hugh Leighton** of Maine, as well as **Raphael Tuck** and others. However, the most intriguing to the author was **The Asheville Postcard Co.** They produced view cards just as the above publishers but on a smaller scale, and were still the biggest postcard publisher and distributor south of New York.

Fortunately for me, the city of Asheville is only seven miles from my home. I "found" the Asheville Post Card Co. in 1972 and for four years spent many delightful hours looking through the remnants of stocks of old postcards which had accumulated in three warehouses since Mr. LeCompte, the owner, founded the company in 1916.

He told me many times how, from 1916 through 1965, he traveled throughout North Carolina, South Carolina, Tennessee, Virginia, Georgia, Alabama, and Florida twice each year taking photographs in all large and small towns along his route. He took pictures of all the important buildings, streets, depots, etc., in each town.

The photos were printed and retouched as needed, and then sent to Curt Teich, A.C. Bosselman, Illustrated Postcard Co., Kraemer Art., etc., who would make several black & white printing proofs of each photo. Upon receipt of the proofs, he would return to each of his stops and take orders from the town merchants. Coloring of the buildings, an important feature, was noted on this trip. Resulting orders were returned by mail.

In anticipation of future sales of a popular view, business being good, Mr. LeCompte would sometimes place an order up to 10,000 copies. Future orders could then be filled from stock. A sizeable portion of business was enhanced by his pictures and cards of tourist courts, filling stations, restaurants, etc., which we now refer to as **Roadside America.** These were given away by each advertiser, and orders of up to 5000 of each view were not uncommon.

File copies of each card, plus the printing proofs (and the color scheme), were saved in the archives section by state and by town. Each town and view were labeled and numbered; e.g., Asheville 2 or Savannah 5. The merchants reordered by these numbers when their stocks were almost depleted. It may be noted that there were several "stock" views of the same scene...usually designated as "A peaceful view in Sumter," with that same peaceful view in Greenville, Greenwood, and so on.

Basically, this is how the tremendous view card business was handled throughout the U.S. Thanks to these photographers, publishers and distributors, histories of small and large towns throughout the country have been recorded for future generations.

Mr. LeCompte was 82 years old in 1972. He still managed the company but the business was poor, as view card and novelty sales were very depressed, unlike the thriving years prior to the Great Depression and just after WWII. He passed away in 1976. The company was sold by the heirs and liquidated a year later.

VIEWS

View cards are classified as to Era for this listing. 1 = Postcard Era - 1900-1915; 2 = White Border Era - 1915-1930; 3 = Linen Era - 1930's-1940's.

The values listed represent views from the more highly populated areas in the Northeast and Middle Atlantic States. For the other areas, which were less densely populated or had fewer views published, prices should be adjusted higher for certain states relative to the percentages listed below.

On the other hand, for big cities such as New York, Washington, D.C., Philadelphia, and the resort areas such as Niagara Falls, plus the tourist attractions of Mt. Vernon, Monticello, and Civil War Battlegrounds, etc., the price structure must be lowered significantly.

Georgia, Indiana, Louisiana, Maine, North Carolina, South Carolina, and Tennessee—add 10% to all price listings.

Florida, Kentucky, Minnesota, Mississippi, Nevada, Oregon, and Washington—add 20%.

California, Colorado, Nebraska, Texas, Wyoming, and Missouri—add 30%.

Arkansas, Idaho, Montana, North and South Dakota, Rhode Island, Wisconsin, and Utah—add 40%.

Alabama, Delaware, New Mexico, and Oklahoma - Add 50%.

Alaska and Hawaii—add 100%.

Airports-1	$5 - 6	$6 - 8
Airports-2	4 - 5	5 - 6
Airports-3	1 - 2	2 - 3
Amusement Parks-1	8 - 10	10 - 15
Amusement Parks-2	6 - 7	7 - 10
Amusement Parks-3	2 - 3	3 - 4
Banks-1	2 - 3	3 - 5
Banks-2	1 - 2	2 - 3
Banks-3	0.50 - 1	1 - 1.50
Birds Eye View-1	3 - 4	4 - 6
Birds Eye View-2	2 - 3	3 - 4
Birds Eye View-3	1 - 1.50	1 .50 - 2
Bridges-1	1 - 2	2 - 3
Bridges-2	1.50 - 2	2 - 2.50

Interior View of Merchants Bank of Winona, Minnesota

Real Photo, 1st Avenue, Cordova, Alaska

Bridges-3	0.50 - 1	1 - 1.50
Bus Stations-1	N/A	N/A
Bus Stations-2	4 - 5	5 - 7
Bus Stations-3	2 - 3	3 - 4
Cemetery-1	5 - 6	6 - 8
Cemetery-2	4 - 5	5 - 6
Cemetery-3	2 - 3	3 - 4
Churches-1	2 - 3	3 - 4
Churches-2	1 - 2	2 - 3
Churches-3	1 - 1.50	1.50 - 2
Colleges-1	2 - 3	3 - 5
Colleges-2	1 - 2	2 - 4
Colleges-3	1 - 1.50	1.50 - 2
County Fair-1	6 - 7	8 - 12
County Fair-2	5 - 6	6 - 8
County Fair-3	3 - 4	4 - 6
Court House-1	3 - 4	4 - 6
Court House-2	2 - 3	3 - 4
Court House-3	1 - 1.50	1.50 - 2
Depots-1	5 - 6	6 - 10
Depots-2	3 - 5	5 - 7
Depots-3	2 - 3	3 - 4
Diners-1	N/A	N/A
Diners-2	N/A	N\A
Diners-3	10 - 12	12 - 25
Fire Department-1	6 - 8	8 - 12

Coal Breaker, Pennsylvania

Fire Department-2	5 - 6	6 - 8
Fire Department-3	3 - 4	4 - 5
Funeral Homes-1	7 - 8	8 - 12
Funeral Homes-2	6 - 7	7 - 9
Funeral Homes-3	4 - 5	5 - 6
Garages/Gas Stations-1	6 - 7	8 - 12
Garages/Gas Stations-2	5 - 6	6 - 8
Garages/Gas Stations-3	4 - 5	5 - 7
General Stores-1	5 - 6	6 - 10
General Stores-2	4 - 5	5 - 7
General Stores-3	2 - 3	3 - 4
Gymnasiums-1	4 - 5	5 - 7
Gymnasiums-2	3 - 4	4 - 5
Gymnasiums-3	1 - 2	2 - 3
Hospitals-1	3 - 4	4 - 6
Hospitals-2	2 - 3	3 - 4
Hospitals-3	1 - 1.50	1.50 - 2
Hotels-1	3 - 4	4 - 6
Hotels-2	2 - 3	3 - 4
Hotels-3	1 - 2	2 - 3
Library-1	3 - 4	4 - 5
Library-2	2 - 3	3 - 4
Library-3	1 - 2	2 - 3
Main Streets-1	5 - 6	6 - 10
Main Streets-2	4 - 5	5 - 7
Main Streets-3	1 - 2	2 - 3

Mills/Plants-1	4 - 5	5 - 10
Mills/Plants-2	3 - 4	4 - 6
Mills/Plants-3	1 - 2	2 - 4
Motels-1	N/A	N/A
Motels-2	4 - 5	5 - 7
Motels-3	1 - 2	2 - 4
Opera-1	5 - 7	7 - 12
Opera-2	4 - 5	5 - 7
Opera-3	2 - 3	3 - 5
Parks-1	1 - 2	2 - 3
Parks-2	1 - 1.50	1.50 - 2
Parks-3	0.50 - 1	1 - 1.50
Post Office-1	3 - 4	4 - 6
Post Office-2	2 - 3	3 - 4
Post Office-3	1 - 1.50	1.50 - 2
Restaurants-1	6 - 7	7 - 10
Restaurants-2	3 - 4	4 - 6
Restaurants-3	2 - 3	3 - 4
Rivers, Creeks-1	1 - 2	2 - 3
Rivers, Creeks-2	1 - 1.50	1.50 - 2
Rivers, Creeks-3	0.50 - 1	1 - 1.50
Roadside Stands-1	N/A	N/A
Roadside Stands-2	4 - 5	5 - 8
Roadside Stands-3	3 - 4	4 - 6

Railroad Station, Chateaugay, New York

Schools-1	2 - 3	3 - 5
Schools-2	1 - 2	2 - 3
Schools-3	1 - 1.50	1.50 - 2
Statues-1	1 - 2	2 - 3
Statues-2	1.50 - 2	2 - 2.50
Statues-3	0.50 - 1	1 - 1.50
Street Scenes-1	4 - 5	5 - 7
Street Scenes-2	3 - 4	4 - 5
Street Scenes-3	1 - 2	2 - 4
W/Parades-1	6 - 7	7 - 10
W/Parades-2	5 - 5	6 - 8
W/Parades-3	2 - 3	3 - 5
Tennis Courts-1	7 - 8	8 - 12
Tennis Courts-2	6 - 7	7 - 9
Tennis Courts-3	3 - 4	4 - 5
Theatres-1	8 - 10	10 - 15
Theatres-2	7 - 8	8 - 10
Theatres-3	4 - 5	5 - 6

This Space For Writing Messages

POST CARD

PLACE STAMP HERE

This side for the Address only

10 Roadside America

The postcards of Roadside America consist of those that were published to advertise a place of business on or near busy highways. They catered primarily to travelers and were usually given to these travelers when they stopped by or were mailed to prospective customers.

Most of the Roadside America cards were issued in the Linen and early Chrome Eras. There has, however, been some overlapping from the White Border Era, especially with filling stations and restaurants. Real Photo views, and any views of diners, are always in great demand and command the highest prices. Super-imposed signs, drawn by the publishers and placed on motel and other businesses, are also very popular.

AUTOMOBILE DEALERSHIPS	$ 4 - 6	$ 6 - 7
Real Photo	8 - 10	10 - 12
CAFE	3 - 4	4 - 6
Real Photo	6 - 8	8 - 12
COFFEE POT CAFE	5 - 7	7 - 9
Real Photo	8 - 10	10 - 12
DINERS	12 - 14	14 - 18
Real Photo	20 - 25	25 - 28
DRIVE-IN RESTAURANTS	5 - 6	6 - 8
Real Photo	8 - 10	10 - 12

Pine View Tourist Court, 10 Miles N. of Georgia/Florida Line

DRIVE-IN THEATER	5 - 6	6 - 9
Real Photo	8 - 10	10 - 15
EXAGGERATED BUILDINGS	5 - 7	7 - 10
Real Photo	10 - 12	12 - 14
FOOD MARKETS	4 - 5	5 - 7
Real Photo	8 - 9	9 - 10

Old Museum Village, Orange County, New York

Real Photo Restaurant, Cabano, Temis, Province of Quebec

FRUIT STANDS	4 - 5	5 - 7
Real Photo	8 - 9	9 - 10
GAS PUMPS	5 - 6	6 - 8
Real Photo	8 - 10	10 - 12
ICE CREAM SHOPS	6 - 7	7 - 10
Real Photo	10 - 12	12 - 16

River Bridge Super Service, Fremont, Ohio

Fort View Court, US 411, Chatsworth, Georgia

MINIATURE GOLF	4 - 5	5 - 7
Real Photo	8 - 10	10 - 12
MOTOR COURT	3 - 4	4 - 5
Real Photo	6 - 8	8 - 9
PECAN STANDS	4 - 5	5 - 7
Real Photo	8 - 10	10 - 12
SANDWICH SHOP	5 - 6	6 - 8
Real Photo	8 - 10	10 - 12
SKATING RINKS	4 - 5	5 - 7
Real Photo	8 - 10	10 - 12
SOUVENIR SHOPS	5 - 6	6 - 7
Real Photo	8 - 9	9 - 10
SWIMMING POOLS	5 - 6	6 - 7
Real Photo	8 - 9	9 - 10
TRADING POST	4 - 6	6 - 7
Real Photo	8 - 10	10 - 12
TRAILER PARK	8 - 10	10 - 12
Real Photo	15 - 18	18 - 22
VEGETABLE MARKET/STAND	5 - 6	6 - 8
Real Photo		

This Space For Writing Messages

POST **C**ARD

PLACE STAMP HERE

11 | Real Photos

This side for the Address only

Real-photo cards have become one of the major collectible groups. Their authenticity and portrayal of life and living as it actually was, plus the fact that many are one-of-a-kind, are determining factors. This has been a new field of activity since earlier collectors completely neglected them, not realizing the true values of these photographic art gems and their place in illustrating the early history of the U.S. after the turn of the century.

As with other postcards, there were publishers of real-photo cards and various processes for developing them, but there also had to be a photographer. The photographer, if in business, usually signed and titled each photo. Avid real-photo collectors seek cards of these photographers the same as other collectors would a signed Clapsaddle.

Photo cards most sought by collectors are those by amateur photographers who happened upon an accident, a disaster, or event... of the train, the new car (with the proud family sitting inside)... or of the baby and her new teddy bear. All of these events give collectors many topics from which to choose.

Clarity and sharpness in the photo image is important so that all detail can be seen and the time era can be identified. It is also important, in most instances, that the photo be identified. Usually this information might be penciled in by the person posting the card if no title is printed.

These elements are very important to collectors, and must be taken into consideration when pricing each card.

Various papers and processes were used for producing real photos, with AZO and VELOX being the dominant ones. Others include EKC, KRUXO, KODAK, CYKO, DARKO, EKKP, and DOPS. These are usually notated in the stamp box on the reverse side. Big publishers, such as **Rotograph** and **Bamforth**, also use the real-photo process on many of their productions, but they do not qualify in this grouping.

Automobiles

Identified - Large Image	$ 18 - 20	$ 20 - 25
Small Image	10 - 12	12 - 15
Unidentified - Large Image	15 - 18	18 - 22
Small Image	8 - 10	10 - 12

Trucks

Identified - Large Image	20 - 25	25 - 30
Small Image	15 - 18	18 - 22
Unidentified - Large Image	15 - 18	18 - 22
Small Image	10 - 12	12 - 15

Delivery Trucks

Large Image, W/Advertising	40 - 50	50 - 60
Small Image, W/Advertising	30 - 35	35 - 40

"1911 Moyer Touring Car Convertible"

Walking From Coney Island to San Francisco

Farm Trucks
    Large Image   20 - 25   25 - 30

Farm Trucks		
Large Image	20 - 25	25 - 30
Small Image	10 - 12	12 - 15
Service Vehicles		
Dump Trucks, etc., Large Image	25 - 30	30 - 35
Small Image	15 - 18	18 - 22
Fire Engines - Large Image	35 - 40	40 - 45
Small Image	15 - 18	18 - 22
Paddy Wagons	20 - 25	25 - 30
Farm Tractors		
Identified - Large Image	20 - 25	25 - 30
Small Image	12 - 16	16 - 20
Unidentified - Large Image	12 - 16	16 - 20
Small Image	8 - 12	12 - 15
Race Cars		
Large Image	15 - 20	20 - 25
Small Image	10 - 12	12 - 16
W/Driver Identified - Large Image	20 - 25	25 - 30
Small Image	15 - 18	18 - 22
Motorcycles		
Identified - Large Image	25 - 30	30 - 35
Small Image	15 - 20	20 - 25
Unidentified - Large Image	15 - 20	20 - 25
Small Image	10 - 12	12 - 15
Bicycles		
Identified - Large Image	25 - 30	30 - 35

Arnold's Ice Cream, Horse Drawn Wagon

Small Image	15 - 18	18 - 22
Unidentified - Large Image	18 - 22	22 - 25
Small Image	10 - 12	12 - 15
Horse Drawn Delivery Wagons		
Ice - Large Image	50 - 60	60 - 75
Small Image	20 - 25	25 - 35
Mail - Large Image	50 - 60	60 - 70
Small Image	20 - 25	25 - 30
Coal - Large Image	50 - 60	60 - 70
Small Image	20 - 25	25 - 30
Others - Large Image	40 - 50	50 - 60
Small Image	20 - 25	25 - 30
Moving Vans/Freight Wagons - Large Image	40 - 50	50 - 60
Small Image	20 - 25	25 - 30
Horse Drawn Sales Wagons		
Ice Cream - Large Image	60 - 70	70 - 85
Small Image	35 - 40	40 - 50
Bakery - Large Image	50 - 60	60 - 70
Small Image	30 - 35	35 - 40
Grocery - Large	50 - 60	60 - 70
Small Image	30 - 35	35 - 40
Others - Large Image	45 - 50	50 - 60
Small Image	25 - 30	35 - 40
Horse & Buggy - Large Image	15 - 18	18 - 25
Small Image	10 - 12	12 - 15

Horse & Wagon, Carts - Large Image	12 - 15	15 - 20
Small Image	8 - 10	10 - 12
Goat Carts, W/Children - Large Image	15 - 20	20 - 25
Oxen Driven Wagons	12 - 15	15 - 20
Fire Engines	12 - 15	15 - 20
Hose Trucks	15 - 18	18 - 22
Horse Driven Fire Engines	18 - 22	22 - 26
Horse Driven Equipment	20 - 22	22 - 30
Trains, W/Engine		
Identified - Large Image	18 - 20	20 - 25
Unidentified - Large Image	10 - 12	12 - 15
Passenger Car Interiors	20 - 25	25 - 30
Repair Shop Interiors	18 - 20	20 - 25
Train Wrecks		
Identified - Large Image	20 - 25	25 - 30
Small Image	15 - 18	18 - 20
Unidentified -Large Image	15 - 18	18 - 22
Train Depots		
Small Town, East	15 - 20	20 - 25

Baby Ruth, Age 19,
Weight 702 Lbs.

Miller Bros. Clothing
Windham, N.Y.

Trolley Car, Liberty Bell Route Limited

Large Town, East	5 - 8	8 - 12
Small Town, West	20 - 25	25 - 30
Large Town, West	10 - 12	12 - 15
Trolley Cars		
Identified - Large Image	20 - 25	25 - 30
Small Image	12 - 15	15 - 18
Unidentified - Large Image	12 - 15	15 - 20
Small Image	8 - 10	10 - 12
Small Image	10 - 12	12 - 15
Airplanes		
Identified - Large Image	15 - 20	20 - 25
Small Image	10 - 12	12 - 15
W/Pilot	20 - 25	25 - 30
Balloons		
Identified - Large Image	20 - 25	25 - 30
Small Image	15 - 20	20 - 25
Unidentified - Large Image	15 - 20	20 - 25
Small Image	10 - 12	12 - 15
Dirigibles		
Identified - Large Image	20 - 25	25 - 30
Small Image	15 - 20	20 - 25
Unidentified - Large Image	15 - 20	20 - 25
Small Image	10 - 12	12 - 15
Ships, Interior Views	10 - 15	15 - 20
Small Business Buildings, Identified		

Bakeries - Exteriors	15 - 20	20 - 25
Interiors	20 - 25	25 - 30
Banks - Exteriors	10 - 12	12 - 15
Interiors	15 - 18	18 - 20
Billiard Parlors - Exteriors	20 - 25	25 - 30
Interiors	25 - 30	30 - 35
Bowling Alley - Exteriors	10 - 12	12 - 18
Interiors	18 - 20	20 - 25
Cigar/Tobacco Store - Interiors	50 - 55	55 - 60
Dairies - Exteriors	10 - 15	15 - 20
Interiors	15 - 20	20 - 25
Drug Stores - Exteriors	12 - 15	15 - 20
Interiors	20 - 25	25 - 30
Fish/Meat Markets - Exteriors	20 - 25	25 - 30
Interiors	30 - 35	35 - 40
General Stores - Exteriors	15 - 20	20 - 25
Interiors	25 - 32	30 - 35
Grocery Stores - Exteriors	15 - 20	20 - 25
Interiors	25 - 30	30 - 35

Little Girl and Doll

Little Girls and Dolls

Ice Cream Parlors - Exteriors	30 - 35	35 - 40
Interiors	40 - 45	45 - 50
Post Office - Exteriors	10 - 12	12 - 15
Interiors	20 - 25	25 - 30
Restaurants - Exteriors	10 - 12	12 - 15
Interiors	15 - 18	18 - 22
Service Stations - Exteriors	15 - 18	18 - 22
Soda Fountains	15 - 18	18 - 22
W/Ice Cream or Coca Cola Signs	20 - 25	25 - 35
Taverns - Exteriors	12 - 15	15 - 18
Interiors	15 - 20	20 - 25
Theaters - Exteriors	20 - 25	25 - 30
Toy Store - Exteriors	20 - 25	25 - 30
Interiors, showing toys	35 - 40	40 - 50
Street Scenes		
Main Streets - Small Towns	8 - 15	15 - 25
Large Towns	6 - 10	10 - 20
Others - Small Towns	6 - 12	12 - 18
Large Towns	5 - 8	8 - 12
Bathing		
Attractive Ladies	8 - 10	10 - 12
Groups	7 - 8	8 - 10
Blacks		
Children	5 - 8	8 - 10
Men/Women	4 - 7	7 - 8
Blacks Working in field, etc.	10 - 12	12 - 15
Musical Groups	10 - 15	15 - 25
Blackface Minstrels	25 - 28	28 - 32
Bands	20 - 25	25 - 30
Baseball Team	20 - 25	25 - 30
Children		
Common	3 - 4	4 - 7
W/Animals	7 - 8	8 - 12
W/Dolls	10 - 15	15 - 18
W/Dolls in Doll Carriage	15 - 18	18 - 25
W/Toys	10 - 15	15 - 18
W/Large Teddy Bears	20 - 25	25 - 35
W/Small Teddy Bears	15 - 18	18 - 22
In Classroom/School	10 - 12	12 - 15
In Costumes	15 - 18	18 - 25
Christmas Trees	15 - 18	18 - 22
W/Gifts under Tree	20 - 25	25 - 30
Circus Related		
Trapeze Artist, Identified	15 - 20	20 - 25

Other Performers	10 - 15	15 - 20
Fat Ladies	15 - 18	18 - 22
Giants, Midgets, Strongmen, etc.	12 - 15	15 - 20
Advertising Circus	20 - 25	25 - 30
Animals - Elephants, etc.	12 - 15	15 - 18
Add $5-8 for Barnum & Bailey Circus.		

Exaggerated

Big Fish	10 - 12	12 - 15
Big Grasshoppers	12 - 14	14 - 18
Farm Products	6 - 8	8 - 12
Big Fruit	6 - 8	8 - 10
Big Animals	7 - 9	9 - 12

Hangings/Lynchings	25 - 30	30 - 40

Adolf Hitler

By Hoffman		
Used, W/Postmark	15 - 18	18 - 22
Unused, no Postmark	12 - 15	15 - 18
Other Publishers		
Used, W/Postmark	16 - 20	20 - 25
Unused, no Postmark	12 - 15	15 - 18

Indians

Identified Chiefs	20 - 25	25 - 30
Others	12 - 15	15 - 18
Unidentified	8 - 10	10 - 12

Trolley Car Wreck, Kingston, New York

Nudes   See "Real Photo Nudes"
Plants, Mills

Small Town		
Exteriors	15 - 20	20 - 25
Interiors	20 - 25	25 - 35
Large Town		
Exteriors	10 - 15	15 - 20
Interiors	18 - 22	22 - 26
Political		
Presidents	15 - 18	18 - 25
President and Running Mate	20 - 22	22 - 30
Losing Candidates	18 - 20	20 - 25
Governors	20 - 25	25 - 30
River Ferries	20 - 25	25 - 30
Billy Sunday	10 - 12	12 - 14
U.S. Flag		
People Dressed or Wrapped in Flag	35 - 40	40 - 50
Uncle Sam in Flag	40 - 45	45 - 55
Rallies, Showing Flag	15 - 20	20 - 25
Orations or Debates, showing Flag	20 - 25	25 - 30
Patriotic Children	15 - 20	20 - 25
Zeppelin	20 - 25	25 - 30

Atlantic Zeppelin Over Munich, 6-9-1924

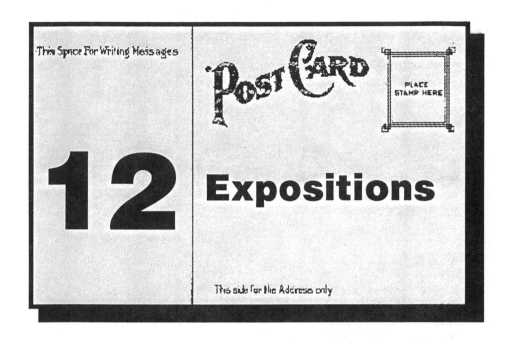

Exposition postcards, heavily collected in the 1970's, now lie dormant with only occasional offerings coming on the market. Most, especially the early rarer issues, are in collections of those who do not wish to part with them. It may be several years before these begin to appear again on the market.

1893 COLUMBIAN EXPOSITION		
Goldsmith Pre-Official, no Seal	$80 - 100	$100 - 120
Officials, Series 1	10 - 12	12 - 16
J. Koehler B&W Issues	35 - 40	40 - 45
PMC or Post Card Backs	15 - 20	20 - 30
Puck Magazine Advertising Cards	135 - 140	140 - 145
Other Advertising Cards	100 - 120	120 - 150
Signed **R. SELINGER**	100 - 115	115 - 140
Anonymous Publishers	100 - 150	150 - 175
1894 CALIFORNIA MID-WINTER EXPO	120 - 130	130 - 140
1895 COTTON STATES & INT. EXPO	125 - 130	130 - 140
1897 TENNESSEE CENTENNIAL EXPO	160 - 170	170 - 190
1898 TRANS-MISSISSIPPI EXPO		
Trans-Mississippi Official Cards	30 - 35	35 - 45
Albertype Co. Views	90 - 100	100 - 110
1898 WORCESTER SEMI-CENTENNIAL	70 - 80	80 - 90
1900 PARIS EXPOSITION		
Scenes	10 - 12	12 - 15

Hold-To-Light	20 - 25	25 - 30
1901 PAN AMERICAN EXPOSITION		
Niagara Envelope Co. B&W	5 - 6	6 - 8
Color	6 - 7	7 - 9
Oversized	70 - 80	80 - 90
1902 SOUTH CAROLINA INTERSTATE		
Albertype Co. Issues	70 - 80	80 - 100
Others	80 - 90	90 - 110
1904 LOUISIANA PURCHASE EXPOSITION		
Buxton & Skinner	6 - 8	8 - 10
Chisholm Bros.	4 - 5	5 - 6
Samuel Cupples	4 - 5	5 - 6
Transparencies	5 - 6	6 - 8
Hold-To-Light	30 - 32	32 - 35
V.O. Hammon	4 - 5	5 - 6
Inside Inn H-T-L	70 - 80	80 - 90
E.C. Kropp	3 - 4	4 - 5
R. Tuck	5 - 8	8 - 12
Advertising Cards	6 - 7	7 - 10
1905 LEWIS & CLARK EXPOSITION		
E.P. Charlton	6 - 7	7 - 8
W. H. Mitchell	6 - 7	7 - 8
B.B. Rich	8 - 10	10 - 12
A. Selige	7 - 8	8 - 10
Advertising Cards	6 - 7	7 - 8
1907 JAMESTOWN EXPOSITION		
A.C. Bosselman	7 - 8	8 - 10
Illustrated Post Card Co.	25 - 30	35 - 40
Jamestown A&V	10 - 12	12 - 14
Battleships	12 - 15	15 - 20
H.C. CHRISTY Army & Navy Girls	40 - 50	50 - 60
60 and 61	50 - 60	60 - 65
R. Tuck Oilettes	6 - 8	8 - 10
Silver Issues	12 - 14	14 - 15
1908 PHILADELPHIA FOUNDERS WEEK		
Illustrated Post Card Co.	6 - 7	7 - 8
Fred Lounsbury	6 - 8	8 - 10
1908 APPALACHIAN EXPO, Knoxville, TN	3 - 4	4 - 6
1909 ALASKA YUKON-PACIFIC EXPOSITION		
Edwin H. Mitchell	3 - 4	4 - 5
Portland Post Card Co.	2 - 3	3 - 4
Advertising Postcards	4 - 5	5 - 8
1909 HUDSON-FULTON CELEBRATION		
J. Koehler	4 - 5	5 - 6

Hudson-Fulton Celebration 1909, Signed B. Wall

Fred Lounsbury	7 - 8	8 - 10
Redfield Floats	5 - 6	6 - 7
R. Tuck	5 - 7	7 - 8
Valentine & Co., S/Wall	5 - 6	6 - 8
1909 PORTOLA FESTIVAL	4 - 5	5 - 6
1915 PANAMA-PACIFIC EXPOSITION	3 - 4	5 - 6
1915 PANAMA-CALIFORNIA EXPOSITION	3 - 4	5 - 6
Pre-Issues	5 - 6	6 - 8
1933 CENTURY OF PROGRESS		
Exhibits	1 - 2	2 - 3
Advertising	2 - 3	3 - 5
Comics	2 - 3	3 - 5
1936 TEXAS CENTENNIAL	2 - 3	3 - 5
1939 NEW YORK WORLD'S FAIR	1 - 3	3 - 6

POSTCARD PUBLISHERS & DISTRIBUTORS

Following are some of the major publishers of postcards world-wide. Minor publishers can be found under each particular listing throughout this book.

A.S.B. – Greetings
Ackerman – Pioneer Views of New York City
Albertype Co. – Pioneer & Expo Views; Local Views
Am. Colortype Co. – Expositions
Am. News Co. – Local Views
Am. Post Card Co. – Comics
Am. Souvenir Co. – Pioneers
Anglo-Am. P.C. Co. (AA) – Greetings, Comics
Art Lithograph Co. – Local Views
Asheville P.C. Co. – Local Views, Comics
Auburn P.C. Mfg. Co. – Greetings, Comics
Austin, J. – Comics
Ballerini & Fratini, Italy – Chiostri, Art Deco
BKWI, German – Artist-Signed, Comics
Bamforth Co. – Comics, Song Cards
Barton and Spooner – Comics, Greetings
Bergman Co. – Comics, Artist-Signed Ladies, etc.
Julius Bien – Comics, Greetings, etc.
B.B. (Birn Brothers) – Greetings, Comics
Bosselman, A.C. – Local Views, Others
Britton & Rey – Expositions, Battleships, etc.
Campbell Art Co. – Comics Rose O'Neill, etc.
Chapman Co. – Greetings, College Girls, etc.

Charlton, E.P. – Expositions, Local Views
Chisholm Bros. – Expositions, Local Views
Conwell, L.R. – Greetings
Crocker, H.S. – Local Views
Davidson Bros. – Greetings and Artist-Signed
Dell Anna & Gasparini, Italy – Art Deco
Delta, Paris – French Fashion
Detroit Pub. Co. – Prolific Publisher, All Types
Faulkner, C.W., British – Artist-Signed, Greetings
Finkenrath, Paul, Berlin (PFB) – Greetings
Gabriel, Sam – Greetings
German-American Novelty Art – Greetings, Comics
Gibson Art Co. – Comics, Greetings
Gottschalk, Dreyfus & Davis – Greetings
Gross, Edward – Artist-Signed
Hammon, V.O. – Local Views
Henderson & Sons – Artist-Signed, Comics
Henderson Litho – Greetings, Comics, Local Views
Huld, Franz – Installment Sets, Expositions, etc.
Ill. Postal Card Co. – Greetings, Artist-Signed and Many Others
Int. Art Publishing Co. – Greetings by Clapsaddle, etc.
Knapp Co. – Artist-Signed
Koeber, Paul C. (P.C.K.) – Comics, Artist-Signed
Koehler, Joseph – H-T-L, Expositions, Local Views
Kropp, E.C. – Local Views, Battleships, etc.
Langsdorf, S. – Alligator and Shell Border Views, Local Views, Greetings
Lapina, Paris – Color Nudes and French Fashion
Leighton, Hugh – Local Views
Leubrie & Elkus (L.&E.) – Artist-Signed
Livingston, Arthur – Pioneers, Local Views
Lounsbury, Fred – Greetings, Local Views, etc.
Manhattan P.C. Co. – Local Views, Comics
Marque L-E, Paris – French Fashion
Meissner & Buch, German – Artist-Signed, Greetings
Metropolitan News Co. – Local Views
Mitchell, Edward H. – Expositions, Battleships, Local Views
Munk, M., Vienna – Artist-Signed, Comics, etc.
Nash, E. – Greetings
National Art Co. – Artist-Signed, Greetings, etc.
Nister, E., British – Artist-Signed, Greetings
Novitas, Germany – Artist-Signed
Noyer, A., Paris – Nudes and French Fashion
Owen, F.A. – Greetings, Artist-Signed
Phillipp & Kramer, Vienna – Artist-Signed, Art Nouveau
Platinachrome – Artist-Signed, Earl Christy, etc.
Reichner Bros. – Local Views
Reinthal & Newman – Artist-Signed, Greetings
Reider, M. – Local Views
Rose, Charles – Greetings, Song Cards, Artist-Signed, Comics
Rost, H.A. – Pioneer Views, Battleships
Roth & Langley – Greetings, Comics
Rotograph Co. – Local Views, Expostiions, Battleships, Artist-Signed, etc.
Sander, P. – Greetings, Comics, Artist-Signed

Santway – Greetings
Sborgi, E., Italy – Famous Art Reproductions
Selige, A. – Expositions, Western Views, People, etc.
Sheehan, M.T. – Local Views, Historical, Artist-Signed
Souvenir Post Card Co. – Local Views, Greetings, etc.
Stecher Litho Co. – Greetings, Artist-Signed
Stengel & Co., Germany – Famous Art Reproductions
Stewart & Woolf, British – Comics, Artist-Signed
Stokes, F.A. – Artist-Signed, Comics
Strauss, Arthur – Local Views, Historical, Expositions
Stroefer, Theo. (T.S.N.), Nurenburg – Artist-Signed, Animals, etc.
Taggart Co. – Greetings
Tammen, H.H. – Expositions, Historical, Local Views
Teich, Curt – Local Views, Artist-Signed, Comics
Tichnor Bros. – Later Local Views, Comics
Tuck, Raphael & Sons, British – Artist-Signed, Views, Comics, Greetings, etc.
Ullman Mfg. Co. – Greetings, Artist-Signed, Comics
Valentine & Sons, British – Artist-Signed, Comics, Views, etc.
Volland Co. – Artist-Signed, Greetings
Whitney & Co. – Greetings, Artist-Signed
Winsch, John – Greetings, Artist-Signed
Wirth, Walter – Pioneer Views

Bibliography

The following publications, all related to the collection and study of postcards, are recommended for further reading.

American Advertising Postcards, Sets and Series, 1980-1920, Fred and Mary Megson, Martinsville, NJ, 1987

The American Postcard Guide to Tuck, Sally Carver, Chestnut Hill, MA, 1979

The American Postcard Journal, Roy and Marilyn Nuhn, New Haven, CT

Bessie Pease Gutmann, Published Works Catalog, Victor J.W. Christie, Park Avenue Publishers, NJ, 1986

Art Nouveau Post Cards, Alan Weill, Image Graphics, NY, 1977

The Collector's Guide to Post Cards, Jane Wood, Gas City, IN

Erotic Postcards, Barbara Jones and William Ouelette, U.K., 1977

Fantasy Postcarads, William Ouelette, New York, 1975

Harrison Fisher, David Bowers, Ellen H. Budd, George M. Budd, 1984

I.P.M. Catalogue of Picture Postcards, J.H.D. Smith, IPM Ltd., U.K.

Official Postcard Price Guide, Dianne Allman, NY, 1990

Philip Boileau, Painter of Fair Women, Dorothy Ryan, Gotham Book Mt., NY, 1981

The Picture Postcard and its Origins, Frank Staff, U.K., 1966

Pictures in the Post, Richard Carline, Gordon Fraser, U.K., 1971

Picture Postcards, Marian Klamkin, David & Charles, U.K., 1974

Picture Postcards in the U.S., 1893-1918, Dorothy Ryan

Picture Postcards of the Golden Age, Tonie & Valmai Holt, U.K.

Pioneer Postcards, J.R. Burdick, Nostalgia Press, 1956

Postcard Collectors Magazine, Bob Hendricks, Pamona, CA, 1954-55

Prairie Fires & Paper Moons: The American Photographic Postcard, 1902-1920, Hal Morgan, Andreas Brown, Boston, 1981

The Postcards of Alphonse Mucha, Q. David Bowers, Mary Martin

Reklame Postkarten, Peter Weiss, Karl Stehle, Munich, Birkhauser Verlag, Basel, Switzerland

Standard Postcard Catalog, James L. Lowe, PA

The Super Rare Postcards of Harrison Fisher, J.L. Mashburn, Enka, NC, World-Comm, 1992

Suomalaista Postikortti Taidetta, Teuvo Tekomonen, Oy KAJ Hellman Ltd., Espoo, Finland, 1984

Till the Boys Come Home, Tonie & Valmai Holt, U.K., 1977

What Cheer News, Mrs. E.K. Austin, Editor, Rhode Island Postcard Club, RI

Periodicals

The Antique Trader Weekly, P.O. Box 1050, Dubuque, IA 52004

Antiques & Auction News, P.O. Box 500, Mt. Joy, PA 17552

Barr's Post Card News, 70 S. 6th St., Lansing, IA 52151

Paper Collectors Marketplace, P.O. Box 127, Scandinavia, WI 54977

Paper Pile Quarterly, P.O. Box 337, San Anselmo, CA 94979

Picture Post Card Monthly, 15 Debdale Ln, Keyworth, Nottingham NG12 5HT, U.K.

Postcard Collector, P.O. Box 37, Iola, WI 54945

Index